JAVA

PROGRAMMING LANGUAGE
HANDBOOK

Anthony Potts

David H. Friedel, Jr.

CORIOLIS GROUP BOOKS

Publisher	Keith Weiskamp
Editor	Keith Weiskamp
Proofreader	Kirsten Dewey
Cover Design	Gary Smith
Interior Design	Michelle Stroup
Layout Production	Kim Eoff
Indexer	Kirsten Dewey

The Coriolis Group
7339 E. Acoma Drive, Suite 7
Scottsdale, AZ 85260
Phone: (602) 483-0192
Fax: (602) 483-0193
Web address: www.coriolis.com

ISBN 1-883577-77-2 : $24.99

Printed in the United States of America

10 9 8 7 6 5 4 3 2 1

To my wife who has been there through it all.
Anthony Potts

To my sister Beth, who has helped make this book possible.
Dave Friedel

Acknowledgments

To Keith Weiskamp who really should be listed as a co-author for all the developmental and editorial work he did for this book.

To John Rodley for helping us get started with Java.

To Neil Bartlett, Alex Leslie, and Steve Simkin for all their help and for letting us have a sneak peek at their book, *Java Programming EXplorer*.

And, to Sun for creating a really cool alternative!

Contents

Chapter 3   Java Language Fundamentals   55

Chapter 8   Threads   203

Chapter 9   The Java AWT   225

Chapter 10   Java Applet Programming Techniques   285

Chapter 13   Networking with Java   345

Foreword

The Crazy Years Are Here Again

By Jeff Duntemann

As a brand new magazine editor at the end of 1984, I surveyed the IBM PC field and commented under my breath, "These are the Crazy Years." The IBM PC world had begun exploding in 1983; *PC Magazine* hit 800 pages; new companies were forming every minute and spending huge amounts of money launching new products into an astonishingly hungry and immature market. The machines of the time were almost unimaginably underpowered. 5Mhz. 8 bits. 256K of RAM. Only rich people had hard drives. And yet everyone spoke of their miserable little IBM PCs as though they could do the work of mainframes— we just hadn't yet figured out quite *how*.

History doesn't repeat itself—but it echoes, it echoes. Here we sit, eleven years later, I'm still a magazine editor (though not nearly as new) and the Crazy Years are back again. This time, plug the Internet into the place the IBM PC occupied in 1984. Our PCs really are mainframes now; those 166 Mhz Pentiums that we take for granted can handle anything we throw at them. What we're enraptured with today is the ability to connect to a server and bounce around the world like manic pinballs, grabbing a Web page here, a shareware file there, a picture of Cindy Crawford somewhere else. New Internet magazines are appearing weekly, enormous sums of money are being spent and earned on Internet technology companies, and Internet books have crowded almost everything else off of the computer book shelves at the superstores. The Internet will become the OS of the future. Applications will be fragmented and distributed around the world; a piece in Britain, a piece in Finland; a piece in Rio. Faithful agent software will wander around the globe, sniffing out what we want and paying for it with digital cash. Our Internet boxes will be our phones, our faxes, our stereos, our game platforms, and our personal bank machines.

Yikes! Aren't we getting maybe just a *little* bit ahead of ourselves?

Sure. *But admitting we're ahead of ourselves doesn't mean that we won't catch up.*

And that's why things are so crazy. Somewhere south of our conscious minds we understand that this is the way the world is going, even if the results in the here and now fall just a touch short of spectacular. We're making this up as we go along—there's no established body of technical knowledge to fall back on—so everything's being tried, and everything's being trumpeted as the ultimate Magic Bullet.

The trick, of course, is to get behind the right bullet. (Which is always better than being in *front* of it...) The game is far from over (especially with that Big Rich Guy still knocking around in the upper left corner of the country, making trouble) but if you want my penny and a half, the bullet to get behind for the Internet game is Java.

You can look at Java in a number of different ways, from C++ with all the barbed wire stripped out of it, to the ultimate global cross-platform integration scripting language. That's a strong element of its success: Good magic bullets are never too specific, or the Atari personal computers (which were muscular game boxes) would have knocked the underpowered but protean IBM PC right out of the ring. Again, there is that never-quite-fully-expressed feeling that Java was created with exactly the *right* balance of power and specificity, and that it can rise to whatever challenges we might put in front of it, given time for us to pry the devil out of the details and toss him in the junk drawer.

No, there isn't enough bandwidth on the Internet to do all we want to do. *This year.*

No, the majority of people do not have fast, always-there connections to the Internet. *This year.*

No, there is no clean, standard, and acceptably secure way for people to pay for electronic deliverables over the Internet. *This year.*

Care to place bets on next year? Or (for higher stakes yet) the year after that?

I didn't think so.

Whatever you do, avoid the Clifford Stoll Trap. Stoll, one of the original architects of the Internet, wrote an entire book about how the Internet was a major shuck, that it was ruining all our lives, that he was giving it up forever, and don't expect him to come back and rescue us from ourselves, farewell, good bye forever, I'm leaving and I'm serious, don't try to stop me, and on and on and on.

We waved good-bye. Now he's gone. And not only is he not especially missed, I doubt that one person in a hundred even remembers who he was. That's how our business works. If you stand back and let the train go by, you will not be missed, and the train generally passes through your station only once.

That's why I encourage you to stick with this stuff, no matter how crazy it gets. As best we can tell right now, Java is the brand of pipe that we'll be using to plumb global communications software for the foreseeable future. No, we don't have the whole foundation poured, and no, we don't have a stack of plans to go by. Still, without the pipes in place, it won't work. You have to develop the skills you'll need to do the work next year and the year after. What better time than now?

You've got the book in hand to take you through the Java language and make it stick. So do it!

Or heads will bounce.

Introducing
Java

Introducing Java

1

Java has swept the computer industry with its promise to deliver executable content to the vast sea of computers connected to the World Wide Web. Here's a look at why you'll want to start developing with this language as soon as you can.

In just a few months, Java has moved from the R&D labs at Sun Microsystems to the center stage of the World Wide Web. Never before had a simple programming language garnered so much attention and captured the imaginations of so many software developers and computer users alike so quickly. Some cynics think that the best part about Java is its name, which is also the reason they think Java gets so much attention in the press. But most experts who follow Web development think that Java is the most significant thing that has been developed or announced for the Web.

Why has Java taken over so quickly? The short answer is found in its platform independence and potential to turn the Web into a much more dynamic and interactive environment—something that is badly needed. Other reasons are because of Java's similarity to C++ and its support of popular object-oriented programming techniques, making it easier for hundreds of thousands of C and C++ programmers to quickly master Java's powerful features.

Our goal in this chapter is to set the stage for Java, exploring where this language has come from and where it is going. We'll introduce the key features of Java, give you some insight into why Java was developed in the first place, and examine some of the key similarities between Java and C++. We think it is important to spend as much time as possible looking at Java through the lenses of a C++ programmer because the syntax and object-oriented features are very similar.

3

The World of Java

"Java may be overhyped, but it also may be as significant to the computer world as television was to broadcasting."
—*U.S. News and World Report*

In the old days of computer languages (less than six months ago), programs were designed to run under a single operating system, more or less, and the name of the game was to create programs that could run as fast as possible. Almost overnight, the World Wide Web and Java have changed this notion of operating system-based language environments to platform independent network-driven languages and systems. Java represents the sea change of distributed programming and application development that is taking place in the computer industry today. Languages like Java are radically shifting the computing burden from local desktop computers to servers that deliver executable content to users.

Programmers have accepted Java very quickly because it provides everything that is needed in a modern day language including:

- Object-Oriented Features
- Multithreading
- Garbage Collection (Automatic Memory Management)
- Networking and Security Features
- Platform Independence (Architecture Neutral)
- Internet/Web Development Features

(If you are unfamiliar with some of this terminology, make sure you read the *Java Jargon Survival Guide* included in this chapter.) Popular languages like Smalltalk and C++ have been moving programmers away from top-down structured programming methods and into the more flexible and adaptable object-oriented paradigm for years. Java greatly contributes to this evolution and even enhances some of the shortcomings found in object-oriented languages like C++.

What is most remarkable about Java is that it is the first language that allows developers to create robust cross-platform networked software for the Internet. Once you start using Java, you can throw away the notion that all software must first be developed on a specific platform to be run on the same platform and then ported if it needs to run on other systems.

If you have seen Java in action by using your Web browser to view Web pages that contain Java applets, you already know some of the types of programs you can write. But Java applets are only half of the story. The Java language can be used to write both applets and standalone applications. Applets are incorporated into Web pages using a special <APPLET> HTML tag and they are downloaded and launched automatically when their pages are displayed by a Java-enabled Web browser. This process is similar to the way in which a Web browser might process and display other elements such as images and hyperlinked text. The big difference with an applet is that the browser processes *dynamic executable content* instead of static data.

A Java application, on the other hand, looks suspiciously like a C++ program. It can run on its own and perform a myriad of tasks from performing calculations to specialized file I/O operations. The only problem with writing Java applications at the moment is that Java is an interpreted language, and thus programs written in Java require the Java Virtual Machine in order to execute. Fortunately, work is underway to develop compilers that enable Java applications to run quicker and more independently.

Java Jargon Survival Guide

Architecture-Natural   This is a term language designers use to describe languages like Java that are truly portable across different operating systems. Programs written in architecture-natural languages typically run under bytecode interpreters that are capable of running on any type of computer.

Bytecodes   The entire language design of Java is based on the notion of bytecode interpreters, which can efficiently run ("interpret") programs at runtime and perform operations like error handling and memory management. To create and use bytecodes, a compiler must first translate a program into a series of codes which are then executed by an interpreter which converts the general bytecode instructions into local actions.

Classes   Java utilizes the basic object technology found in C++, which in turn was heavily influenced by Smalltalk. Object-oriented features are implemented in these languages using basic building blocks called *classes*. Essentially, a class is a structure that allows you to combine data and the code that must operate on the data under one roof. Once classes have been defined, they can easily be used to derive other classes.

Distributed Programming   This emerging field of software development involves the techniques of writing programs that can be executed across networks like the Internet. In traditional programming, applications run on a single computer and only data is distributed across networks. In distributed programming, programs can be downloaded from networks and executed at the same time. As you might guess, this approach opens the door wide for ways in much software can be shared and distributed.

Garbage Collection   This is the memory management technique that Java programs use to handle dynamic memory allocation. In traditional compiled languages like C and C++, memory for dynamic variables and objects (pointers), must be allocated and deallocated manually by the programmer. In Java, memory allocation is handled by the Java runtime environment, thus eliminating the need for explicit memory allocation and pointers. Garbage collection is one key feature that many programmers claim make "Java a better and safer C++."

HotJava   This is Sun's Web browser written in the Java language. It contains the Java Virtual Machine and can download and play any Java applet. Originally, HotJava was the rage on the Web but since Netscape has licensed and incorporated the Java Virtual Machine into Netscape Navigator, most Web users have forgotten about HotJava.

Java Applet   These are small programs written in Java that can execute remotely over networks. They are downloaded from the Web via a Java-enabled Web browser and then they are executed from within the shell of the browser. An applet can be anything from animations to search engines to games. In the short time that Java has been available, hundreds of applets have appeared on the Web written by programmers from all around the world.

Java Virtual Machine   This is the code that serves as the engine or interpreter for Java programs. Any application that is capable of running Java programs requires the use of the Java Virtual Machine (VM). The process for running a Java applet involves compiling the applet into a sequence of bytecodes which are then interpreted by the Java VM at runtime. Sun has aggressively licensed the Java VM to many companies, such as Netscape, Oracle, and Borland, to help expand the developer base for Java.

Java-Enabled   A term used to indicate if Internet applications like Web browsers are capable of running Java applications, in particular, Java applets.

JavaScript   This is an object-oriented scripting language developed by both Sun and Netscape. The language was designed to be used as a scripting language to customize Netscape browsers and control Java applets running under Netscape. Originally, Netscape called their scripting language "LiveScript" but the name was changed to JavaScript. Rumor has it that Netscape's stock rose $20 per share in one day after announcing the name change. You can think of JavaScript as the "glue" between Java applets and Netscape browser features such as plug-ins, HTML, and special events.

Just-in-Time Compiler   This is new compiler technology that is being developed for Java so that Java applications can be custom compiled for a particular platform as they are downloaded from networks.

Methods   These are the functions (operations) that are included in Java classes to operate on data.

Multithreading   To allow Java applications and applets to run efficiently even tough they must be executed by a Java interpreter, Java supports a technique called *multithreading* that allows different processes to execute at the same time.

The Java Development Platform

As we've mentioned, a Java-enabled browser such as HotJava or Netscape 2 is needed in order to run Java applets. You can also use the *appletviewer* utility which is provided with Sun's Java Development Kit (JDK). For any Java programming that you wish to do, you'll need the JDK because it provides the compiler for compiling Java applets and applications (*javac*), an interpreter for running standalone Java applications (*java*), and a debugger (*jdbg*). But don't be surprised to find that each of these development tools are somewhat primitive and must be run from the command line. In the near future, we should have much better Java visual development tools. If you don't currently have the JDK, you can visit Sun's Java Web site to download a copy (http://www.javasoft.com/). The syntax and command options for using the tools in the JDK are presented with the Java Programming Language reference card included at the end of this book.

All of the tools included in the JDK are designed to support Sun's notion of what the Java language is all about including:

- A compiler for the Java language that generates architecture-neutral bytecodes
- The Java Virtual Machine that interprets bytecodes at runtime.
- A set of class libraries to help Java programmers create applications. Some of these libraries include interface tools, I/O, applet development, networking, and so on.
- A Java runtime environment that supports bytecode verification, multithreading, and garbage collection
- Java development support tools including a debugger, documentation generator, and so on.

The Roots of Java

"Java has become perhaps the first programming language to move the stock market."
—*Application Development Trends*

Whether or not you believe all the hype surrounding Java, no one will deny that Java is going places. Already numerous major software and hardware companies have licensed Java, including Netscape, IBM (Lotus), Borland, Adobe, Fujitsu, Mitsubishi, Symantec, Spyglass, Macromedia, and even Microsoft. But before we look at the key elements of Java and where it is going, let's explore its roots to give you some perspective. Like many great technological creations, Java's development progressed with a number of twists and turns in the road.

The origins of Java began in April 1991 with a small development team at Sun headed by James Gosling. Gosling had developed quite a reputation in the past as a legendary Unix programmer for creating the first C version of a popular Unix editor named *Emacs*. He also developed the innovative Postscript-based windowing environment for Sun OS called *NEWS*. In the early days, Gosling's team operated as an independent unit from Sun. They went by the name "the Green group" and Sun eventually set this group up as a separate company called *First Person*. (Don't you wish you owned stock in this company?) Their initial charter was to develop software that could be sold to consumer electronics companies. Sun felt that many consumer-driven technologies, such as PDAs, set-top boxes, and so on, were up and coming technologies worth pursuing to enhance their base of software sales.

Soon after the Green group set up shop, they discovered that the success of creating widely-distributed software for consumer products would only come if a platform-independent development environment were created. They began work in this area by trying to extend existing C++ development tools and compilers but this turned out to be a dead end of sorts because of the complexity of C++. C and C++ have always been promoted as highly portable languages, but when it comes right down to it, trying to create general purpose, portable, and robust code in these languages is not so easy.

When you run into a wall in software development, the best thing to do is develop a language that provides the solutions you need. And that's exactly what Gosling and the Green group did. Their new language was originally called *Oak*—named after a tree outside Gosling's office. Because Oak could not be trademarked by Sun, a new name emerged—Java—after a brainstorming session or two.

The overriding goal of Java's developers was simple but ambitious: *Design a programming language that can run on anything connected to a network*. This would include Sun workstations, PCs, Macs, PDAs, and even television sets and toasters. To meet these goals, they borrowed heavily from existing languages such as C++, Objective-C, Smalltalk, Eiffel, and Cedar-Mesa. Java's developers also wanted to make sure their language achieved an entirely new level of robustness, not found in languages like C++ because of all the dangerous features like pointers, operator overloading, and dynamic memory allocation. One writer in a popular computer developer's journal summed this goal up nicely when he wrote that Java's developers wanted to "get rid of all the complicated, dangerous, and/or stupid crud in C++." The end result is that you won't find features like the following in Java:

- Header files
- #defines
- typedefs or structs

- Pointer arithmetic
- Multiple inheritance of classes
- General functions (Only methods are supported)

On May 23, 1995, Sun introduced the Java language and its corresponding browser *HotJava*. The language and its associated development tools only took about four years to create, but as the Green group proved, four years was ample time to create a new standard for the rest of the world to follow. Soon after the announcement of Java, alpha versions of the language started appearing across the World Wide Web. Another noteworthy date to mark on your calendar is December 7, 1995—the date Microsoft agreed to license Java, an endorsement that has helped to accelerate Java's popularity. (If you owned any of Sun's stock, you probably noticed that their stock increased by $336 million on that day!)

The Power of Distributed Software

"I have seen the future of the World Wide Web, and it is executable content."
—Ray Valdes, *Dr Dobb's Developer Update*

Before Java was unleashed on the world, most Web development and interactivity was accomplished using Common Gateway Interface (CGI) scripting. For the past year, the key scripting contender has been Perl. The processing model for CGI is completely client-server based. For example, a user on a client computer running a software program like Netscape fills out a form on a Web page and the data is sent to a server. Then, the server reads and processes the data and sends a response back to the client. The disadvantage of this approach is that the client operates almost like a dumb terminal; most of the key processing tasks are performed by a central computer—the server. And if the server is busy (which happens a lot in the Web world), the client must wait *and wait and wait.*

In the world of distributed software, networks are used to send executable code, often called *executable content*, to client computers which are capable of running the software locally. For many software developers and users, this is a dream come true. In fact over the past year, many leading software development companies have been trying to create standards for delivering executable content. Some of the more noteworthy attempts include Macromedia's Shockwave, NEXT's WebObjects, and Microsoft's new ActiveX controls.

The visual benefits of running distributed software like Java applets are only the tip of the iceberg. Of course, it is impressive to see a well-designed animated applet dance across a Web page as its code is being downloaded across a network and executed locally, but Java programmers are already looking forward to the day in the not so distant future when they can develop major applications that can run across networks. This dynamic flexibility will open up new possibilities for both updatable entertainment and business-related software. And the best part is that programmers will no longer have to write applications that they have to port to multiple platforms. The same program written in Java can run on any type of computer that can connect to a network and run the Java Virtual Machine.

But the best part is that you can use Java today in its current form and take advantage of some of the key benefits the distributed software paradigm has over the CGI client-server approach:

Develop Interactive Web Interfaces   With Java you can create much more interactive interfaces to the Web than you can with CGI languages like Perl. Applets that you customize for Web pages can allow users to move objects on the screen, view animations, and control multimedia features, such as sound and music.

Utilize Local Resources   With the CGI model, a server is limited to processing the data it has on hand. With Java, on the other hand, you can write applications that truly take advantage of resources available on a user's local system. For example, a Java program might use local hardware features in a way that a CGI program never could. The Java approach allows the local computer to take full control over how and where code is executed.

Greater Internet/Web Access   One of the biggest problems with the Internet and the Web is that content is scattered all over the place in a somewhat chaotic fashion. Using Java, you can write better front-ends to the Web, such as agents and search engines, to better access the Web.

Reduce the Cost of Distributing Software   The software industry has rapidly turned into a "hits" based business, which means that computer software outlets typically only carry the major blockbuster products. One of the reasons this has occurred is that the cost and risks of selling and distributing software have greatly increased over the past five years. With distributed software, users can purchase and download the software they need instead of having to order from a direct mail catalog or buying it in a store. This approach of getting software from a publisher or developer to a user also is ideal for updating software. If you need a new version of your favorite tax program to get your taxes done by April 15, you can simply point to the right place on the Web and quickly access the software you need.

The Challenges of Security

Along with the promises and opportunities of distributed software, come the risks of security. Think about it. The programs you run on your desktop computer are ones that you've decided to buy or download. Once you install them, you can check them for viruses and remove them if they cause problems on your system. Distributed programs such as Java applets, on the other hand, reside on someone else's computer. When you run them you are essentially downloading executable code from another computer, of which you have no control over.

Fortunately, the underlying philosophy behind Java's design is security. Bytecodes that are downloaded from a network are passed to a bytecode verifier which attempts to weed out bad code that could damage a local computer. Because Java has no pointers or programmer-driven memory allocation routines, Java code is less likely to go off track and crash a local computer due to illegal memory access operations. The absence of pointers also keeps troublesome hackers from writing code that accesses a local computer's system memory to get unauthorized privileges.

By design, the Java Virtual Machine assumes that code downloaded from a network should be trusted less than code that is resident on a local computer. To enhance security, Java provides built-in classes that check for security related conflicts. As a final measure, Java allows its user *layer of security* to be configurable. For example, a user can specify exactly which directories applets can read from and write to. Applets can also be limited to accessing sockets on other machines.

Java and C++

If you haven't noticed already, Java is very similar to C++. If you are an accomplished C++ programmer, moving to Java will be easy for you. However, there are a few important things you should know that we will present in this chapter. If you are new to both C++ and Java, you may have a little more catching up to do to understand the object-oriented nature of the Java language.

Object-Oriented Quick Tour

Let's start by looking at some key object-oriented programming issues. First of all, C++ is not a "true" object-oriented (OO) language but Java is much closer. Why? Because *everything* in Java is a class and *all* method calls are done via a method invocation of a Java class object. In C++ you can use stand-alone functions, header files, global variables, and so on. This is an extremely important point, so don't gloss over it. The only thing in Java not placed in a class is interfaces, although they are used like classes but without implementations.

This strict OO nature means that you won't be able to port C++ code as easily. You will need to change the basic structure of your C++ applications, although you should be able to keep the logic as long as you are not using any of the features that have been removed.

What's Missing?

As we've mentioned, one of big goals for the developers of Java was to look at all the other programming languages and pull the best features of each and dump the rest. Since C/C++ has such a large installed base of programmers, it is obvious why they chose to mimic so much of its syntax and structure. There are, however, several features that C++ has that Java does not implement. Many of these subtractions were made for security reasons, since Java was designed as a Web language. Other features were left out because the Java creators thought they were to difficult to use or just plain useless. Let's look at some of the important subtractions.

Gone: Pointers

Pointer arithmetic is the bane of everyone who hates C++. For the few programmers who have mastered pointers, we salute you. For the rest of us, good riddance. The major reason pointers are not used with Java is security. If a Java applet had the ability to access memory directly, it could easily cause some real problems. By forcing the Java interpreter to handle memory allocation and garbage collection, it relieves you of a big burden and lessens the chance that anyone can do bad things to your computer through a Java program.

There are a few areas where pointers seem necessary for performing certain operations. But since we don't have them in Java, we need to find a way around them. In Java, objects are passed as arguments directly instead of passing a pointer to an object's memory space. You must also use indices to manipulate arrays rather than accessing the values directly.

Gone: Header Files

To C++ users, header files are a mainstay of programming life. However, if you look closely at how most programmers use header files, you'll find that the biggest use is for prototyping and documentation. To examine the interface to a certain member function, you can read a header file and find the function. By just looking at the header files from a C++ class, you can figure out a lot about what that class does—without ever seeing any of the implementation.

In Java there is no way to do this since the implementation for classes and methods must reside in the same place. The implementation always follows the declaration in Java. Of course, you can add all the comments you want to aid in understanding your code, but your code may run on for pages and pages. It is not always easy to look at a Java class and understand how it can be used.

So, why doesn't Java use header files? There are two reasons. First, it is not possible to use a library that declares a method but does not implement it. Second, it is more difficult to program using files that are out of synchronization with the implementation.

Gone: Multiple Inheritance

Very often in object-oriented programming, an object needs to inherit the functionality of more than one class. In C++ this is accomplished using multiple inheritance, a technique allowing a single class to subclass as many classes as it needs. Multiple inheritance can get extremely complicated and is one of the leading causes of C++ bugs (and programmer suicide). Java's answer to multiple inheritance is *interfaces*. Interfaces are the only item in Java that are not a class. They are simply templates for a class to follow. They list method declarations with no implementation (no guts). Any class that implements an interface *must* use the methods declared in the interface.

Interfaces work well, but they do have some limitations. The big drawback is that you must write the code for each method that an interface declares. Multiple inheritance in C++ allows you to override the methods that you chose and then you can just use the parent's implementation of the methods for the others.

Interfaces are much easier to understand and master than multiple inheritance. Check Chapter 6 for an in-depth look at interfaces. With the right programming strategy, you can get almost all of the functionality of multiple inheritance. And hopefully, you won't have all the problems.

What's New?

Since Java is supposed to be the next step in the evolution of programming languages you would expect some advancements. Most of the new features focus on security and making programming easier.

Garbage Collection

When you finish using a resource in a C++ program, you must explicitly tell the computer when to release the memory it was using. This is accomplished with pointers. Since Java does not use pointers for security reasons, it needs a way to clean up resources when they are not needed any more. That's where garbage collection comes in.

Garbage collection is a threaded run-time environment that keeps track of all the parts of your program and automatically de-allocates the memory used when the memory is no longer needed. For example, when you declare a variable, memory is allocated to store its value. The garbage collection engine looks at what scope of the program is seen by this variable. When the program leaves that scope, the memory is cleared.

Lets look at a specific example. Here is a simple **for** loop:

```
for (int x; x < 10; ++x) System.out.println(x);
```

The integer we are using to count to ten is actually declared within the declaration of the loop. As soon as the expression is met and the loop ends, the **x** variable's memory space is cleared and put back into the shared memory pool. This same idea works at all levels of the Java environment.

Security

Security was an issue that the creators of C++ did not have to deal with—they left that up to individual programmers. However, since Java is designed to be a distributed programming language, security is a prime concern. Java includes many features that aid in preventing security problems. The omission of pointers is a key issue that reduces security risks. The functionality you lose is made up for in the robustness of your applications and applets. Now, it's just up to browser creators to develop programs that can't be hacked!

Exceptions

Exceptions are not really new—they were used in C++. However, using them was difficult at best. In Java, exceptions are used heavily. Exceptions are error conditions that are not expected during the course of a standard program run. Situations like missing files will result in exceptions in Java.

In Java, exceptions are actually part of the language; they have their own classes, interfaces, and so on. In C++, exceptions were more of an add-on that was never fully implemented. Look at Chapter 7 for a detailed look at exceptions.

Strings versus Character Arrays

In C++, strings are simply arrays of characters. In Java, strings can be handled as strings. They are not officially a primitive type but are in fact a class which is instanced as an object whenever you use strings. So, whenever you handle strings, you are actually handling a **String** object that has its own methods. Instead of calling methods that act upon your string (C++), you are actually calling methods *of* your string object that act upon itself.

If you choose to, you could still use an array of **chars** to act like a string, but you would lose much of the easy functionality built in to the **String** class.

The Super Class

If you have used C++ much, you are familiar with the **this** keyword that is used to reference the current object. Java implements the **this** operator to, but also adds the **super** operator, which tells Java to find the class that our current class extended. You can use **super** to make explicit calls to the superclass of the current class.

New Modifiers

In C++, modifiers are used quite heavily. Java takes many of the C++ modifiers and adds new ones. Most of the new modifiers are needed to help support security issues. Table 1.1 provides a list of the new modifiers:

Table 1.1	Some of the New Java Modifiers
Modifier	**Descriptions**
abstract	Used to define classes and methods that *must* be subclassed or overridden to be useful.
synchronized	Tells Java that a method can only be called by one object at a time.
native	Used to create calls to languages like C.
final	Tells Java that a class cannot be subclassed.

The instanceof Operator

The **instanceof** operator is an extremely handy operator to use when you are dealing with objects and you are not sure of their type. You will probably find yourself using this operator most often in conjunction with the Abstract Windows Toolkit (AWT).

Helper Programs

The Java Developer's Kit (JDK) ships with two helpful programs: *javadoc* and *javap*. *javadoc* is an automatic documentation program that creates HTML files automatically to list your classes methods, interfaces, variables, and so on. We discuss this program in greater detail in Chapter 3 so we won't repeat it here. The entire API documentation that shipped with the 1.0 JDK was created using this program. *Javadoc* can only be used with source files.

Another useful utility is *javap*, a disassembler program that prints class signatures. *javap* is used with the compiled class files. When *javap* is run, it outputs a simple listing of a classes public methods and variables. Here is an example:

```
Compiled from /home/weisblat/C.java
private class C extends java/lang/Object {
    static int a;
    static int b;
    public static void main(java/lang/String []);
    public C();
    static void ();
}
```

As you can see, this program can be very useful when trying to figure out how to use a class that has little documentation or that you do not have the source for.

2

Writing Your First
Java Applet

Writing Your First Java Applet

The best way to learn the elements of the Java language is to dive in head first and create a real-world applet.

Before we get into the down and dirty details behind the Java language, let's create a simple program that will introduce you to many of the basic concepts of Java.

Once we decided to put a tutorial program at the beginning of this book, we tried to find one that included many of the major programming elements that you will encounter while coding your own programs. We had to decide if the program would be an application or an applet. Applications and applets are very different things. Creating one over the other is not as simple as changing a couple of lines of code and recompiling. Java applications are free-standing programs; therefore, they must create their own "space" to work within. Java applets, on the other hand, are run from within another program, usually a Web browser. Applets have many parts of their code already written for them and ready to go. For example, if you wanted to display a graphic in a stand-alone Java application, you would first have to create a window to run the program in, a frame, then the graphics you might need. With an applet, most of that work is done for you. A simple call to a graphic method can load an image into your applet's space.

Does that mean that applets are better? Not necessarily, they are simply "different." Both applets and applications have their place in the programming world. The one you use depends on your needs and the needs of the people who will use your programs.

We decided to use an applet as a tutorial mostly because of their emerging popularity. Java applets are popping up on the Web faster than Trekies show up at a Star Trek convention. The concepts and programming techniques we present as we discuss our applet can be used in any program you create. We'll start out by showing you the code for the applet and then we'll take it apart, piece-by-piece. As we dissect it, you'll begin to see how straightforward the Java language really is.

Introducing the TickerTape Applet

Our first applet is called TickerTape. It scrolls a custom message across the applet space (like a ticker tape). You will be able to specify a couple of parameters, including the text that is displayed and the speed at which the text moves across the screen.

The best part about this applet is that it will introduce you to a number of Java programming language features all at once, including:

- Comments
- Packages
- Classes
- Class Inheritance
- Variables
- Parameters
- Constructors
- Threads
- Overriding Methods
- Graphic Double-Buffering
- Basic Operators
- Interfaces
- Exceptions

And, here is the moment we've been waiting for—the applet itself:

```
// TickerTape Applet

import java.applet.*;
import java.awt.*;
```

```
// TickerTape Class
public class TickerTape extends Applet implements Runnable {
    // Declare Variables
    String inputText;
    String animSpeedString;
    Color color = new Color(255, 255, 255);
    int xpos;
    int fontLength;
    int fontHeight;
    int animSpeed;
    Font font;
    Thread ttapeThread = null;
    Image im;
    Graphics osGraphics;
    boolean suspended = false;

    // Initialize Applet
    public void init(){
        inputText = getParameter("TEXT");
        animSpeedString = getParameter("SPEED");
        animSpeed = Integer.parseInt(animSpeedString);
        im=createImage(size().width, size().height);
        osGraphics = im.getGraphics();
        xpos = size().width;
        fontHeight = 4 * size().height / 5;
        font = new Font("Helvetica", 1, fontHeight);
    }

    // Override Applet Class' paint method
    public void paint(Graphics g){
        paintText(osGraphics);
        g.drawImage(im, 0, 0, null);
    }

    // Draw background and text on buffer image
    public void paintText(Graphics g){
        g.setColor(Color.black);
        g.fillRect(0, 0, size().width, size().height);
        g.clipRect(0, 0, size().width, size().height);
        g.setFont(font);
        g.setColor(color);
        FontMetrics fmetrics = g.getFontMetrics();
        fontLength = fmetrics.stringWidth(inputText);
        fontHeight = fmetrics.getHeight();
        g.drawString(inputText, xpos, size().height - fontHeight / 4);
    }
```

```
// Start Applet as thread
public void start(){
    if(ttapeThread == null){
        ttapeThread = new Thread(this);
        ttapeThread.start();
    }
}


// Animate coordinates for drawing text
public void setcoord(){
    xpos = xpos - animSpeed;
    if(xpos <- fontLength){
        xpos = size().width;
    }
}


// Change coordinates and repaint
public void run(){
    while(ttapeThread != null){
        try {Thread.sleep(50);} catch (InterruptedException e){}
        setcoord();
        repaint();
    }
}


// Re-paint when buffer is updated
public void update(Graphics g) {
    paint(g);
}


// Handle mouse clicks
public boolean handleEvent(Event evt) {
    if (evt.id == Event.MOUSE_DOWN) {
        if (suspended) {
            ttapeThread.resume();
        } else {
            ttapeThread.suspend();
        }
    suspended = !suspended;
    }
    return true;
}


// Stop thread then clean up before close
public void stop(){
    if(ttapeThread != null)
```

```
        ttapeThread.stop();
      ttapeThread = null;
   }

} // End TickerTape
```

Before we discuss how the program works, why don't you try it out and see how it looks. You can type the code in for yourself and compile it or head up to the Coriolis Group Web site at *http://coriolis.com* and download this applet as well as all the other code examples listed in this book (look in the "What's Free" section). You can also view this entire chapter on-line by going into the Coriolis books section on the site and searching for this book. There you can choose the "sample chapter" option where you will see this chapter.

Running the Applet

Because our program is set up to be an applet, it cannot run on its own. It needs the help of a Web browser. To run the program from your personal system, you'll need to follow these steps:

1. Use a text editor to type in the applet code. Save the file as TickerTape.java.
2. Compile the program. This will create the file TickerTape.class. To compile the program, you'll need access to the Java Developer's Kit.
3. Move the file into the same directory where you store your HTML files.
4. Create an HTML (HyperText Markup Language) file or edit an existing one, and add the following instructions:

```
<APPLET CODE=TickerTape.class WIDTH=600 HEIGHT=50>
<PARAM NAME=TEXT VALUE="The Java TickerTape Applet...">
<PARAM NAME=SPEED VALUE="4">
</APPLET>
```

Recall that HTML is the language used to create Web pages. Each statement in the language specifies one specific formatting, file processing or hypertext (linking) operation, such as loading and displaying a graphic image, defining a hypertext link, displaying a word or sentence in bold, or loading and playing a Java applet. (We'll look at the HTML instructions for playing our applet in much more detail in a moment.) If you are creating a new HTML file, you might want to name it TTAPE.HTML.

5. Start a Web browser like Netscape 2 that is capable of running Java applets. Then, load in the HTML file you just created. Keep in mind that not all Web browsers can run Java applets. If nothing happens after you load in the HTML file, first check to make sure that you entered the HTML instructions carefully. Then, check to make sure that you are using a Java-playable browser.

After you open the HTML file that includes the required instructions, you should see a screen similar to one shown in Figure 2.1. Once you get the applet to run, you can experiment with it by changing the text and speed parameters. Just replace the strings listed after each **VALUE** statement. For example, if you changed the third HTML statement to be:

```
<PARAM NAME=TEXT VALUE="Buy stock in Java">
```

You would see the string "Buy stock in Java" scrolled across the screen. For the **SPEED** parameter, lower numbers produce slower but smoother animation and higher numbers create faster but sometimes jerky animation.

Even if you have created Web pages using HTML instructions, you might be unfamiliar with the Java applet-specific HTML tags. (If you need to brush up on the general techniques of creating Web pages with HTML, we suggest you get a copy of a good tutorial book such as The Coriolis Group's *Netscape and*

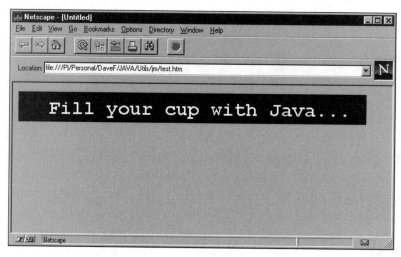

Figure 2.1

The TickerTape applet in action.

HTML Explorer.) The **<APPLET>** ... **</APPLET>** tag pair tells a Java-enabled Web browser, such as Netscape 2, that a specified applet should be loaded and played. Notice that in our example, one HTML line does this work for us:

```
<APPLET CODE=TickerTape.class WIDTH=600 HEIGHT=50>
```

The **CODE** parameter specifies the name of the applet—in this case it is the name of our file, *TickerTape.class.* If you used a different filename, you would need to change this instruction. The **WIDTH** and **HEIGHT** parameters specify the width and height of the window or "space" that will be used to play the applet. The dimensions are specified in units of screen pixels. Since our applet needs to simulate a ticker tape-like device, we've defined it to be very wide but short. The other HTML instructions, **<PARAM>**, are used to specify the parameters for our applet:

```
<PARAM NAME=TEXT VALUE="The Java TickerTape Applet...">
<PARAM NAME=SPEED VALUE="4">
```

Notice that each parameter has a name and a value. The name must correspond with the name of the parameter used in the Java applet. The **VALUE** clause handles the work of assigning the parameter a default value. Later in this chapter we'll show you how parameters are processed using special Java functions. If you change the values for either of these parameters and reload the HTML file, you'll see the effect of the changes immediately.

Where's the Main Program?

After taking a quick look at our applet, the first question you might have is where the heck is the main program? That is, which code is executed first? If you have experience programming with a language like C/C++ or Pascal, you're probably looking for a program entry point like this:

```
main()  // The starting point for a C++ program
{
    inputText = getParameter("TEXT");
    animSpeedString = getParameter("SPEED");
    animSpeed = Integer.parseInt(animSpeedString);
    im=createImage(size().width, size().height);
    ...
}
```

Don't look too hard because you won't find such a "main function" in a Java applet. Instead, Java applets really are designed to run "inside" another application—in our case the Netscape browser. You can think of an applet as if it were a plug-in or component. This means that the routines and methods in a Java applet are executed by the controlling program (the browser). Let's step through our applet to better understand how this process works.

The TickerTape applet contains a number of functions, which are actually called methods in Java. (This terminology is borrowed directly from C++.) Take a moment to look over the applet and you'll find methods like **init()**, **paintText()**, **start()**, **run()**, **stop()**, and so on. Some of these are standard Java applet methods (they have names and perform operations that are pre-defined); and others are user-defined (we made them up). When the applet runs, the browser running the applet knows which methods are used and in which order to call them. Figure 2.2 shows the order of how the methods are called. Notice, first that the browser calls the **init()** method. Each statement in **init()** executes until the method

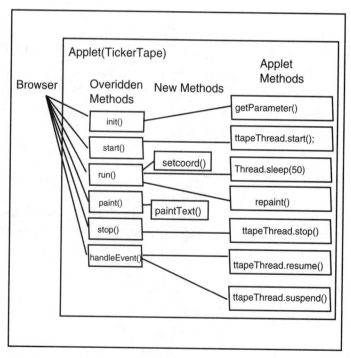

Figure 2.2

How the methods are controlled in the Java applet.

finishes. If you look closely, you'll see that **init()** doesn't call any of the other **TickerTape** class methods. What gives?

To understand what happens next, keep in mind that the browser is the controlling program—not the applet itself. After **init()** is called, the **start()** method is then called by the Web browser. **start()** sets up TickerTape as a thread. You'll learn more about threads later on, but for now you can think of a thread as a mechanism for handing off control. If the applet were not set up as a thread, it would run inefficiently and the browser performance would suffer as well. Once the TickerTape applet is set up as a thread, the browser will know what to do when events occur such as the mouse button being clicked, a window being moved, and so on.

After **start()** has done its job of setting up the thread, typically the **run()** method would be called next by the browser. This methods acts as a loop that keeps the program in motion—in other words, it drives the operations to make our text move across the screen. Table 2.1 provides a summary of each of the key methods used in the TickerTape applet. The methods like **paint()**, which are standard Java applet methods, can be redefined to perform different operations. For ex-

Table 2.1	Methods Used in the TickerTape Applet
Method	**Description**
init()	A standard Java applet method that is used to initialize variables and objects defined for the TickerTape applet.
paint()	A standard Java applet method that is called whenever a browser has recognized that something has changed, such as a window being moved or resized, text being drawn on a window, and so on.
paintText()	A user defined method that refreshes text for the ticker tape in a buffer.
start()	A standard Java applet method that turns the applet into a thread.
setcoord()	A user defined method that is called by the **run()** method at every program cycle to update the position of the text.
run()	A standard Java applet method that serves as the heart of the program. Without the **run()** method, the applet would not perform any actions.
update()	A standard Java applet method that calls the **paint()** method to update the screen.
handleEvent()	A standard Java applet method that process mouse activity.
stop()	A standard Java applet method that stops the thread, which in turn terminates the execution of the applet.

ample, in our TickerTape applet we redefine **paint()** to process updates to the screen in a more efficient way. We could add additional features (code) to this method to handle other tasks such as adding a border around the ticker tape, adding a frame counter, and so on.

Introducing Java Comments

Like any good programming language, Java allows you to include comments along with your programming statements. You can see Java's connection to C/C++ right off, since it supports both the C and C++ comment styles. For example:

```
int i; /* This is a C-style comment */

int i; // This is a C++-style comment
```

Java also provides a new type of comment syntax that can be used to automatically generate formatted documentation. This new syntax looks like this:

```
/** Documentation comment. Comments listed between these symbols will be
used to automatically create documentation. */
```

Back to our program, the first line of the code is actually just a comment that tells us about the program:

```
// TickerTape Applet
```

Although Java allows us to use any or all of these styles within a single program, we will only use the // notation in our TickerTape program. After all, we don't want to make things more complicated than they need to be.

What's in a Package?

The next two lines of our applet are used to reference *packages* that contain *classes* that contain the *methods* we wish to use. This may sound like a mouthful, but the concepts involved are actually quite simple. Here's the code in question:

```
import java.applet.*;
import java.awt.*;
```

Packages are used to group related classes for use in other programs. This is a direct extension of the object-oriented techniques that languages like C++ provide for programmers.

There are several class packages that come with Java. Table 2.2 provides the current set of them.

By default, every Java application imports the classes contained within the java.lang package, so you do not have to manually import this package.

The Import Statement for C Users

Using the **import** statement to include packages is similar in concept to using the **include** statement in C to include header files.

Java Note

If you look closely at our **import** statements in the TickerTape program, you'll notice that the * character is used. This character tells the Java byte-code compiler to use all the classes stored within the package. You could also specify which classes to use; but since you usually need many classes within a single package, it is easier to simply use the asterisk. Also, the Java compiler is smart enough to figure out which classes are used and which ones aren't so that using the asterisk does not eat up any additional memory.

In our program we import the **applet** package because we are creating an applet. We also need to import the **awt** package because we want to use its graphics

Table 2.2	Standard Java Classes
Java Class	**Description**
java.lang	Contains essential Java classes.
java.io	Contains classes used to perform input/output to different sources.
java.util	Contains utility classes for items such as tables and vectors.
java.net	Contains classes that aid in connecting over networks. These can be used in conjunction with java.io to read and write information to files over a network.
java.awt	Contains classes that let you write platform-independent graphic applications. It includes classes for creating buttons, panels, text boxes, and so on.
java.applet	Contains classes that let you create Java applets that will run within Java-enabled browsers.

capabilities. This package contains the classes we need so that we can display our ticker tape-like graphics.

The AWT package was developed to aid in creating windowed applications and applets. It does for Java what Visual C++ does for C. Instead of having to manually define graphical user elements like buttons, windows, and menus, and then manually having to write code to handle mouse events, the AWT package takes care of it for you.

The Mystery of the AWT Package

Now that you know a bit about the Java programming language, it's time for a little quiz. What does AWT stand for?

A. Another Window Toolkit

B. Abstract Window Types

C. Abstract Window Toolkit

D. Advanced Window Toolikit

E. Abstract Windowing Toolkit

The answer is C. (If you guessed right, you may have a future in Java programming after all.) According to the official AWT tutorial, this acrynom stands for the *Abstract Window Toolkit.* (Another Window Toolkit came in a close second.) We think all the extra names came about because the name got passed on from programmer to programmer without the aid of any official documentation. As people referred to the package, using different names, no one knew who was correct anymore.

Classes, Inheritance, and Interfaces

If you have done any programming in C++, you already know how important classes are. Java is no exception. Most of the Java programming work you will be doing involves writing classes from scratch and deriving more powerful classes from your existing classes.

To see how classes are defined in Java, let's return to our TickerTape program. After the two key packages have been included, we define our first class:

```
// TickerTape Class
public class TickerTape extends Applet implements Runnable {
    // Declare Variables
    String inputText;
    String animSpeedString;
    Color color = new Color(255, 255, 255);
    int xpos;
    ...
```

We're not showing the complete class here but it contains the following components:

- Definition
- Variables
- Methods

The first line of code that actually sets up the class definition is illustrated in Figure 2.3. Let's take a close look at each section.

Class Modifier   A class modifier tells the Java compiler how and where a class can be used. The two main types of classes are called *public* and *private*. A **public** class can be accessed from other packages, either directly or by using an **import** statement. If you omit the **public** modifier at the beginning of the class definition, the class would become private and use of the class would be limited to the package in which it is declared.

The two other modifiers that can be used to define classes are **abstract** and **final**. We'll cover these class modifiers in detail in Chapter 4.

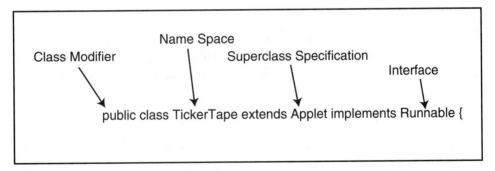

Figure 2.3

Setting up a class definition in Java.

Name Space   The name space in a class declaration is simply the name of the class. In our case the name space is "TickerTape."

Superclass   The keyword **extends** indicates that we are inheriting all of the methods, variables, and field declarations from the **Applet** class. **Applet** becomes the superclass of our TickerTape class. This means that we can use any of the methods and variables from the **Applet** class.

If we did not include the superclass specifier, the program would derive itself from the **Object** class by default.

Java Note

Applet Package vs. Applet Class

Don't get confused by the **applet** *package* and the **Applet** *class.* At the beginning of the program we imported the **applet** package with the **import** command. This gave us access to all the classes within the package, which in turn means that we can then subclass the **Applet** class.

The **applet** package has other classes in it that help in creating applets. The **Applet** class has methods in it that we *must* use in all applets.

Interface   An *interface* is a collection of method declarations, but without implementations. An interface simply sets up a template that all classes that use it must follow. For instance, if we set up an interface that has two methods, **start** and **stop**, then any class that implements that interface must have **start** and **stop** methods within it.

The interface **Runnable** is used here via the **implements** keyword. Interfaces solves some of the same problems that are solved by multiple-inheritance in C++. You can implement many interfaces if you want. Here's an example:

```
TickerTape extends Applet implements Runnable, Stoppable, Pausable
```

Once again, you *must* implement every method in the interface you are using. Interface **Runnable** contains only the method **run()**.

Types, Objects, and Constructors

Now that we have declared the class for our TickerTape applet we need to set up a few variables that we will need to store various strings, numbers, dimensions, and so on. Table 2.3 lists the basic types supported by the Java language.

Let's now use a few of these data types to declare our variables. These variables will be the ones that are used throughout our class, so we place them directly after the class declaration as shown here:

```
public class TickerTape extends Applet implements Runnable {
   String inputText;
   String animSpeedString;
   Color color = new Color(255, 255, 255);
   int xpos;
   int fontLength;
   int fontHeight;
   2int animSpeed;
   Font font;
   Thread ttapeThread = null;
   Image im;
   Graphics osGraphics;
   boolean suspended = false;
```

Let's take a few of these variable declarations and break them down into their components. As shown in Figure 2.4, a standard variable declaration consists of a data type, variable name, and optional value.

Table 2.3	The Basic Data Types Supported by Java
Data Type	**Description**
boolean	A true or false value. You cannot convert between booleans and any other basic types.
byte	8-bit signed value
short	16-bit signed value
char	16-bit unicode character
int	32-bit signed value
float	32-bit IEEE754 floating-point
double	64-bit IEEE754 floating-point
long	64-bit signed value

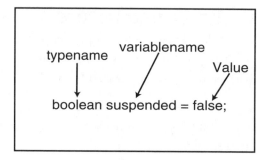

Figure 2.4

Standard Java variable declaration.

The *typename* in a standard declaration needs to be one of the basic Java types listed in Table 2.3. One potential problem to watch out for here is capitalization. Spelling boolean with a capital B can really cause some errors. With the current state of Java debuggers, don't expect them to help much.

The *variableName* can be any ASCII string. You can even make the variablename the same as the class name. Be careful though; this can get very confusing. Variable names are also case-sensitive. This means the variable String1 is different from the variable string1. You also cannot include spaces or any other whitespace characters in your variable names.

When you declare a variable, you can also assign it a value at the same time. This is a very useful feature that was introduced with the C language, which Java heavily steals from. You can even perform a calculation or call a method to obtain values while you are declaring a variable. However, the value sections of any declaration do not need to be set when they are declared—they can be given values later in your program. Here are some examples:

```
// declare a variable and assign a value
int xpos = 10;

// use a calculation in a declaration
int fontLength = 30 + xpos;

// call a method to obtain a value during a declaration
int fontHeight = getvalue();
```

Variables can also use modifiers like classes do. However, there are several more modifiers for variables, including **static**, **final**, **transient**, and **volatile**. We'll cover all of the variable modifiers in detail in Chapter 4.

VARIABLE DECLARATIONS USING A CONSTRUCTOR

If you look closely at the variable declarations in the TickerTape class, you'll see that most of them are quite simple. But there is one that looks a little different:

```
Color color = new Color(255, 255, 255);
```

In this declaration, a device called a constructor is used. The constructor actually serves as a special type of method that is responsible for initializing new objects. Constructors are used to create custom and/or complex objects other than the basic types. In this case, the **Color** constructor (a method in the AWT package) is passed the three integers (255,255,255). Then a value "java.awt.Color[r=255,g=255,b=255]" is returned to the variable **color**. The actual components used in this type of declaration are illustrated in Figure 2.5.

This constructor initializes an instance of the variable **color** that represents a color by its RGB values.

Thank Goodness for Garbage Collection

One of the biggest headaches in creating large programs with languages like C or C++ is keeping track of resources and disposing of them when they are not needed. An unruly C program that does not properly clean up after itself can quickly eat up a lot of memory (and a lot of your time trying to debug it). For example, if you write a C++ program that allocates a big block of memory for a dynamic data structure, but you forget to release the memory after the data structure is no longer used, your program could make a mess of things. Or if you use pointers in a program and you don't allocate, access, manage, or release them properly, you could end up spending a number of late nights debugging your code. The trouble with these type of resource allocation problems is that they

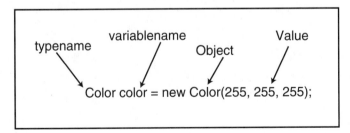

Figure 2.5

Using a constructor in a variable declaration.

are very difficult to detect. Anyone who is active in the software development industry is keenly aware of intermittent errors in their software that can cause their release dates to slip. Every year millions of dollars are spent and lost because of extensive software testing that is required to find the errors caused by troublesome pointers and mismanaged memory allocation.

So is there is a solution to this crippling problem? The answer is *garbage collection.* Garbage collection is not a new invention, recently created for Java programmers. It has been around for years; in fact, programmers who have used languages like Lisp, Smalltalk, and Prolog, have been writing amazing programs that really push this technology to the limit. The basic idea behind garbage collection is to offload the work of managing memory and other resources to the program itself. If memory is needed for a new data structure or object, the program automatically takes care of this task and automatically releases the resources when they are no longer needed. This frees the programmer from a number of complex tasks, such as declaring pointers to access memory, passing pointers as arguments to functions, setting up memory buffers to swap the contents of data structures, and so on.

Of course there is a price to pay for all of this convenience. Programming languages that use garbage collection tend to be bigger and run slower than programs written in "the programmer does it all by hand" languages such as C and C++.

In developing Java, the language designers at Sun wanted to make it as flexible yet robust as possible. They reasoned that a smart compiler, even for a language that has a syntax like C++, could figure out for itself which program elements require memory allocation and perform memory management operations automatically. In Java, memory taken up by objects, methods, and variables is allocated and then cleared when those items are no longer needed. This garbage collection was designed not only to make life easier for programmers but because it is required for creating programs that can run on many different platforms and allocate memory in the same way.

Using Methods

Now we're ready to get into the meat of our program by exploring the implementation section of the applet:

```
public void init(){
   inputText = getParameter("TEXT");
```

```
    animSpeedString = getParameter("SPEED");
    animSpeed = Integer.parseInt(animSpeedString);
    im=createImage(size().width, size().height);
    osGraphics = im.getGraphics();
    xpos = size().width;
    fontHeight = 4 * size().height / 5;
    font = new Font("Helvetica", 1, fontHeight);
}
```

We learned earlier that this code actually shows the definition of what is called a *method*. (We'll be looking at methods in more detail a little later.) The method defined here is named **init**(). As we discussed earlier, it is the starting point for all applets. *Remember that it is called by the browser whenever the applet is first loaded.* You can think of this method as serving a similar role to the one carried out by a **main**() function in a C program. When the applet is first loaded into a runtime environment like a Web browser, the program execution will begin with the first statement in the **init**() method.

The **public** modifier in front of this method tells us that this method may be called from any object, and the **void** modifier states that the applet will not return any values.

Init() performs a number of tasks. First, it loads in the two parameters used by the applet. Then, it calculates the animation speed for the ticker tape using the **SPEED** parameter. The remaining statements in this method are needed to set up variables to support the graphics and text fonts used in the applet. Let's look at all of this code in a little more detail.

PROCESSING PARAMETERS

Many times when you create applets you will want the user to be able to specify options such as font size or animation speed. If we were creating an application, instead of an applet, these values could be passed as command line arguments. Applets do not have command line arguments, but they do have parameters. As we introduced earlier, parameters are embedded in HTML tags that reside between the opening and closing **<APPLET>** tags like this:

```
<APPLET CODE=TickerTape.class Width=600 Height=50>
<PARAM NAME=TEXT VALUE="The Java TickerTape Applet...">
<PARAM NAME=SPEED VALUE="4">
</APPLET>
```

The idea behind parameters is very similar to arguments, but parameters allow you a little more flexibility. Since parameters have a name associated with them, they can be put in any order. It is also easier to determine if a parameter has been left out and if so, which one.

When a **getParameter**() method executes in a applet, the method searches a parameter list to locate a parameter with the corresponding **NAME** field. In our applet, we need to read in the text that will be displayed in the applet and a speed setting that effects how fast the text scrolls across the screen. Thus, notice that the **init**() method contains two calls to **getParameter**():

```
inputText = getParameter("TEXT");
animSpeedString = getParameter("SPEED");
```

After these methods are called, the variable **inputText** will contain the string "The Java TickerTape Applet..." and **animSpeedString** will contain the value "4." But there is one catch: *All parameters must be read in as strings.* Since the variable we declared for animation speed **animSpeed** in the **TickerTape** class is an integer

```
int animSpeed;
```

we need to convert the speed parameter from a string to its integer representation. To perform the conversion, we use the **parseInt**() method of the **Integer** class that resides in the java.lang package. (Make sure that you use the correct capitalization here, or you will get errors when you try and compile the program.) The code that performs this operation looks like this:

```
animSpeed = Integer.parseInt(animSpeedString);
```

Notice that the syntax for calling this method involves using the name of the **Integer** class. The **parseInt**() method takes a string as its argument and returns a 32-bit signed integer. For larger numbers you could use the **parseLong**() method that can return a 64-bit signed integer. The value of the converted string, 4, is stored in the variable **animSpeed**—right where we want it.

COMPLETING THE INITIALIZATIONS

To code our applet so that it provides smooth animation, we use a popular programming trick called *buffering.* The idea is that we don't want to write every pixel on the screen as changes occur. With buffering, we send data to a holding area that is constructed until we are ready to update the screen. Then, we blast the entire contents of the image buffer to the screen at once. To understand how this process works in more detail, see the sidebar *Double Buffering*.

Fortunately, an image buffer is easy to set in a Java applet. In fact, we only need a few lines of code. The following two lines in **init**() perform the work of setting up the image buffer component that will store all the changes we make to the graphics until we want to blast it onto the screen:

```
im=createImage(size().width, size().height);
osGraphics = im.getGraphics();
```

This code creates a graphics object called **im** with a width and height equal to the size of the applet. We use the **size().width** and **size().height** objects to return information about the applet's client space. In this case, **size().width** and **size().height** will always be equal to the width and height values we used when we called the applet in our HTML file:

```
<APPLET CODE=TickerTape.class Width=600 Height=50>
```

Our final bit of business for creating the buffer is to use the **getGraphics**() method to initialize the graphics and clear the buffer.

The next two lines of code in **init**() are used to set the values of the **xpos** and **fontHeight** variables.

```
xpos = size().width;
fontHeight = 4 * size().height / 5;
```

The **xpos** variable will be used to track the current position of the left side of the text. We start the applet with **xpos** equal to the width of the applet (**size().width**) so that as it starts, the text begins scrolling from off of the applet. Figure 2.6 shows how this process works for scrolling the text to the left.

The **fontHeight** variable is used to store the height of the text. In this case, we are setting the height of the text to be 80% of the height of the applet. By doing this, we allow the HTML programmer to change the size of the applet and have the size of the text reflect that change. You could also use another parameter to input the size of the text, but our method is simpler and saves a step or two. Figure 2.7 shows you how all the applet and text sizes correspond with each other.

Figure 2.6

Starting the text off of the visible part of the applet.

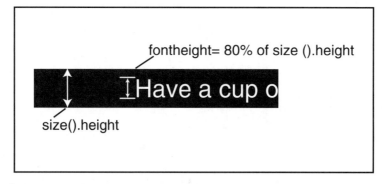

Figure 2.7

Coordinates in our applet.

The final line of code in **init()** is used to initialize our **font** object:

```
font = new Font("Helvetica", 1, fontHeight);
```

Recall that we already created this variable in our declaration section at the beginning of the applet (the **TickerTape** class) but we gave it no value. Here we are setting up the name of the font (Helvetica), the style (sum of constants PLAIN, BOLD, and/or ITALIC), and the size (points or pixels).

Notice also that we are using a constructor again. Recall that the **new** statement tells Java that we want a "new" object, in this case with all the characteristics of the standard **Font** class.

Java Note

Using Fonts with Java Applets

Here is something you should keep in mind when using different fonts with your Java applets: *Not all fonts will work with Java.* Be careful when you choose a font name that it is a standard font. You may have strange fonts on your system that are not available to everyone else, so choose them wisely. If your applet requests a font that is not present on the user's system, it will use a default font.

Methods and Method Overriding

As we've seen, methods are the object-oriented equivalent to functions in C. They are much more powerful, however, because they allow you to access the internal components of an object. For example, in our TickerTape applet, we use methods like **init()**, **paint()**, and **paintText()** to access some of the key data elements like **animSpeed** (the animation speed for a ticker tape), **font** (the font used to display text), and **xpos** (the position of the ticker tape text). Because of the object-oriented nature of the Java language, we are able to organize our programs in such a way that details can be hidden away and protected from being accessed by only those parts of the program that need to have access. In the world of object-oriented programming, this technique is called *encapsulation.*

But hiding details and controlling access is only part of the story. The real power of object-oriented programming comes from the ability to take existing code and derive new code from it. Most programmers spend way too much time writing the same functions or routines over and over again, changing them ever so slightly so that they can be used in different applications.

To take advantage of the potential of object-oriented programming, Java, like its C++ counterpart, supports a concept called *method overriding*. The idea behind method overriding is that you can take an existing method and derive a new one from it. The new method would have the same name as the original but its behavior—the actions it performs—could be entirely different.

As you've learned already, Java applets provide a number of methods that are predefined for you. Some of these include **init()**, **paint()**, **start()**, and **stop()**. When you create an applet, it becomes your job to decide which methods to override and how to make them do what you need.

Method Overriding with Classes

The technique of method overriding has quite an impact on how you use classes in Java to derive other classes. Whenever you "subclass" a class, you also have access to all the original class' methods. Many times though, the whole point of subclassing is to change how the class interacts or responds to certain events. For example, let's say you created a class to process mouse events. In particular, you could define a class that responds to a mouse click by performing the action of playing a sound, among other things. Now, maybe you want another class that will perform another action, such as displaying a graphic, when a mouse button is clicked. You could either create a new class and duplicate your work or use the sound class as a base class and simply use method overriding to create a new method to respond to the user input.

In the new class, all you have to do is create a method with the same name as the corresponding method in the superclass. Of course, you must change its behavior (how it reacts to the user input—displaying a graphic instead of playing sound).

When working with applets, you will be doing a lot of method overriding because the **Applet** class that you extend already has many methods built into it. Many of these methods perform little, if anything; but they need to be there to capture all the possible calls the browser may send.

INTRODUCING THE paint() METHOD

Now that you know a little about method overriding, we are ready to dig in and look at the **paint()** method. This method is called by the browser whenever the browser thinks something needs to be repainted. Events that might trigger the **paint()** method include displaying text or graphics, re-sizing a component, and so on. Since we don't "write" directly to our applet, it will never initiate the **paint()** method on its own; so we will call it later. We use method overriding to create our own **paint()** method that will handle all the painting chores that would usually be handled automatically by Java.

For our applet we only need two calls in the **paint()** method:

```
public void paint(Graphics g){
   paintText(osGraphics);
   g.drawImage(im, 0, 0, null);
}
```

The declaration of the argument **Graphics g** may look a little strange. It sets up the applet background to be printed to. (Java will set up the device context of the applet itself as **g**.) The first line of this method calls another method, **paintText**(), which prints the text onto the buffer image. The **paintText**() method is a *user-defined* method that takes a single argument. In this case that argument is the graphics object we want the text drawn onto—the **osGraphics** object.

Finally, we call the **drawImage**() method that copies the buffer data (**im**) onto the applet space on the browser (**g**) for the user to see.

Double Buffering

Double buffering is an extremely powerful concept that has helped make some of today's flicker-free animation and game play possible. It reduces flicker by performing all the graphics functions on a hidden image that resides in memory instead of drawing directly to the screen. Then, the entire image is displayed all at once instead of having to update the screen every time a new bit of graphics is drawn.

If we removed the double buffering technique from our applet, you would see the screen flicker every time the text moved even a little bit. (As an experiment, you might want to try changing the applet code so that the double buffering gets disabled.) If we were drawing any extra graphics or additional text, you would also see flickers for each of those events. These flashes and flickers occur because the screen is updated multiple times during the drawing of the object and the Applet class' **paint**() method clears the screen before it redraws it. With text, the screen can sometimes be redrawn for each letter! This causes the flicker and can actually slow things down if you are drawing many items.

Double buffering improves performance because the graphics can be drawn into memory faster than they can be drawn onto the screen. Even with the extra step of blasting the graphics to the screen, double buffering is still much faster. Figure 2.8 illustrates how double-buffering speeds display by reducing calls to the **paint()** method.

The double buffering technique we used in our TickerTape applet is very general, and you can apply it to many of the applets that you write that need to perform flicker free animation. We suggest you experiment with these concepts—you may come up some of your own for writing optimized applets.

Graphic Methods

Now that we are aware of the basics involved in overriding methods, let's return to our applet and explore the other methods used to perform all of the graphics drawing operations. Our next step is to see how the applet will print our text onto the image buffer. This work is accomplished by the user-defined **paintText**() method:

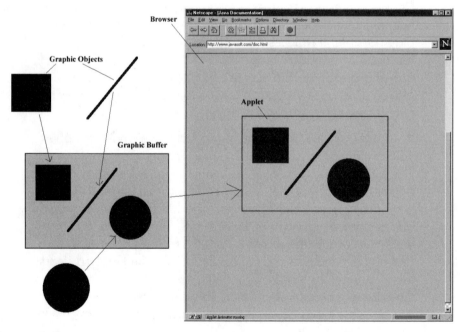

Figure 2.8
Double buffering the applet display to reduce flicker.

```
public void paintText(Graphics g){
   g.setColor(Color.black);
   g.fillRect(0, 0, size().width, size().height);
   g.clipRect(0, 0, size().width, size().height);
   g.setFont(font);
   g.setColor(color);
   FontMetrics fmetrics = g.getFontMetrics();
   fontLength = fmetrics.stringWidth(inputText);
   fontHeight = fmetrics.getHeight();
   g.drawString(inputText, xpos, size().height - fontHeight / 4);
   }
```

First, keep in mind that **paintText()** is a method that we created from scratch. In other words, we did not create this method by overriding one that already exists with Java.

This set of method calls found in **paintText()** start by setting the current pen color to black by using the **setColor()** method. Then, we call the **fillRect()** method to draw a filled rectangle that fills the applet. Next, comes the **clipRect()** method that tells Java to clip any data or graphics that are written outside the given boundaries, which in this case is the same as the size of the black rectangle. This set of initializations is illustrated in Figure 2.9.

Next we set the font of the graphics buffer equal to the font we set up in the **init()** method. We also need to change the pen color to something other than black so that our text shows up. For this task, we use the **color** object we set up earlier.

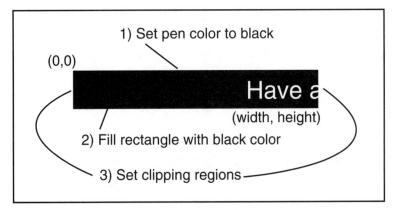

Figure 2.9

Setting up the rectangle for displaying the ticker tape text.

```
g.setFont(font);
g.setColor(color);
```

Now that we are set to print, we need to determine where to print. Recall that we previously initialized a variable named **xpos** to keep track of the text position. Thus, we can use this variable to tell us where to begin printing. Now we need to find out how tall and long the text we want to print is. We will use this data to center the text vertically and to tell us how long the text is so we can reset the location of the text when it is done scrolling.

To accomplish these tasks, we use the **FontMetrics** constructor. Using font metrics is an easy way to gather information about the physical characteristics of text as it is related to certain components at certain font sizes, types, and so on:

```
FontMetrics fmetrics = g.getFontMetrics();
fontLength = fmetrics.stringWidth(inputText);
fontHeight = fmetrics.getHeight();
```

To actually print the text onto the graphics buffer, we use the **drawString()** method. This method takes several arguments as shown:

```
g.drawString(inputText, xpos, size().height - fontHeight / 4);
```

First, we must tell **drawString()** what string we want to print. In this case, **inputText**. Next, we tell it where to start printing along the x-coordinate. Finally we send it the vertical component to tell it where the bottom of the text should be. Figure 2.10 illustrates how **drawString()** sets up the required components. Here, we want the height to be a quarter of the difference of the height of the applet and the height of the text. This does a nice job of centering at any applet size.

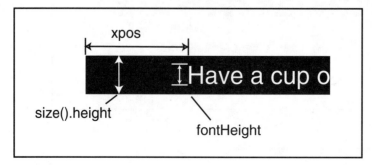

Figure 2.10

Placing text in the buffer with drawString().

In looking over the call to the **drawString**() method, don't get confused by the use of **g** as the name of our graphic object. In the **paint**() method we used the **g** variable to reference the applet's device context. Here you should notice that **g** is referencing the **osGraphics** object we created to act as an image buffer. This is an example of how scoping works with variables in Java. Scoping is basically the same as it is in other languages but we wanted to make sure you were aware of what is going on here. Since the **g** variable is not declared anywhere outside the methods, but simply declared within the method declaration as an argument, it is available only to the method where it was created.

Working with Threads

Now we get to a complex but powerful part of Java—*threads*. As we mentioned earlier, a thread is a special type of process that is used by a Java interpreter to control how a particular applet is executed. Fortunately, our TickerTape applet only needs a single thread to run smoothly, so our job is easy here. In Chapter 8 we will cover threads in much more detail, but for now we need to cover some basics so that you can follow the magic that is occurring in our TickerTape applet.

Here are the three methods that are responsible for handling our thread:

```
public void start(){
   if(ttapeThread == null){
      ttapeThread = new Thread(this);
      ttapeThread.start();
   }
}


public void run(){
   while(ttapeThread != null){
      try {Thread.sleep(50);} catch (InterruptedException e){}
      setcoord();
      repaint();
   }
}

public void stop(){
   if(ttapeThread != null)
      ttapeThread.stop();
   ttapeThread = null;
}
```

As you might have guessed, each of these methods is predefined in Java and they have been overridden by our applet. The **start()** method is called after the **init()** method finishes; **start()** actually belongs to the applet. It is called whenever the applet is started, such as when the Web page the applet is assigned to is first loaded and every time the page is referenced again from a Web browser.

The **start()** method checks to see if the thread for the applet has been created by asking if the thread is equal to a null value. (A null value indicates that it has not been created.) If the thread has not been created, Java creates a new thread using the **this** keyword to tell Java to turn the current applet class we are running into a thread. Then, **start()** calls the *start()* method of the thread to initiate its execution. We know this sounds weird! But make sure you understand that this **start()** method is different then the **start()** method of the applet. Otherwise, you might think this call will create an infinite loop.

The **run()** thread method is called repeatedly as the thread runs. It is the only method that we were required to have because of the use of the **runnable** interface:

```
public void run(){
    while(ttapeThread != null){
        try {Thread.sleep(50);} catch (InterruptedException e){}
        setcoord();
        repaint();
    }
}
```

We use the **sleep()** method to pause the thread for a few milliseconds to slow it down a little. This gives us a refresh rate of ten frames per second maximum. It also gives the thread time to check for mouse clicks.

We then increment the **xpos** object to facilitate animation by calling the user-defined **setcoord()** method. Here we also need to stop and check to see if the text has gone completely off the left edge of the applet. We do this by checking to see if **xpos** is less than negative **fontLength**:

```
public void setcoord(){
    xpos = xpos - animSpeed;
    if(xpos < -fontLength){
        xpos = size().width;
    }
}
```

Finally, we come to the **stop**() thread method, which is called whenever someone leaves the current Web page the applet is assigned to or otherwise closes the applet.

```
public void stop(){
   if(ttapeThread != null)
      ttapeThread.stop();
   ttapeThread = null;
}
```

In **stop**(), we check again to see if the thread is equal to **null**. If the thread is active, we stop it using the thread's **stop**() method. Then, we kill the thread by setting it equal to **null**. You may think that garbage collection would take care of killing the thread for us, but this is one case where you would not want to rely on garbage collection. Why? There may be situations where you want to keep a thread active as people move from page to page in the browser (of course, closing the browser will kill all applet threads).

At this point, the applet is ready to run. However, it would be nice to be able to start and stop the TickerTape with a mouse click, so let's add support for user input.

Threading Java Applets

Trying to understand, not to mention program, multitasking and threaded applications is tricky until you get a good grasp of the basics. One good place to start is to try to understand why threading is required in the first place.

Making your applets use threads is extremely important. If you don't use them and your applets are not very "friendly," the browser's performance can suffer dramatically. What causes this? Current browsers like Netscape 2.0 give applets as much of the system resources it can. So, if you create an applet that uses a loop to control its operations, the applet would suck up all the processing time the browser can give it. The net effect is that the browser becomes very unresponsive.

If you are creating a sample applet that only performs a single operation and requires little or no interaction, you may not need to use threading. For example, assume you are creating an applet that simply plays a sound when you click on something. When this applet is not playing a sound, it is not doing anything other than waiting. Thus, it is not using resources and it does not need to be a thread. However, if the same program had a loop that checked to see when the sound stopped playing, then displayed a message, the loop used to wait for the end of the sound could use considerable resources no matter how simple it is. Instead of using a controlling loop, you would want to set up the applet as a thread—just as we've done with the TickerTape applet.

In setting up threads the method you will use most is **run()**. This method is called by the browser every cycle. If you have multiple applets or multiple classes, each with its own **run()** method, they will all be called at the same time.

How does the browser know to call the **run()** method? That's where interfaces come in. If you want the **run()** method to be called by the browser then you *must* implement the **runnable** interface, as we've done with our TickerTape applet. By doing this, the browser can query the applet to see if it has implemented the **runnable** interface. If it has, the browser knows it can call the **run()** method of the applet.

Processing User Input

Allowing people to gain control over a program is a very powerful means of interacting with users. Simply being able to start and stop the TickerTape applet is enough to give people the feeling of interactivity rather than passive viewing.

Here is the code that adds user interaction to our applet:

```
public boolean handleEvent(Event evt) {
    if (evt.id == Event.MOUSE_DOWN) {
        if (suspended) {
            ttapeThread.resume();
        } else {
            ttapeThread.suspend();
        }
        suspended = !suspended;
    }
    return true;
}
```

This **handleEvent**() method can be used for everything from mouse clicks to key presses, to drag and drop functions. It is automatically called by the browser whenever it senses that the user is trying to interact with the applet. The argument **evt** is the crucial part of this method. It tells us what event has occurred and allows us to react accordingly.

Since we are filtering for all mouse clicks, we simply use an **if..then** statement to check and see it the **evt** argument ever equals **Event.MOUSE_DOWN**. When it does, we know that a button has been pressed. Since Java is a cross-platform language, we do not have the ability to determine which button was pressed, just that one was indeed pressed. If you are a Windows programmer only, it may be possible to create code in C that detects the other mouse button clicks and then passes that on to a Java program, but that's more than we can get into here.

When we receive the word that a button has been pressed, we check to see if the TickerTape is in motion (**suspended** is False or True). If it is not in motion, we start it by calling the thread's **suspend**() method. If it is already suspended, we use the thread's **resume**() method to start it back up again. Finally, we switch the **suspended** Boolean object to be the opposite of what it was before the mouse button was pressed.

One Last Thing

If this is your first time working with Java, we need to fill you in on how to compile your applet. The process of compiling takes your source code (.java file) and turns it into bytecodes (.class file). The bytecodes are an interim form of the code that can be read by many different operating systems. The bytecodes will then be used by the Java Virtual Machine (VM) built in to the Web browser that actually interprets the code and runs the program.

The Java compiler is activated by executing the JAVAC program. You also need to supply a few arguments including the name of the file you are compiling and whether or not you want to use the debugger.

Here are a few different compile commands that will all work for the TickerTape applet:

```
javac TickerTape     // Standard compile
javac TickerTape -g  // Compile with debugging information on
javac TickerTape -d c:\java  // Compiles the file to the c:\java directory
// Overrides your default classpath
javac TickerTape -classpath .;c:\java\classes
```

If you do not have the Java Development Kit (JDK), check the Javasoft site (http://www.javasoft.com). Read the online instructions to learn how to install the JDK. Check out the resource guide from Appendix A for more information.

That's It—Run It

Go ahead and compile the complete program, then run it. How does it look? Try changing the parameters and the applet size. Does the text scale to the height of the applet? If something does not work correctly go back and verify that all your code is correct, recompile, and run the applet again. Make sure that when you recompile an applet that you restart your browser. Many browsers, including Netscape 2.0, do not reload Java applets when you hit the reload button. They *do* however reread the HTML file. So, if you only made changes to the parameters or size of the applet then you do not need to restart the browser.

Well, what do you think? Is Java going to rule the world? We can't answer that, but in just a few pages we have shown you how to create a fairly useful applet that can be put to use immediately.

Now that we have hit many of the basics of Java programming, let's look at the details of the language. Over the next several chapters we will delve into the Java language and explore the details of its structure and syntax.

3

Java Language Fundamentals

Java Language Fundamentals

The language building blocks of Java are similar to those found in C++, but keep a close eye out because there are some subtle differences.

After following the ticker tape adventure in the previous chapter, you should now have a basic understanding of the Java language and its grammar—at least you'll know how to write a simple applet that can scroll text across the screen! Unfortunately, we covered a number of Java programming features very quickly, and we didn't get a chance to explain the main language features in sufficient detail. In this chapter and the ones that follow, we'll slow down the pace a little and uncover the key Java language features that you'll need to know to write useful Java programs. In particular, we'll explain the basic Java language components in this chapter—everything from comments to variable declarations. Then we'll move ahead and cover operators, expressions, and control structures in Chapter 4.

For those of you who are already familiar with programming, especially C or C++ programming, this chapter and Chapter 4 should serve as a good hands-on review. As we discuss Java, we'll point out the areas in which Java differs from other languages. If you don't have much experience using structured programming languages, this chapter will give you a good overview of the basic components required to make programming languages like Java come alive.

The actual language components featured in this chapter include:

- Comments
- Identifiers
- Keywords
- Data types
- Variable declarations

What Makes a Java Program?

Before we get into the details of each Java language component, let's stand back ten steps and look at how many of the key language components are used in the context of a Java program. Figure 3.1(shown later) presents a complete visual guide. Here we've highlighted components such as variable declarations, Java keywords, operators, literals, expressions, and control structures. As we work our way through the next two chapters, you'll learn how these components are defined and used.

In case you're wondering, the output for this program looks like this:

```
Hello John my name is Anthony
That's not my name!
Let's count to ten....
1 2 3 4 5 6 7 8 9 10
Now down to zero by two.
10 8 6 4 2 0
Finally, some arithmetic:
10 * 3.09 = 30.9
10 * 3.09 = 30 (integer cast)
10 / 3,09 = 3.23625
10 / 3.09 = 3 (integer cast)
```

Lexical Structure

The lexical structure of a language refers to the elements of code that make the code easy for us to understand, but have no effect on the compiled code. For example, all the comments you place in a program to help you understand how it works are ignored by the Java compiler. You could have a thousand lines of comments for a twenty line program and the compiled *bytecodes* for the program would be the same size if you took out all the comments. This does not mean that *all* lexical structures are optional. It simply means that they do not effect the bytecodes.

The lexical structures will discuss include:

• Comments

• Identifiers

• Keywords

• Separators

Comments

Comments make your code easy to understand, modify, and use. But adding comments to an application only after it is finished is not a good practice. More often than not, you won't remember what the code you write actually does after you get away from it for a while. Unfortunately, many programmers follow this time-honored tradition. We suggest you try to get in the habit of adding comments as you write your code.

Java supports three different types of comment styles. The first two are taken directly from C and C++. The third type of comment is a new one that can be used to automatically create class and method documentation.

COMMENT STYLE #1

```
/* Comments here... */
```

This style of commenting comes to us directly from C. Everything between the initial slash-asterisk and ending asterisk-slash is ignored by the Java compiler. This style of commenting can be used anywhere in a program, even in the middle of code (not a good idea). This style of commenting is useful when you have multiple lines of comments because your comment lines can wrap from one line to the next, and you only need to use one set of the /* and */ symbols. Examples:

```
/*
This program was written by Joe Smith.
It is the greatest program ever written!
*/

while (i <= /* comments can be placed here */ maxnum)
{
   total += i;
   i++;
}
```

In the second example, the comment line is embedded within the program statement. The compiler skips over the comment text, and thus the actual line of code would be processed as:

```
while (i <= maxnum)
...
```

```
/**
 * Sample Java Application                    ——— unique Java style comment
 * @author Anthony Potts
 * @version 1.0
 */                          ┌— superclass
                                                    ——— standard C++ style comment
class Test extends Object { // Begin Test class
    // Define class variables
    static int i = 10;                  ——— standard data type
    static final double d = 3.09;       ——— variable

                                        ——— literal

    /*
    The main() method is automatically called when
    the program is run. Any words typed after the program
    name when it is run are placed in the args[] variable
    which is an array of strings.
    For this program to work properly, atleast one word must
    be typed after the program name or else an error will occur.
    */
    public static void main(String args[]) {
        Test thisTest = new Test(); // Create instance (object) of class
        String myName = "Anthony";              ——— declaration and assignment
        boolean returnValue;                ——— assignment operator

                                                    ——— string data type

        System.out.println("Hello " + args[0] + " my name is " + myName);


        if(thisTest.sameName(args[0], myName)) {
            System.out.println("Your name is the same as mine!");
        } else {
            System.out.println("That's not my name!");
        }


        System.out.println("Let's count to ten....");

                                            ——— increment operator
        for (int x = 1; x < 11; x++) {
            System.out.print(x + " ");
        }                                       ——— expression
```

variable declarations

if-then-else control structure

while control statement —

logical expression

```
    System.out.println("\nNow down to zero by two.");

    while ( i > -1) {
        System.out.print(i + " ");
        i -= 2;
    }

    System.out.println("\nFinally, some arithmetic:");

    thisTest.doArithmetic();———— method call
}

// This method compares the two names sent to it and
// returns true if they are the same and false if they are not
public boolean sameName(String firstName, String secondName) {
    if (firstName.equals(secondName)) {
        return true;
    } else {
        return false;
    }
}

// This method performs a few computations and prints the result
public void doArithmetic(){
    i = 10;
    System.out.println(i + " * " + d + " = " + (i * d));
    System.out.println(i + " * " + d + " = " +
                            (int)(i * d) + " (Integer)");
    System.out.println(i + " / " + d + " = " + (i / d));
    System.out.println(i + " / " + d + " = " +
                            (int)(i / d) + " (Integer)");
    }
} // End of class
```

method modifier — `public`

returns value to calling class

assignment expression

Figure 3.1

A visual guide to the key Java language components.

Programmers occasionally use this style of commenting while they are testing and debugging code. For example, you could comment out part of an equation or expression:

```
sum = i /* + (base - 10) */ + factor;
```

COMMENT STYLE #2

```
// Comment here...
```

This style of commenting is borrowed from C++. Everything after the double slash marks is ignored by the Java compiler. The comment is terminated by a line return, so you can't use multiple comment lines unless you start each line with the double-slash. Examples:

```
// This program was written by Joe Smith.
// It is the greatest program ever written!

while (i <= // this won't work maxnum)
{
    total += i;
    i++;
}

base = 20;
// This comment example also won't work because the Java
    compiler will treat this second line as a line of code
value = 50;
```

The comment used in the second example won't work like you might intend because the remainder of the line of code would be commented out (everything after i <=). In the third example, the second comment line is missing the starting // symbols, and the Java compiler will get confused because it will try to process the comment line as if it were a line of code. Believe it or not, this type of commenting mistake occurs often—so watch out for it!

COMMENT STYLE #3

```
/** Doc Comment here... */
```

This comment structure may look very similar to the C style of commenting, but that extra asterisk at the beginning makes a huge difference. Of course, remember that only one asterisk must be used as the comment terminator. The

Java compiler still ignores the comment; but another program called JAVADOC.EXE that ships with the Java Development Kit uses these comments to construct HTML documentation files that describe your packages, classes, and methods as well as all the variables they use.

Let's look at the third style of commenting in more detail. If implemented correctly and consistently, this style of commenting can provide you with numerous benefits. Figure 3.2 shows what the output of the JAVADOC program looks like when run on a typical Java source file.

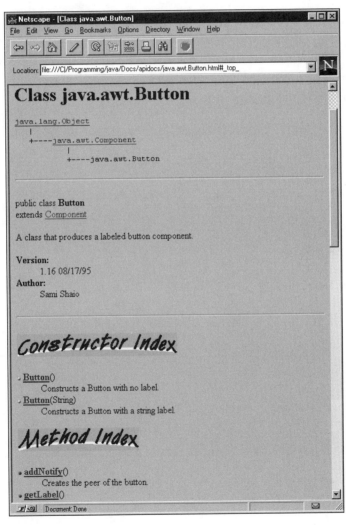

Figure 3.2

Sample output from the JAVADOC program.

If you have ever looked at the Java API documentation on Sun's Web site, Figure 3.2 should look familiar to you. In fact, the entire API documentation was created this way.

JAVADOC will work if you have created comments or not. Figure 3.3 shows the output from this simple application:

```
class HelloWorld {
    public static void main(String args[]) {
        System.out.println("Hello World");
    }
}
```

To add a little more information to our documentation, all we have to do is add this third style of comments. If we change the little HelloWorld application and add a few key comments, the code will look like this:

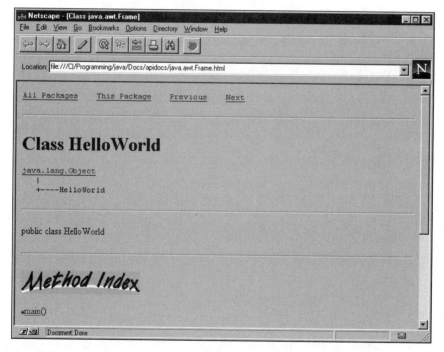

Figure 3.3

Simple output from the JAVADOC program.

```
/**
 * Welcome to HelloWorld
 * @author Anthony Potts
 * @version 1.1
 * @see java.lang.System
 */
class helloworld {
    /**
     * Main method of helloworld
     */
    public static void main(String args[]) {
        System.out.println("Hello World!");
    }
}
```

If you now run JAVADOC, the browser will display what you see in Figure 3.4. As you can see, this gives us much more information. This system is great for producing documentation for public distribution. Just like all comments though, it is up to you to make sure that the comments are accurate and plentiful enough to be helpful. Table 3.1 lists the tags you can use in your class comments.

Identifiers

Identifiers are the names used for variables, classes, methods, packages, and interfaces to distinguish them to the compiler. In the sample program from Chapter 2 the identifier for the applet's class was **TickerTape**. We also used identifiers like **fontHeight** and **fontWidth** to name some of the variables.

Identifiers in the Java language should always begin with a letter of the alphabet, either upper or lower case. The only exceptions to this rule are the underscore symbol (_) and the dollar sign ($), which may also be used. If you try to use any other symbol or a numeral as the initial character, you will receive an error.

After the initial character you are allowed to use numbers, but not all symbols. You can also use almost all of the characters from the Unicode character set. If you are not familiar with the Unicode character set or you get errors, we suggest that you stick with the standard alphabetic characters.

The length of an identifier is basically unlimited. We managed to get up to a few thousand characters before we got bored. It's doubtful you will ever need nearly that many characters, but it is nice to know that the Java compiler won't limit

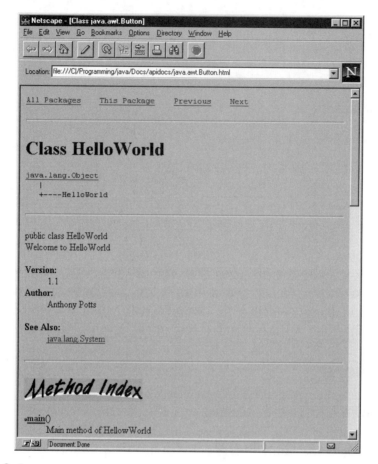

Figure 3.4
The new JAVADOC output.

you if you want to create long descriptive names. The only limit you may encounter involves creating class names. Since class names are also used as file names, you need to create names that will not cause problems with your operating system or anyone who will be using your program.

You must also be careful not to use any of the special Java keywords listed in the next section. Here are some examples of valid identifiers:

```
HelloWorld     $Money      TickerTape
_ME2           Chapter3    ABC123
```

Table 3.1 Tags Used in Class Comments

Tag	Description
@see *classname*	Adds a hyperlinked "See Also" to your class. The *classname* can be any other class.
@see *fully-qualified-classname*	Also adds a "See Also" to the class, but this time you need to use a fully qualified class name like "java.awt.window."
@see *fully-qualified-classname#methodname*	Also adds a "See Also" to the class, but now you are pointing to a specific method within that class.
@version *version-text*	Adds a version number that you provide. The version number can be numbers or text.
@author *author-name* -	Adds an author entry. You can use multiple author tags.
	The tags you can use in your method comments include all of the "@see" tags as well as the following:
@param *paramter-name description...*	Used to show which parameters the method accepts. Multiple "@param" tags are acceptable.
@return *description...*	Used to describe what the method returns.
@exception *fully-qualified-classname description...*	Used to add a "throw" entry that describes what type of exceptions this method can throw. Multiple "@exception" tags are acceptable. (Don't worry about exceptions and throws too much yet. We will discuss these in detail in Chapter 7.)

And here are some examples of invalid identifiers:

```
3rdChapter     #Hello    -Main
```

COMMON ERRORS WITH USING IDENTIFIERS

As you are defining and using identifiers in your Java programs, you are bound to encounter some errors from time-to-time. Let's look at some of the more common error messages that the Java compiler displays. Notice that we've included the part of the code that is responsible for generating the error, the error message, as well as a description of the message so that you can make sense of it.

Code Example:

```
public class 1test {
}
```

Error Message:

```
D:\java\lib\test.java:1: Identifier expected.
```

Description:

An invalid character has been used in the class identifier. You will see this error when the first character is invalid (especially when it is a number).

Code Example:

```
public class te?st {
}
```

Error Message:

```
D:\java\lib\test.java:1: '{' Expected
```

Description:

This is a common error that occurs when you have an invalid character in the middle of an identifier. In this case, the question mark is invalid, so the compiler gets confused where the class definition ends and its implementation begins.

Code Example:

```
public class #test {
}
```

Error Message:

```
D:\java\lib\test.java:1: Invalid character in input.
```

Description:

Here, the error stems from the fact that the initial character is invalid.

Code Example:

```
public class catch {
}
```

Error Message:

```
D:\java\lib\test.java:1: Identifier expected.
```

Description:

This error shows up when you use a protected keyword as an identifier.

Keywords

In Java, like other languages, there are certain *keywords* or "tokens" that are reserved for system use. These keywords can't be used as names for your classes, variables, packages, or anything else. The keywords are used for a number of tasks such as defining control structures (*if, while,* and *for*) and declaring data types (*int, char,* and *float*). Table 3.2 provides the complete list of the Java keywords.

Table 3.2	Java Language Keywords
Keyword	**Description**
abstract	Class modifier
boolean	Used to define a boolean data type
break	Used to break out of loops
byte	Used to define a byte data type
byvalue *	Not implemented yet
cast	Used to translate from type to type
catch	Used with error handling
char	Used to define a character data type (16-bit)
class	Used to define a class structure
const *	Not implemented yet
continue	Used to continue an operation
default	Used with the switch statement
do	Used to create a do loop control structure
Double	Used to define a floating-point data type (64-bit)
else	Used to create an else clause for an if statement
extends	Used to subclass
final	Used to tell Java that this class can not be subclassed
finally that	Used with exceptions to determine the last option before exiting. It guarantees code gets called if an exception does or does not happen.
float	Used to define a floating-point data type (32-bit)
for	Used to create a for loop control structure
future *	Not implemented yet
generic *	Not implemented yet
goto *	Not implemented yet
if	Used to create an if-then decision-making control structure
implements	Used to define which interfaces to use
import	Used to reference external Java packages
inner	Used to create control blocks
instanceof	Used to determine if an object is of a certain type
int	Used to define an integer data type (32-bit values)
interface	Used to tell Java that the code that follows is an interface

continued

Table 3.2	Java Language Keywords (Continued)
long	Used to define an integer data type (64-bit values)
native	Used when calling external code
new	Operator used when creating an instance of a class (an object)
null	Reference to a non-existent value
operator *	Not implemented yet
outer	Used to create control blocks
package	Used to tell Java what package the following code belongs to
private	Modifier for classes, methods, and variables
protected	Modifier for classes, methods, and variables
public	Modifier for classes, methods, and variables
rest *	Not implemented yet
return	Used to set the return value of a class or method
short	Used to define an integer data type (16-bit values)
static	Modifier for classes, methods, and variables
super	Used to reference the current class' parent class
switch	Block statement used to pick from a group of choices
synchronized	Modifier that tells Java that only one instance of a method can be run at one time. It keeps Java from running the method a second time before the first is finished. It is especially useful when dealing with files to avoid conflicts.
this	Used to reference the current object
throw	Statement that tells Java what exception to pass on an errors
transient	Modifier that can access future Java code
try	Operator that is used to test for exceptions in code
var *	Not implemented yet
void	Modifier for setting the return value of a class or method to nothing
volatile	Variable modifier
while	Used to create a while loop control structure.

The words marked with an asterisk (*) are not currently used in the Java language, but you still can't use them to create your own identifiers. More than likely they will be used as keywords in future versions of the Java language.

Literals

Literals are the values that you assign when entering explicit values. For example, in an assignment statement like this:

```
i = 10;
```

the value 10 is a literal. But do not get literals confused with types. Even though they usually go hand in hand, literals and types are not the same.

Types are used to define what type of data a variable can hold, while literals are the values that are actually assigned to those variables.

Literals come in three flavors: numeric, character, and boolean. Boolean literals are simply True and False

NUMERIC LITERALS

Numeric literals are just what they sound like—numbers. We can subdivide the numeric literals further into *integers* and *floating-point* literals.

Integer literals are usually represented in *decimal* format although you can use the *hexadecimal* and octal format in Java. If you want to use the hexadecimal format, your numbers need to begin with an 0x or 0X. Octal integers simply begin with a zero (0).

Integer literals are stored differently depending on their size. The **int** data type is used to store 32-bit integer values ranging from -2,147,483,648 to 2,147,483,648 (decimal). If you need to use even larger numbers, Java switches over to the **long** data type, which can store 64 bits of information for a range of - 9.223372036855e+18 to 9.223372036855e+18. This would give you a number a little larger than 9 million trillion—enough to take care of the national debt! To specify a **long** integer, you will need to place an "l" or "L" at the end of the number. Don't get confused by our use of the terms **int** and **long**. There are many other integer data types used by Java, but they all use **int** or **long**literals to assign values. Table 3.3 provides a summary of the two integer literals.

Table 3.3 Summary of Integer Literals		
Integer Literals Ranges	**Negative Minimum**	**Positive Maximum**
int data type	-2,147,483,648	2,147,483,648
long data type	-9.223372036855e+18	9.223372036855e+18

Here are some examples of how integer literals can be used to assign values in Java statements:

```
int i;
i = 1;  // All of these literals are of the integer type
i= -9;
i = 1203131;

i = 0xA11;  // Using a hexadecimal literal
i = 07543;  // Using an octal literal

i = 4.5;   // This would be illegal because a floating-point
          // literal can't be assigned to an integer type
long lg;
lg = 1L;     // All of these literals are of the long
          // integer type
lg = -9e15;
lg = 7e12;
```

The other type of numeric literal is the floating-point literal. Floating-point values are any numbers that have anything to the right of the decimal place. Similar to integers, floating-point values have 32-bit and 64-bit representations. Both data types conform to IEEE standards. Table 3.4 provides a summary of the two floating-ponit literals.

Here are some examples of how floating-point literals can be used to assign values in Java statements:

```
float f;
f = 1.3;  // All of these literals are of the floating-point
        // type float (32-bit)
f = -9.0;
f = 1203131.1241234;


double d;
d = 1.0D;  // All of these literals are of the floating-
        // point type double(32-bit)
d = -9.3645e235;
d = 7.0001e52D;
```

Table 3.4 Summary of Floating-Point Literals		
Floating-Point Ranges	**Negative Minimum**	**Positive Maximum**
float data type	1.40239846e-45	3.40282347e38
double data type	4.94065645841246544e-324	1.79769313486231570e308

CHARACTER LITERALS

The second type of literal that you need to know about is the *character literal.* Character literals include single characters and strings. Single character literals are enclosed in single quotation marks while string literals are enclosed in double quotes.

Single characters can be any one character from the Unicode character set. There are also a few special two-character combinations that are non-printing characters but perform important functions. Table 3.5 shows these special combinations.

The string character literal are any number of characters enclosed in The character combinations from Table 3.5 also apply to strings. Here are some examples of how character and string literals can be used in Java statements:

Table 3.5 Special Character Combinations in Java		
Character Combination	**Standard Designation**	**Description**
\	<newline>	Continuation
\n	NL or LF	New Line
\b	BS	Backspace
\r	CR	Carriage Return
\f	FF	Form Feed
\t	HT	Horizontal Tab
\\	\	Backslash
\'	'	Single Quote
\"	"	Double Quote
\xdd	0xdd	Hex Bit Pattern
\ddd	0ddd	Octal Bit Pattern
\uddd	0xdddd	Unicode Character

```
char ch;
ch = 'a';   // All of these literals are characters
ch = \n;    // Assign the newline character
ch = \';    // Assign a single quote
ch = \x30;  // Assign a hexadecimal character code

String str;
str = "Java string";
```

Operators

Operators are used to perform computations on one or more variables or objects. You use operators to add values, comparing the size of two numbers, assigning a value to a variable, incrementing the value of a variable, and so on. Table 3.6 lists the operators used in Java. Later in this chapter, we'll explain in detail how each operator works; and we'll also explain operator precedence.

Table 3.6 Operators Used in Java

Operator	Description
+	Addition
-	Subtraction
*	Multiplication
/	Division
%	Modulo
++	Increment
—	Decrement
>	Greater than
>=	Greater than or equal to
<	Less than
<=	Less than or equal to
==	Equal to
!=	Not equal to
!	Logical NOT
&&	Logical AND
||	Logical OR
&	Bitwise AND

continued

Table 3.6	Operators Used in Java (Continued)
^	Bitwise exclusive OR
|	Bitwise OR
~	Bitwise complement
<<	Left shift
>>	Right shift
>>>	Zero fill right shift
=	Assignment
+=	Assignment with addition
-=	Assignment with subtraction
*=	Assignment with multiplication
/=	Assignment with division
%=	Assignment with modulo
&=	Assignment with bitwise AND
|=	Assignment with bitwise OR
^=	Assignment with bitwise exclusive OR
<<=	Assignment with left shift
>>=	Assignment with right shift
>>>=	Assignment with zero fill right shift

Separators

Separators are used in Java to delineate blocks of code. For example, you use curly brackets to enclose a method's implementation, and you use parentheses to enclose arguments being sent to a method. Table 3.7 lists the seperators used in Java.

Table 3.7	Separators Used in Java
Separator	**Description**
( )	Used to define blocks of arguments
[ ]	Used to define arrays
{ }	Used to hold blocks of code
,	Used to separate arguments or variables in a declaration
;	Used to terminate lines of contiguous code

Types and Variables

Many people confuse the terms *types* and *variables*, and use them synonymously. They are, however, not the same. Variables are basically buckets that *hold information*, while types *describe what type of information* is in the bucket.

A variable must have both a type and an identifier. Later in this chapter we will cover the process of declaring variables. For now, we just want to guide you through the details of how you decide which types to use and how to use them properly.

Similar to literals, types can be split into several different categories including the numeric types—**byte**, **short**, **int**, **long**, **float**, and **double**—and the **char** and **boolean** types. We will also discuss the string type. Technically, the string type is not a type—it is a class. However, it is used so commonly that we decided to include it here.

All of the integer numeric types use signed two's-complement integers for storing data. Table 3.8 provides a summary of the ranges for each of the key Java data types.

byte

The **byte** type can be used for variables whose value falls between -256 and 255. **byte** types have an 8-bit length. Here are some examples of byte values:

```
-7        5        238
```

short

The **short** numeric type can store values ranging from -32768 to 32767. It has a 16-bit depth. Here are some examples:

```
-7       256      -29524
```

Table 3.8	Summary of the Java Data Types	
Data Type	**Negative Minimal**	**Positive Maximal**
byte	-256	255
short	-32768	32767
int	-2147483648	2147483647
long	-9223372036854775808	9223372036854775807
float	1.40239846e-45	3.40282347e38
double	4.94065645841246544e-324	1.79769313486231570e308
boolean	False	True

int

The **int** data type takes the **short** type to the next level. It uses a 32-bit signed integer value that takes our minimal and maximal value up to over 2 billion. Because of this tremendous range, it is one of the most often used data types for integers.

Often, unskilled programmers will use the **int** data type even though they don't need the full resolution that this data type provides. If you are using smaller integers, you should consider using the **short** data type. The rule of thumb to follow is *if you know exactly the range of values a certain variable will store, use the smallest data type possible.* This will let your program use less memory and therefore run faster, especially on slower machines or machines with limited RAM.

Here are some examples of **int** values:

```
-7      256     -29523234      1321412422
```

long

The **long** data type is the mother of all integer types. It uses a full 64-bit data path to store values that reach up to over 9 million trillion. But be extremely careful when using variables of the **long** type. If you start using many of them or God forbid, an array of **long**s, you can quickly eat up a ton of resources.

Java Note

The Danger of Using long

Java provides useful garbage collection tools, so when you are done with these large data types, they will be disposed of and their resources reclaimed. But if you are creating large arrays of **long** integers you could really be asking for trouble. For example, if you created a two-dimensional array of **long** integers that had a 100x100 grid, you would be using up about 100 kilobytes of memory.

Here are some examples of **long** values:

```
-7      256     -29523234      1.835412e15      -3e18
```

float

The **float** data type is one of two types used to store floating-point values. The **float** type is compliant with the IEEE 754 conventions. The floating-point types of Java can store gargantuan numbers. We do not have enough room on the page to physically show you the minimal and maximal values the **float** data type can store, so we will use a little bit of tricky sounding lingo taken from the Java manual.

"The finite nonzero values of type **float** are of the form s * m * 2e , where s is +1 or -1, m is a positive integer less than 2^24 and e is an integer between -149 and 104, inclusive."

Whew, that's a mouthful. Here are a few examples to show you what the **float** type might look like in actual use:

```
-7F    256.0  -23e34    23e100
```

double

As if the **float** type could not hold enough, the **double** data type gives you even bigger storage space. Let's look again at Sun's definition of the possible values for a **double**.

"The finite nonzero values of type **float** are of the form s * m * 2e , where s is +1 or -1, m is a positive integer less than 2^53 and e is an integer between -1045 and 1000, inclusive."

Again, you can have some truly monstrous numbers here. But when you start dealing with hard core programming, this type of number becomes necessary from time to time, so it is wise to understand its ranges. Here are a few examples:

```
-7.0D  256.0D -23e424 23e1000
```

boolean

In other languages, the **boolean** data type has been represented by an integer with a nonzero or zero value to represent True and False, respectively. This method works well because it gives the user the ability to check for all kinds of values and perform expression like this:

```
x=2;
if x then...
```

This can be handy when performing parsing operations or checking string lengths. In Java, however, the **boolean** data type has its own True and False literals that do not correspond to other values. In fact, as you will learn later in this chapter, Java does not even allow you to perform casts between the **boolean** data type and any others. There are ways around this limitation that we will discuss in a few pages when we talk about conversion methods.

char

The **char** data type is used to store single characters. Since Java uses the Unicode character set, the **char** type needs to be able to store the thousands of characters, so it uses a 16-bit signed integer. The **char** data type has the ability to be cast or converted to almost all of the others, as we will show you in the next section.

string

The **string** type is actually not a primitive data type; it is a class all its own. We decided to talk about it a little here because it is used so commonly that it might as well be considered a primitive. In C and C++, strings are stored in arrays of chars. Java does not use the **char** type for this but instead has created its own class that handles strings. In Chapter 5, when we get into the details of declaring variables within classes, you will see the difference between declaring a primitive variable and declaring an instance of a class type.

One big advantage to using a class instead of an array of **char** types is that we are more or less unlimited in the amount of information we want to place in a string variable. In C++, the array of chars was limited, but now that limitation is taken care of within the class, where we do not care how it is handled.

Variable Declarations

Declaring variables in Java is very similar to declaring variables in C/C++ as long as you are using the primitive data types. As we said before, almost everything in Java is a class—except the primitive data types. We will show you how to instantiate custom data types (including strings) in Chapter 5. For now, let's look at how primitive data types are declared.

Here is what a standard declaration for a primitive variable might look like:

```
int i;
```

We have just declared a variable "i" to be an integer. Here are a few more examples:

```
byte i, j;
int a=7, b = a;
float f = 1.06;
String name = "Tony";
```

These examples illustrate some of the things you can do while declaring variables. Let's look at each one individually.

```
int i;
```

This is the most basic declaration, with the data type followed by the variable you are declaring.

```
byte i, j;
```

In this example, we are declaring two byte variables at one time. There is no limit to the number of variables you can declare this way. All you have to do is add a comma between each variable you wish to declare of the given type, and Java takes care of it for you.

You also have the ability to assign values to variables as you declare them. You can even use a variable you are declaring as part of an expression for the declaration of another variable in the same line. Before we confuse you more, here is an example:

```
int i = 1;
int j = i, k= i + j;
```

Here we have first declared a variable **i** as **int** and assigned it a value of 1. In the next line, we start by declaring a variable **j** to be equal to **i**. This is perfectly legal. Next, on the same line, we declare a variable **k** to be equal to **i** plus **j**. Once again, Java handles this without a problem. We could even shorten these two statements to one line like this:

```
int i = 1, j = i, k= i + j;
```

One thing to watch out for is using variables *before* they have been declared. Here's an example:

```
int j = i, k= i + j;  // i is not defined yet
int i = 1;
```

This would cause an "undefined variable" error because Java does not know to look ahead for future declarations. Let's look at another example:

```
float f = 1.06;
```

Does this look correct? Yes, but it's not. This is a tricky one. By default, Java assumes that numbers with decimal points are of type **double**. So, when you try and declare a **float** to be equal to this number, you receive the following error:

```
Incompatible type for declaration. Explicit cast needed to convert double
to float.
```

Sounds complicated, but all this error message means is that you need to explicitly tell Java that the literal value 1.06 is a **float** and not a **double**. There are two ways to accomplish this. First, you can *cast* the value to a **float** like this:

```
float f = (float)1.06;
```

This works fine, but can get confusing. Java also follows the convention used by other languages of placing an "f" at the end of the literal value to indicate explicitly that it is a float. This also works for the double data type, except that you would use a "d." (By the way, capitalization of the f and d does not make a difference.)

```
float f = 1.06f;
double d = 1.06d;
```

You should realize that the "d" is not needed in the **double** declaration because Java assumes it. However, it is better to label all of your variables when possible, especially if you are not sure.

We will cover variables and declarations in more detail in Chapter 5, but you should have enough knowledge now to be able to run a few basic programs and will delve deeper into the Java fundamentals and look at operators, expressions, and control statements.

Using Arrays

It's difficult to imagine creating any large application or applet without having an array or two. Java uses arrays in a much different manner than other languages. Instead of being a structure that holds variables, arrays in Java are actually objects that can be treated just like any other Java object.

The powerful thing to realize here is that because arrays are objects that are derived from a class, they have methods you can call to retrieve information about the array or to manipulate the array. The current version of the Java language only supports the **length** method, but you can expect that more methods will be added as the language evolves.

One of the drawbacks to the way Java implements arrays is that they are only one dimensional. In most other languages, you can create a two-dimensional array by just adding a comma and a second array size. In Java, this does not work. The way around this limitation is to create an array of arrays. Because this is easy to do, the lack of built-in support for multi-dimensional arrays shouldn't hold you back.

Declaring Arrays

Since arrays are actually instances of classes (objects), we need to use constructors to create our arrays much like we did with strings. First, we need to pick a variable name and declare it as an array object and also specify which data type the array will hold. Note that an array can only hold a single data type—you can't mix strings and integers within a single array. Here are a few examples of how array variables are declared:

```
int intArray[];
String Names[];
```

As you can see, these look very similar to standard variable declarations, except for the brackets after the variable name. You could also put the brackets after the data type if you think this approach makes your declarations more readable:

```
int[] intArray;
String[] Names;
```

Sizing Arrays

There are three ways to set the size of arrays. Two of them require the use of the **new** operator. Using the **new** operator initializes all of the array elements to a default value. The third method involves filling in the array elements with values as you declare it.

The first method involves taking a previously declared variable and setting the size of the array. Here are a few examples:

```
int intArray[];          // Declare the arrays
String Names[];

intArray[] = new int[10];      // Size each array
Names[] = new String[100];
```

Or, you can size the array object when you declare it:

```
int intArray[] = new int[10];
String Names[] = new String[100];
```

Finally, you can fill in the array with values at declaration time:

```
String Names[] = {"Tony", "Dave", "Jon", "Ricardo"};
int[] intArray = {1, 2, 3, 4, 5};
```

Accessing Array Elements

Now that you know how to initialize arrays, you'll need to learn how to fill them with data and then access the array elements to retrieve the data. We showed you a very simple way to add data to arrays when you initialize them, but often this just is not flexible enough for real-world programming tasks. To access an array value, you simply need to know its location. The indexing system used to access array elements is zero-based, which means that the first value is always located at position 0. Let's look at a little program that first fills in an array then prints it out:

```
public class powersOf2 {

    public static void main(String args[]) {
        int intArray[] = new int[20];
        for (int i = 0; i < intArray.length; i++) {
```

```
        intArray[i] = 1;
        for(int p = 0; p <  i; p++) intArray[i] *= 2 ;
    }
    for (int i = 0; i < intArray.length; i++)
        System.out.println("2 to the power of " + i + " is " +
            intArray[i]);
  }
}
```

The output of this program looks like this:

```
2 to the power of 0 is 1
2 to the power of 1 is 2
2 to the power of 2 is 4
2 to the power of 3 is 8
2 to the power of 4 is 16
2 to the power of 5 is 32
2 to the power of 6 is 64
2 to the power of 7 is 128
2 to the power of 8 is 256
2 to the power of 9 is 512
2 to the power of 10 is 1024
2 to the power of 11 is 2048
2 to the power of 12 is 4096
2 to the power of 13 is 8192
2 to the power of 14 is 16384
2 to the power of 15 is 32768
2 to the power of 16 is 65536
2 to the power of 17 is 131072
2 to the power of 18 is 262144
2 to the power of 19 is 524288
```

So, how does the program work? We first create our array of integer values and assign it to the **intArray** variable. Next, we begin a loop that goes from zero to **intArray.length**. By calling the **length** method of our array, we find the number of indexes in the array. Then, we start another loop that does the calculation and stores the result in the index specified by the **i** variable from our initial loop.

Now that we have filled in all the values for our array, we need to step back through them and print out the result. We could have just put the **print** statement in the initial loop, but the approach we used gives us a chance to use another loop that references our array.

Here is the structure of an index call:

```
arrayName[index];
```

Pretty simple. If you try and use an index that is outside the boundaries of the array, a run-time error occurs. If we change the program to count to an index of 21 instead of the actual array length of 20, we would end up getting an error message like this:

```
java.lang.ArrayIndexOutOfBoundsException: 20
        at powersOf2.main(powersOf2.java:10)
```

This is a pretty common error in any programming language. You need to use some form of exception handling to watch for this problem unless you are positive you can create code that never does this (in your dreams). See Chapter 7 for additional information on exception handling.

Multidimensional Arrays

Multidimensional arrays are created in Java in using arrays of arrays. Here are a few examples of how you can implement multidimensional arrays:

```
int intArray[][];
String Names[][];
```

We can even do the same things we did with a single dimension array. We can set the array sizes and even fill in values while we declare the arrays:

```
int intArray[][] = new int[10][5];
String Names[][] = new String[25][3];

int intArray[][] = {{2, 3, 4} {1, 2, 3}};
String Names[][] = {{"Jon", "Smith"}{"Tony", "Potts"}{"Dave", "Friedel"}};
```

We can also create arrays that are not "rectangular" in nature. That is, each array within the main array can have a different number of elements. Here are a few examples:

```
int intArray[][] = {{1, 2} {1, 2, 3} {1, 2, 3, 4}};
String Names[][] = {{"Jon", "Smith"} {"Tony","A", "Potts"} {"Dave", "H",
  "Friedel", "Jr."}};
```

Accessing the data in a multidimensional array is not much more difficult than accessing data in a single-dimensional array. You just need to track the values for each index. Be careful though, as you add dimensions, it becomes increasingly easy to create out of bounds errors. Here are a few examples of how you can declare multidimensional arrays, assign values, and access array elements:

```
int intArray[][] = new int[10][5];            // Declare the arrays
String Names[][] = new String[25][3];

intArray[0][0] = 5;        // Assign values
intArray[7][2] = 37;
intArray[7][9] = 37;       // This will cause an out of bounds error!
Names[0][0] = "Bill Gates";
// Access an array element in a Java statement
System.out.println(Names[0][0]);
```

We will cover variables and declarations in more detail in Chapter 5, but you should have enough knowledge now to be able to run a few basic programs and get the feel for Java programming.

Using Command-Line Arguments

Programming with command-line arguments is not a topic you'd typically expect to see in a chapter on basic data types and variable declarations. However, because we've been using command-line arguments with some of the sample programs we've been introducing, we thought it would be important to discuss how this feature works in a little more detail.

Command-line arguments are only used with Java applications. They provide a mechanism so that the user of an application can pass in information to be used by the program. Java applets, on the other hand, read in parameters using HTML tags as we learned in Chapter 2. Command-line arguments are common with languages like C and C++, which were originally designed to work with command-line operating systems like Unix.

The advantage of using command-line arguments is that they are passed to a program when the program *first* starts, which keeps the program from having to query the user for more information. Command-line arguments are great for passing custom initialization data.

Passing Arguments

The syntax for passing arguments themselves to a program is extremely simple. Just start your programs as you usually would and add any number of arguments to the end of the line with each one separated by a space. Here is a sample call to a program named "myApp":

```
Java myApp open 640 480
```

In this case, we are calling the Java run-time interpreter and telling it to run he class file "myApp." We then are passing in three arguments: "open," "640," and "480."

If you wanted to pass in a longer string with spaces as an argument, you could. In this case, you enclose the string in quotation marks and Java will treat it as a single argument. Here is an example:

```
Java myApp "Nice program!" "640x480"
```

Once again the name of the program is "myApp." However, this time we are only sending it two arguments: "Nice program!" and "640x480." Note that the quotes themselves are not passed, just the string between the quotes.

Reading in Arguments

Now that we know how to pass arguments, where are they stored? How can we see them in our application? If you'll recall, all applications have a **main()** method. You should also notice that this method has an interesting argument structure:

```
public static void main(String args[]) {
   ...
}
```

Here, **main()** indicates that it takes an array named **args[]** of type **String**. Java takes any command-line arguments and puts them into the **args[]** string array. The array is dynamically resized to hold just the number of arguments passed, or zero if none are passed. Note that the use of the **args** identifier is completely arbitrary. You can use any word you want as long as it conforms to the Java naming rules. You can even get a little more descriptive, like this:

```
public static void main(String commandLineArgumentsArray[]) { ...
```

That may be a bit much, but you will never get confused as to what is in the array!

Accessing Arguments

Once we've passed in the arguments to an application and we know where they are stored, how do we get to them? Since the arguments are stored in an array, we can access them just like we would access strings in any other array. Let's look at a simple application that takes two arguments and prints them out:

```
class testArgs {
    public static void main(String args[]) {
        System.out.println(args[0]);
        System.out.println(args[1]);
    }
}
```

If we use this command line statement to run the application

```
java testArgs hello world
```

we'd get this output:

```
hello
world
```

Now, try this command line:

```
java testArgs onearg
```

Here is the result:

```
onearg
java.lang.ArrayIndexOutOfBoundsException: 1
        at testArgs.main(testArgs.java:4)
```

What happened? Since we only were passing a single argument, the reference to **args[1]** is illegal and produces an error.

So, how do we stop from getting an error? Instead of calling each argument in line, we can use a **for** loop to step through each argument. We can check the **args.length** variable to see if we have reached the last item. Our new code will also recognize if no arguments have been passed and will not try and access the array at all. Enough talking, here is the code:

```
class testArgs {
    public static void main(String args[]) {
        for (int i = 0; i < args.length; i++) {
            System.out.println(args[i]);
        }
    }
}
```

Now, no matter how many arguments are passed (or none) the application can handle it.

Indexing Command-Line Arguments

Java Note

Don't forget that Java arrays are zero based, so the first command-line argument is stored at position 0 not position 1. This is different than some other languages like C where the first argument would be at position 1. In C, position 0 would store the name of the program.

Dealing with Numeric Arguments

One more thing we should cover here is how to deal with numeric arguments. If you remember, all arguments are passed into an array of strings so we need to convert those values into numbers.

This is actually very simple. Each data type has an associated class that provides methods for dealing with that data type. Each of these classes has a method that creates a variable of that type from a string. Table 3.9 presents a list of those methods.

Make sure you understand the difference between the **parse*()** methods and the **valueOf()** methods. The parsing methods return just a value that can be plugged into a variable or used as part of an expression. The **valueOf()** methods return an *object* of the specified type that has an initial value equal to the value of the string.

Table 3.9 Classes and Their Associated Methods for Handling Data Types

Class	Method	Return
Integer	parseInt(String)	An integer value
Integer	valueOf(String)	An **Integer** object initialized to the value represented by the specified String
Long	parseLong(String)	A long value
Long	valueOf(String)	A **Long** object initialized to the value represented by the specified String
Double	valueOf(String)	A **Double** object initialized to the value represented by the specified String
Float	valueOf(String)	A **Float** object initialized to the value represented by the specified String

4

Operators,
Expressions,
and Control
Structures

Operators, Expressions, and Control Structures

*To build useful Java programs you'll need to
master the art of using operators, expressions, and control structures.*

Now that you know about the types of data you can use in Java, you need to learn how to manipulate your data. The tools for manipulating data fall into three categories—operators, expressions, and control structures—each playing a more powerful role as you move up the ladder. In this chapter, we'll discuss each of the key Java operators—everything from assignment statements to bitwise operators. Although Java operators are very similar to C/C++ operators, there are a few subtle differences which we'll point out. Next, we'll show you the basics for creating expressions with Java. Finally, in the last part of the chapter, we'll investigate the world of Java control structures.

Using Java Operators

Operators allow you to perform tasks such as addition, subtraction, multiplication, and assignment. Operators can be divided into three main categories: *assignment, integer,* and *boolean operators.* We'll explore each Java operator in detail by examining each of the three categories. But first, let's cover operator precedence.

Operator Precedence

As you are writing your code, you need to keep in mind which operators have precedence over the others—the order in which operators take effect. If you are an experienced programmer or you can remember some of the stuff you learned in your high school algebra classes, you shouldn't have any problem with understanding the principles of operator precedence. The basic idea is that the outcome or result of an expression like this

```
x = 5 * (7+4) - 3;
```

is determined by the *order in which the operators are evaluated* by the Java compiler. In general, all operators that have the same precedence are evaluated from left to right. If the above expression were handled in this manner, the result would be 36 (multiply 5 by 7, add 4, and then subtract 3). Because of precedence, we know that some operators, such as (), are evaluated before operators such as *. Therefore, the real value of this expression would be 52 (add 7 and 4, multiply by 5, and then subtract 3).

The actual rules for operator precedence in Java are nearly identical to those found in C/C++. The only difference is that C/C++ includes a few operators, such as ->, that are not used in Java. Table 4.1 lists the major operators in order of precedence. Notice that some operator symbols such as (-) show up twice.

Table 4.1 Operator Precedence with Java	
Operators	**Operator Type**
() [] .	Expression
++ -- ! - ~	Unary
* / %	Multiplicative
+ -	Additive
<< >> >>>	Shift
< <= > >=	Relational (inequality)
== !=	Relational (equality)
&	Bitwise ADD
^	Bitwise XOR
|	Bitwise OR
&&	Logical AND
||	Logical OR
?:	Conditional
= *= /= %= += -= <<= >>= &= |= ^=	Assignment

The reason for this is because the operator has different meanings depending on how it is used in an expression. For example, in an expression like this

```
x = 7 + -3;
```

the (-) operator is used as a unary operator to negate the value 3. In this case, it would have a higher precedence than a standard additive operator (+ or -). In an expression like this, on the other hand,

```
x = 7 - 3 + 5;
```

the (-) operator is used as a binary additive operator, and it shares the same precedence with the (+) operator.

Java Note

Which Operators Are Missing?

If you are an experienced C/C++ programmer, you're probably wondering what operators used in C/C++ are not available in Java. The ones missing are the four key data access and size operators shown in Table 4.2. These operators are not needed because Java does not support pointers and does not allow you to access memory dynamically. As we learned in Chapter 2, Java uses garbage collection techniques to provide its own internal system of memory management.

Assignment Operators

The most important and most often used operator is the assignment operator (=). This operator does just what it looks like it should do; it takes whatever variable is on the left and sets it equal to the expression on the right:

```
i = 35;
```

Table 4.2 C/C++ Operators Missing from Java

Operator	Description
*	Performs pointer indirection
&	Calculates the memory address of a variable
->	Allows a pointer to select a data structure
sizeof	Determines the size of an allocated data structure

The expression on the right can be any valid Java expression—a literal, an equation with operands and operators, a method call, and so on. When using an assignment operator, you must be careful that the variable you are using to receive the expression is the correct size and type to receive the result of the expression on the right side. For example, statements like the following could cause you a lot of headaches:

```
short count;
// This number is way too big for a short type!
count = 500000000000;

char ch;
// Oops! We should be assigning a character here
ch = 100;
```

In the first example, the variable **count** is declared as a **short**, which means that the variable can only hold a number as large as 32767. Obviously, the number being assigned to the variable is way too large. In the second example, the variable **ch** expects to receive a character but in reality is assigned something else entirely.

If you look closely at the last line in Table 4.1, you'll see that Java offers a number of variations of the standard assignment statement. They are all borrowed from the C language. An assignment statement like this

```
num *= 5;
```

would be equivalent to this expression:

```
num = num * 5;
```

The combination assignment operators turn out to be very useful for writing expressions inside loops that perform counting operations. Here's an example:

```
While (i <= count)
{
   i += 2;   // Increment the counting variable
   ...
}
```

In this case **i** is used as the loop "counting" control variable, and it is incremented by using a combination assignment statement.

Integer Operators

In the category of integer operators, there are two flavors to choose from: *unary* and *binary*. A unary operator performs a task on a single variable at a time. Binary operators, on the other hand, must work with two variables at a time. Let's start with the unary operators.

UNARY OPERATORS

There are four integer unary operators: negation, bitwise complement, increment, and decrement. They are used without an assignment operation. They simply perform their operation on a given variable, changing its value appropriately.

NEGATION (-)

Unary negation changes the sign of an integer. You must be careful when reaching the lower limits of integer variables because the negative limit is always one greater than the positive limit. So, if you had a variable of type **byte** with a value of -256 and you performed a unary negation on it, an error will occur because the **byte** data type has a maximum positive value of 255. Here are some examples of how this operator can be used:

```
- k;
-someInt;
x = -50 + 10;
```

As we learned earlier, the negation operator is at the top end of the precedence food chain; thus, you can count on operands that use it to be evaluated first.

BITWISE COMPLEMENT (~)

Performing a bitwise complement on a variable flips each bit of the variable—all 1s become 0s and all 0s become 1s. For strict decimal calculations, this operator is not used very often. But if you are working with values that represent bit settings, such as an index into a color palette, this type of operator is invaluable. Here is an example of the unary complement operator in action:

```
// input: byte type variable bitInt = 3 (00000011 in binary)
~bitInt;
// Output: bitInt = 252 (11111100 in binary)
```

INCREMENT (++) AND DECREMENT (- -)

The increment and decrement operators are very simple operators that simply increase or decrease an integer variable by 1 each time they are used. These operators were created as a shortcut to saying x=x+1. As we've already mentioned, they are often used in loops where you want a variable incremented or decremented by one each time a loop is completed. Here is an example of how each operator is used:

```
++intIncrement;
--intDecrement;
```

BINARY OPERATORS

When you need to perform operations that involve two variables, you will be dealing with binary operators. Simple addition and subtraction are prime examples of binary operators. These operators do not change the value of either of the operands, instead they perform a function between the two operands that is placed into a third. Table 4.3 lists the complete set of the binary integer operators. Let's look at each of these operators in detail.

ADDITION, SUBTRACTION, MULTIPLICATION, AND DIVISION

These operators are the standard binary operators that we have all used since we started programming. We won't explain the theory behind algebra be-

Table 4.3   The Binary Integer Operators

Operator	Description
+	Addition
-	Subtraction
*	Multiplication
/	Division
%	Modulus
&	Bitwise AND
|	Bitwise OR
^	Bitwise XOR
<<	Left Shift
>>	Right Shift
>>>	Zero-Fill Right Shift

cause we assume you already know this stuff. We will, however, give you a few examples:

```
// X=12 and Y=4
Z = X + Y; // Answer = 16
Z = X - Y; // Answer = 8
Z = X * Y; // Answer = 48
Z = X / Y; // Answer = 3
```

MODULUS

The modulus operator divides the first operand by the second operand and returns the remainder:

```
// X=11 and Y=4
Z = X % Y; // Answer = 3
```

BITWISE OPERATORS

The bitwise binary operators perform operations at the binary level on integers. They act much like custom *if..then* statements. They compare the respective bits from each of the operands and set the corresponding bit of the return variable to a 1 or 0 depending on which operator is used. The AND operator works as follows: "if both bits are 1 then return a 1, otherwise return a 0." The OR operators works like this: "if either bit is a 1 then return a 1, otherwise return a 0." Finally, the XOR operator works like this: "if the bits are different return a 1, if they are the same return a 0." Table 4.4 provides a set of examples that illustrate how each bitwise operator works.

And here are some code examples to show you how to incorporate bitwise operators into your Java statements:

```
// X=3 (00000011)
// Y=2 (00000010)
Z = X & Y; // Answer: Z = 2X 00000011
      //          Y 00000010
      //          Z 00000010

Z = X | Y; // Answer: Z = 3X 00000011
      //          Y 00000010
      //          Z 00000011

Z = X ^ Y; // Answer: Z = 1X 00000011
      //          Y 00000010
      //          Z 00000001
```

Table 4.4	Using the Java Bitwise Operators		
Operand 1	**Operand 2**	**Bitwise Operator**	**Return**
1	1	AND	True
1	0	AND	False
0	1	AND	False
0	0	AND	False
1	1	OR	True
1	0	OR	True
0	1	OR	True
0	0	OR	False
1	1	XOR	False
1	0	XOR	True
0	1	XOR	True
0	0	XOR	False

Boolean Operators

The boolean data type adds several new operators to the mix. All of the operators that can be used on boolean values are listed in Table 4.5.

BOOLEAN NEGATION (!)

Negation of a boolean variable simply returns the opposite of the boolean value. As you might have guessed, boolean negation is a unary operation. Here's an example:

```
// Bool1 = True
!Bool1; // Answer: Bool1 = False
```

LOGICAL AND (&), OR (|), & XOR (^)

The AND, OR, and XOR operators work identically to the way they do with integer values. However, they only have a single bit to worry about:

```
Bool2 = true;
Bool3 = true;
```

Table 4.5 Java Boolean Operators

Operator	Operation
!	Negation
&	Logical AND
|	Logical OR
^	Logical XOR
&&	Evaluation AND
||	Evaluation OR
==	Equal to
!=	Not Equal to
&=	And Assignment
|=	OR Assignment
^=	XOR Assignment
?:	Ternary (Conditional)

```
Bool4 = False;
Bool5 = False;
Bool1 = Bool2 & Bool3; // Answer: Bool1 = True
Bool1 = Bool2 & Bool4; // Answer: Bool1 = False
Bool1 = Bool2 | Bool3; // Answer: Bool1 = False
Bool1 = Bool2 | Bool4; // Answer: Bool1 = True
Bool1 = Bool3 ^ Bool4; // Answer: Bool1 = False
Bool1 = Bool4 ^ Bool5; // Answer: Bool1 = True
```

EVALUATION AND (&&) AND OR (||)

The evaluation AND and OR are a little different than the logical versions. Using these operators causes Java to avoid evaluation of the righthand operands if it is not needed. In other words, if the answer can be derived by only reading the first operand, Java will not bother to read the second. Here are some examples:

```
// op1 = True op2 = False
result = op1 && op2; // result=False-both ops are evaluated
result = op2 && op1; // result=False-only first op is evaluated

result = op1 || op2; // result=True-only first op is evaluated
result = op2 || op1; // result=True-both ops are evaluated
```

Equal to (==) and Not Equal to (!=)

These operators are used to simply transfer a boolean value or transfer the opposite of a boolean value. Here are a few examples:

```
op1 = True;
if (result == op1); // Answer: result = true
if (result != op1); // Answer: result = false
```

Assignment Boolean Operators (&=), (|=), (^=)

Boolean assignment operators are a lot like the assignment operators for integers. Here is an example of an assignment being used on both an integer and a boolean so that you can compare the two:

```
i    += 5;      // Same as int = int + 5
bool &= true;   // Same as bool = bool & true
bool |= true;   // Same as bool = bool | true
bool ^= false; // Same as bool = bool ^ false
```

Ternary Operator

This powerful little operator acts like an extremely condensed *if..then* statement. If you look at the example below you will see that if the operand is True, the expression before the colon is evaluated. If the operand is False, the expression after the colon is evaluated. This type of coding may look a little strange at first. But once you understand the logic, you'll begin to see just how useful this operator can be. In the following example, the parentheses are not actually needed, but when you use more complicated expressions they will make the code much easier to follow:

```
// op1 = True op2 = False
op1 ? (x=1):(x=2); // Answer: x=1
op2 ? (x=1):(x=2); // Answer: x=2
```

Floating-Point Number Operators

Almost all of the integer operators work on floating-point numbers as well, with a few minor changes. Of course, all the standard arithmetic operators (+, -, *, /) work as well as the assignment operators (+=, -=, *=, /=). Modulus (%) also works; however, it only evaluates the integer portion of the operands. The increment and decrement operators work identically by adding or subtracting 1.0 from the integer portion of the numbers. Be careful when using relational operators on floating-point numbers. Do not make assumptions about how the numbers will behave just because integers behave a certain way. For example, just because an expression like a==b may be true for two floating-point values, don't assume that an expression like a<b || a>b will be true. This is because floating-point values are not ordered like integers. You also have to deal with the possibility of a floating-point variable being equal to negative or positive infinity, **-Inf** and **Inf**, respectively. You can get a positive or negative **Inf** when you perform an operation that returns an overflow.

Using Casts

In some applications you may need to transfer one type of variable to another. Java provides us with *casting* methods to accomplish this. Casting refers to the process of transforming one variable of a certain type into another data type.

Casting is accomplished by placing the name of the data type you wish to cast a particular variable into in front of that variable in parentheses. Here is an example of how a cast can be set up to convert a **char** into an **int**:

```
int a;
char b;
b = 'z';
a = (int) b;
```

Since the variable **a** is declared as an **int**, it expects to be assigned an **int** value. The variable **b**, on the other hand, is declared as a **char**. To assign the contents of **b** to **a**, the cast is used on the right side of the assignment statement. The contents of **b**, the numeric value of the character 'z' is safely assigned to the variable **a** as an integer. If you wanted to, you could perform the cast in reverse:

```
short a;
char b;
a = 40;
b = (char) a;  // Convert value 40 into a character
```

Casting is extremely simple when you are using the primitive data types—**int, char, short, double,** and so on. You can also cast classes and interfaces in Java, which we'll show you how to do in Chapter 5.

The most important thing to remember when using casts is the space each variable has to work with. Java will let you cast a variable of one data type into a variable of a different data type if the size of the data type of the target variable is smaller than the other data type, but you may not like the result. Does this sound confusing? Let's explain this a little better. If you had a variable of type **long**, you should only cast it into another variable of type **float** or **double** because these data types are the only other two primitives with at least 64-bits of space to handle your number. On the other hand, if you had a variable of type **byte**, then you could cast it into any of the other primitives except boolean because they all have more space than the lowly **byte**. When you are dealing with **double** variables, you are stuck, since no other data type offers as much space as the **double**.

If you have to cast a variable into another variable having less space, Java will do it. However, any information in the extra space will be lost. On the plus side though, if the value of a larger variable is less than the maximum value of the variable you are casting into, no information will be lost.

Writing Expressions and Statements

So far we've been more or less looking at operators, literals, and data types in a vacuum. Although we've used these components to write expressions, we haven't formally defined what Java expressions are. Essentially, expressions are the Java statements that make your code work; they are the guts of your programs. A basic expressions contains *operands* and *operators*. For example, in this expression

```
i = x + 10;
```

the variable x and the literal 10 are the operands and + is the operator. The evaluation of an expression performs one or more operations that return a result. The data type of the result is always determined by the data types of the operands(s).

When multiple operands are combined, they are referred to as a *compound expression*. The order in which the operators are evaluated is determined by the precedence of the operators that act upon them. We discussed precedence earlier and showed you the relative precedence of each Java operator.

The simplest form of expression is used to calculate a value, which in turn is assigned to a variable in an assignment statement. Here are a few assignment statements that use expressions that should look very familiar to you by now:

```
i = 2;
thisString = "Hello";
```

Here are a few assignment statements that are a little more involved:

```
Bool1 != Bool2;
i += 2;
d *= 1.9
Byte1 ^= Byte2;
```

An assignment expression involves a variable that will accept the result, followed by a single assignment operator, followed by the operand that the assignment operator is using.

The next step up the ladder is to create expressions that use operators like the arithmetic operators we have already discussed:

```
i = i + 2;
thisString = "Hello";
```

Expressions with multiple operands are probably the most common type of expressions. They still have a variable that is assigned the value of the result produced by evaluating the operands and operators to the right of the equal sign. You can also have expressions with many operators and operands like this:

```
i = i + 2 - 3 * 9 / 3;
thisString = "Hello" + "World, my name is " + myName;
```

The art of programming in Java involves using operators and operands to build expressions, which are in turn used to build *statements*. Of course, the assignment statement is just one type of statement that can be constructed. You can also create many types of control statements, such as while and for loops, if-then decision making statements, and so on. (We'll look at all of the control statements that can be written in Java in the last part of this chapter.)

There are essentially two types of statements you can write in Java: *simple* and *compound*. A simple statement performs a single operation. Here are some examples:

```
int i;      // Variable declaration
i = 10 * 5; // Assignment statement
if (i = 50) x = 200;  // if-then decision statement
```

The important thing to remember about simple statements in Java is that they are *always* completed with a semicolon (;). (Some of the others like class declarations and compound if..else statements don't need semicolons, but if you leave it off the end of an expression, you'll get an error.)

Compound statements involve the grouping of simple statements. In this case, the characters ({ }) are used to group the separate statements into one compound statement. Here are a few examples:

```
while (x < 10)
{
    ++x;
    if (sum < x) printline();
}

if (x < 10)
{
    i = 20;
    p = getvalue(i);
}
```

Notice that the (;) terminating character is not used after the final (}). The braces take care of this for us.

Control Flow Statements

Control flow is what programming is all about. What good are basic data types, variables, and casting if you don't have any code that can make use of them? Java provides several different types of control flow structures. These structures provide your application with direction. They take an input, decide what to do with it and how long to do it, and then let expressions handle the rest.

Let's look at each of these structures in detail. If you have done any programming before, all of these should look familiar. Make sure you study the syntax so that you understand exactly how they work in Java as compared to how they work in other languages.

Table 4.6 lists all of the standard control flow structures, and it shows you what the different parts of their structure represent.

if..else

The **if..else** control structure is probably used more than all the others combined. How many programs have you written that didn't include one? Not very many, we'll wager.

Table 4.6 Control Flow Structures	
Structure	**Expression**
if..else	**if** (*boolean = true*) *statement*
	else *statement;*
while	**while** (*boolean = true*) *statement;*
do..while	**do** *statement* **while** (*boolean = true*);
switch	**switch** (*expression*) {
	case *expression: statement;*
	case *expression: statement;*
	...
	default: *statement;*
	}
for	**for** (*expression1; expression2; expression3*)
	statement;
label	**label:** *statement*
	break *label;*
	continue *label;*

In its simplest terms, the **if..else** structure performs this operation: if *this* is true then do *that* otherwise do *something else*. Of course, the "otherwise" portion is optional. Since you probably already know what **if..else** statements are used for, we will just show you a few examples so you can see how they work in Java.

Here is the structure labeled with standard terms:

```
if (boolean) statement
else statement;
```

Here is a sample of what an **if..else** statement might look like with actual code:

```
if (isLunchtime) {
   Eat = true;
   Hour = 12;
}
else {
   Eat = False;
   Hour = 0;
}
```

You can also use nested **if..else** statements:

```
if (isLunchtime) {
    Eat = true;
    Hour = 12;
}
else if (isBreakfast) {
        Eat = true;
        Hour = 6;
    }
    else if (isDinner) {
            Eat = true;
            Hour = 18;
        }
        else {
            Eat = false;
            Hour = 0;
        }
```

The curly braces are used when multiple statements need to take place for each option. If we were only performing a single operation for each part of the **if..else** statement, we would not need the braces. Here is an example of an **if..else** statement that uses curly braces for one part but not the other:

```
if (isLunchtime) {
    Eat = true;
    Hour = 12;
}
else Eat = False;
```

while and do..while

The **while** and **do..while** loops perform the same function. The only difference is that the **while** loop verifies the expression *before* executing the statement, and the **do..while** loop verifies the expression *after* executing the statement. This is a major difference that can be extremely helpful if used properly.

Here are the structures labeled with standard terms:

```
while (boolean) {
    statement;
}
```

```
do {
   statement
} while(boolean);
```

while and **do..while** loops are used if you want to repeat a certain statement or block of statements until a certain expression becomes false. For example, assume you wanted to send e-mail to all of the people at a particular Web site. You could set up a **while** loop that stepped through all the people, one-by-one, sending them e-mail until you reached the last person. When the last person is reached, the loop is terminated and the program control flow moves on to the statement following the loop. Here is what that loop might look like in very simple terms:

```
boolean done = false;

while (!done){
   emailUser();
   goNextuser();
   if (noNewuser) done = true;
}
```

switch

The **switch** control flow structure is useful when you have a single expression with many possible options. The same thing can be done using recursed **if..else** statments, but that can get very confusing when you get past just a few options. The **if..else** structure is also difficult to change when it becomes highly nested.

The **swtich** statement is executed by comparing the value of an initial expression or variable with other variables or expressions. Let's look at the labeled structure:

```
switch(expression) {
   case expression: statement;
   case expression: statement;
   case expression: statement;
   default: statement;
}
```

Now let's look at a real piece of code that uses the **switch** structure:

```
char age;
```

```
System.out.print("How many computers do you own? ");
age = System.in.read();
switch(age) {
    case '0':
        System.out.println("\nWhat are you waiting for?");
        break;
    case '1':
        System.out.println("\nIs that enough these days?");
        break;
    case '2':
        System.out.println("\nPerfect!");
        break;
    default:
        System.out.println("\nToo much free time on you hands!");
}
```

The **break** statement is extremely important when dealing with **switch** structures. If the **switch** finds a case that is true, it will execute the statements for that case. When it is finished with that case, it will move on to the next one. This process continues until a match is found or the **default** statement is reached. The **break** statement tells the **switch** "OK, we found a match, let's move on."

The **default** clause serves as the "catch-all" statement. If all of the other cases fail, the **default** clause will be executed.

for

for loops are another programming standard that would be tough to live without. The idea behind a **for** loop is that we want to step through a sequence of numbers until a limit is reached. The loop steps through our range in whatever step increment we want, checking at the beginning of each loop to see if we have caused our "quit" expression to become true.

Here is the labeled structure of a **for** loop:

```
for (variable ; expression1 ; expression2);
```

The variable we use can either be one we have previously created, or it can be declared from within the **for** structure. Expression1 from the above example is the expression we need to stay true until the loop is finished. More often than not, this expression is something like x<10 which means that we will step through the loop until x is equal to 10 at which time the expression (x<10) becomse false and drops us out of the loop.

Here is an example of a **for** loop that actually works:

```
for (int x = 0 ; x < 10 ; x++) {
    System.out.println(x);
}
```

If you put this code into an empty **main** method you should get the following output:

```
0
1
2
3
4
5
6
7
8
9
```

For loops are used for many different applications. They are a necessity when dealing with arrays and can really help when creating lookup tables or indexing a database.

labels

Java **labels** provide a means of controlling different kinds of loops. Sometimes, when you create a loop, you need to be able to break out of it before it finishes on its own and satisfies its completion expression. This is where **labels** come in very handy.

The key to **labels** is the **break** statement that you learned to use with the **switch** statement. You can also use the **break** statement to exit out of any loop. It is great for breaking out of **for** loops and **while** loops especially.

However, sometimes you have embedded loops and you need to be able to break out of a certain loop. A great example of this is two embedded **for** loops that are setting values in an array. If an error occurs or you get a strange value, you may want to be able to break out of one loop or another. It gets confusing if you have all these embedded loops and break statements all over with no apparent link to one loop or another. **labels** rectify this situation.

To use a label, you simply place an identifier followed by a colon at the beginning of the line that initiates a loop. Let's look at an example before we go further:

```
outer: for (int x = 0 ; x < 10 ; x++) {
    inner: for (int y = 0 ; y < 10 ; y++) {
    System.out.println(x + y);
       if (y=9) {
          break outer:
       } else {
          continue outer:
       }
    }
}
```

Labels are probably new to most of you, so you may not see a need for them right away. However, as your programs become more complicated you should think about using lables where appropriate to make your code simple and more readable.

Moving Ahead

We covered a lot of ground in this chapter and the previous one. If you are new to Java programming and have little C or C++ background, make sure you understand these concepts well so that you do not get confused in the upcoming chapters.

Let's now move on and discuss another basic structure of Java programming. In fact, we would have to call it the basic structure of Java programming—the class.

5

Java Classes
and Methods

Java Classes and Methods 5

Classes are the key Java components that give the language its object-oriented personality.

If you have some experience programming in a language like C++, you are probably familiar with the power and flexibility that classes provide. They are ideal for plugging general information into a template-like structure for reusing over and over. For example, if you are developing an interactive drawing package, you could create standard classes for some of the fundamental drawing operations and then use those classes to create more sophisticated drawing tasks. If you are new to the world of object-oriented programming (OOP), you'll soon discover that classes are the essential building blocks for writing OOP applications. At first glance, Java classes look and operate like C++ classes; but there are some key differences which we'll address in this chapter.

We'll start by looking at the basics of classes. You'll quickly learn how classes are defined and used to derive other classes. The second half of the chapter covers *methods*—the components used to breathe life into classes.

Understanding Classes

In traditional structured programming languages like C or Pascal, everything revolves around the concepts of algorithms and data structures. The algorithms are kept separate from the data structures, and they operate on the data to perform actions and results. To help divide programming tasks into separate units, components like functions and procedures are defined. The problem with this programming paradigm is that it doesn't allow you to easily create code that can be reused and expanded to create other code.

115

To solve this problem, object-oriented programming languages like Smalltalk and C++ were created. These languages introduced powerful components called *classes* so that programmers could combine functions (operations) and data under one roof. This is a technique called *encapsulation* in the world of object-oriented programming. Every language that uses classes defines them in a slightly different way; however, the basics concepts for using them remain the same. The main advantages of classes are:

- They can be used to define abstract data types
- Data is protected or hidden inside a class so other classes cannot access it
- Classes can be used to derive other classes
- New classes derived from existing classes can inherit the data and methods already defined—a concept called *inheritance*.

As you'll learn in this chapter, the techniques for defining and using Java classes are adapted from techniques found in the C++ language. In some cases, the Java syntax will look very similar to C++ syntax, but in other cases you'll find a number of differences, including new keywords that have been added to Java for declaring classes and methods; restrictions, such as the elimination of pointers; and different scoping rules that determine how classes can be used in an application.

Declaring a Class

If you recall from Chapter 2, we created a class named **TickerTape**, which controlled how text scrolled across the screen. Let's take a step back and look at the full declaration used to define classes in Java:

```
[Doc Comment] [Modifier] class Identifier
[extends Superclassname]
[implements Interfaces] {
    ClassBody;
}
```

Of course, keep in mind that you won't always use all of the clauses, such as *Doc Comment, Modifier,* **extends**, and so on. For example, here's an example of the world's smallest class definition:

```
class Atom_ant {
    int a = 1;
}
```

This class has an identifier, **Atom_ant**, and a body, **int a = 1;**. Of course, don't try to compile this at home as is because it will only result in an error. Why? Well, even though it is a valid class, it is not capable of standing on its own. (You would need to set it up as an applet or a main program to make it work.)

A class declaration provides all of the information about a class including its internal data (*variables*) and functions (*methods*) to be interpreted by the Java compiler. In addition, class declarations provide:

- Programmer comments
- Specifications of the other classes that may reference the class
- Specifications of the superclass the class belongs to (the class's parent)
- Specifications of the methods the class can call

Using a Class

Before we move on and look at all of the other components used to declare classes, let's return to our simple class declaration to see how classes are used in Java programs. Once a class has been declared, you need to use it to create an object. This process is called making an "instance of" a class. In a Java program it requires two steps. First, you declare an object variable using a syntax that looks just like a variable declaration, except the class name is used instead of the name of a primitive data type. For example, this statement would use the **Atom_ant** class we defined earlier to declare an object from the class definition:

```
Atom_ant crazyant;
```

Once the object has been declared, in this case **crazyant**, you then create an instance of it in a Java application by using the **new** operator:

```
crazyant = new Atom_ant();
```

Now the object **crazyant** can access all of the components in a **Atom_ant** class, thus making it an instance of an **Atom_ant** class. To see how this works in context, let's expand our example:

```
class Atom_ant {  // Simple class
   int a = 1;
}
```

```
public class Bug {
   int i = 10;
   Atom_ant crazyant;  // Declare an object

   public static void main (String args[]) {
      // Create an instance of Atom_ant called crazyant
      crazyant = new Atom_ant();
      System.out.println("There are " + bug.i + " bugs here but only " +
         crazyant.i + " atom ant.");
   }
}
```

The output produced by this example would be:

```
There are 10 bugs here but only 1 atom ant.
```

The main class, **Bug**, creates an instance of the **Atom_ant** class—the **crazyant** object. Then it uses the object to access the data member, **a**, which is assigned a value in the **Atom_ant** class. Notice that the dot operator (.) is used to access a member of a class.

Java Note

Object Declaration Time Saver

In Java, you can both declare an object variable and create an instance all in one statement. Here's an example of how it is done:

```
Atom_ant crazyant = new Atom_ant();
```

Notice that the class **Atom_ant** is used to declare the object variable **crazyant** and then the **new** operator is used to create an instance of **Atom_ant**.

Components of a Class Declaration

Let's look at the components of the class declaration in a little more detail. As you recall from our first example, the only really necessary part of a class declaration is its name or *identifier*. However, whenever you need to reference your class in your program to reuse it, you'll need to reference it by its *fully qualified name*. This name is the package name, or group of classes from which it came, followed by the identifier. For example, if *Atom_ant* is the class name and it belongs to a package named *molecule*, its fully qualified name would be *molecule.Atom_ant*.

Documentation Comment

The *Doc Comment* clause of the class declaration is provided as an aid to help other programmers who might need to use your class. It allows you to write your documentation while you're writing the code. The comments you include as part of this clause can easily be converted into easy to read HTML pages. However, keep in mind that your HTML pages will only be as good as your comments. (To brush up on how to write comments for Java programs, make sure you read Chapter 3.)

Let's look at an example to see how the *Doc Comment* feature works. This class definition

```
/**
* Atom ant is the world's smallest super hero,
  so we gave him a class by himself.
* @author Dave Friedel
*/
class Atom_ant {
   int i = 1;
}
```

uses *Doc Comment* style comments to produce the HTML page shown in Figure 5.1. Notice how the comments are formatted and used to document the class. In this case, **Atom_ant** is a subclass under the **java.lang.Object** class—the default parent for all classes.

In case you're wondering, the **@author** notation is a special type of comment tag that allows you to personalize your class. These tags are explained in more detail in Chapter 3.

Class Modifiers

Modifiers define the rules for how classes are used in Java applications. They determine how other packages, or classes of other groups can interact with the current class. There are three kinds of modifiers that can be used in a class declaration:

- public
- abstract
- final

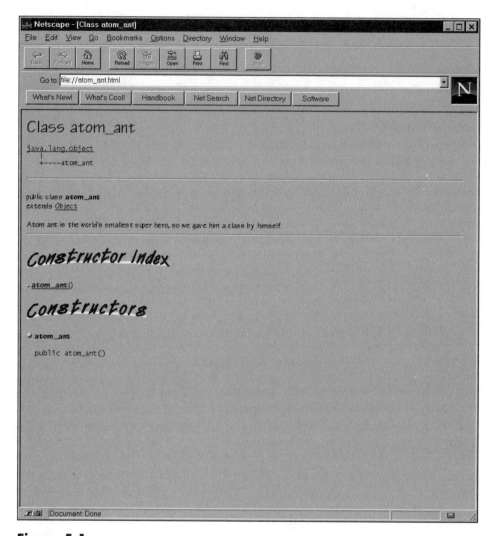

Figure 5.1

The HTML documentation created for the Atom_ant class.

If you don't use one of these modifiers when declaring a class, Java will automatically decide that only other classes in the current package may access the class. Let's look at how each of these modifiers are used.

PUBLIC CLASS

The **public** modifier is used to define a class that can have the greatest amount of access by other classes. By declaring a class as **public**, you allow all other classes and packages to access its variables, methods, and subclasses. However, *only one public class is allowed in any single Java applet or a single source code file.* You can think of the one public class in an applet as serving the role that the **main**() function does in a C/C++ program.

The source code for an applet must be saved as *ClassName.java*, where *ClassName* is the name of the single public class defined in the applet. Recall that when we created the TickerTape applet in Chapter 2, the single public class was defined as

```
public class TickerTape extends Applet implements Runnable {...
```

and the name of the file was TickerTape.java.

Let's look at another example of how the **public** modifier is used to define a Java class:

```
// Filename: Atom_ant.java
public class Atom_ant {
   public static void main (String args[]) {
      System.out.println("Hello World");
   }
}
```

In this case, **Atom_ant** is the name of the class and the filename for the applet is Atom_ant.java.

ABSTRACT CLASS

The **abstract** modifier is used to declare classes that serve as a shell or placeholder for implementing methods and variables. When you construct a hierarchy of classes, your top most class will contain the more general data definitions and method implementations that represent your program's features. As you work your way down the class hierarchy, your classes will start to implement more specific data components and operations. As you build your hierarchy, you may need to create more general classes and *defer* the actual implementation to later stages in the class hierarchy. This is where the abstract class comes in. This approach allows you to reference the operations that you need to include without having to restructure your entire hierarchy.

The technique of using abstract classes in Java is commonly referred to as *single inheritance* by C++ programmers. (By the way, limited multiple inheritance techniques can also be implemented in Java by using interfaces. We'll cover this topic in more detail in Chapter 6.)

Any class that is declared as an abstract class must follow certain rules:

- No objects can be instantiated from an abstract class
- Abstract classes must contain at least one declaration of an abstract method or variable
- All abstract methods that are declared in an abstract class must be implemented in one of the subclasses beneath it
- Abstract classes cannot be declared as final or private classes

Let's look at an example of how an abstract class is defined and used to help create other classes:

```
abstract class Quark extends Atom_ant {
    ...
    abstract void abstract_method1();
    abstract void abstract_method2();
    void normal_method();
    ...
}

public class Aparticles extends Quark {
    public void abstract_method1() {
        ... // Definition of the method
    }
}

public class Bparticles extends Quark {
    public void abstract_method2() {
    ... // Definition of the method
    }
}
```

Here, the class **Quark** is declared as an abstract class and it contains two methods that are declared as abstract methods. The subclasses **Aparticles** and **Bparticles** are located beneath the class **Quark** in the hierarchy of classes. Each one defines a method based on one of the abstract methods found in the **Quark** class. A compile-time error would occur if we had failed to define both of the abstract methods in the **Quark** class. All abstract methods must be defined in the subclasses that are derived from abstract classes.

Java Note

Restrictions in Declaring Abstract Classes

An abstract class cannot be defined as a final class (using the **final** keyword) because the Java compiler will always assume that the abstract class will be used to derive other classes— other subclasses will follow it. (As you'll see in the next section, a final class defines the end of the line for a class hierarchy.) Furthermore, you cannot used a **private** modifier in an abstract class's method declarations because this modifier restricts methods from being used by any other classes except the class they are defined in.

FINAL CLASS

The **final** modifier is used to declare a class that will not be used to derive any other classes. The final class is like the last station on a railway line. By its position in a class hierarchy, a final class cannot have any subclasses beneath it. In **final** class declarations, you cannot use the **extends** clause because the Java compiler always assumes that a final class cannot be extended. Here's an example of what would happen if you tried to declare a final class and then use it in another class declaration:

```
final class Molecule extends Element {
    static String neutron = "molecule";
}

class Atom_ant extends Molecule {
    static String proton = "atom_ant";
}



Compiling...
E:\java\jm\element.java
E:\java\jm\element.java:12: Can't subclass final classes: class
Moleculeclass Atom_ant extends Molecule {      ^1 errorsCompile Ended.
```

In this case, **Molecule** has been defined as a final class. But notice that the second class definition, **Atom_ant**, attempts to use **Molecule** as its parent. The Java compiler catches this illegal declaration and provides the appropriate warning.

Class Identifiers

Each class you define in a Java program must have its own unique identifier. The class's identifier or name directly follows the **class** keyword. The rules for naming classes are the same as those used to name variables. To refresh your memory, identifiers should always begin with a letter of the alphabet, either upper or lower case. The only exception to this rule is the underscore symbol (_) and the dollar sign ($), which may also be used. The rest of the name can be defined using characters, numbers, and some symbols.

Since class names are also used as file names, you need to create names that will not cause problems with your operating system or anyone who will be using your program.

Extending Classes

In most Java applets and programs you write, you will have a number of classes that need to interact each other—in many cases classes will be derived from other classes creating hierarchies. The keyword that handles the work of helping you extend classes and create hierarchies is named appropriately enough, **extends**.

In a class hierarchy, every class must have a parent—except the class that is at the top. The class that serves as a parent to another class is also called the superclass of the class it derives—the class that takes the position immediately above the class. Let's look at an example. As Figure 5.2 indicates, the classes *911*, *944*, and *928* all belong to the superclass *Porsche*. And *Porsche* belongs to the superclass *sportscar*, which in turn belongs to the superclass *automobile*.

When you derive a class from a superclass, it will inherit the superclass's data and methods. (For example, *911* has certain characteristics simply because it is derived from *Porsche*.) To derive a class from a superclass in a class declaration hierarchy, you will need to use the **extend** clause followed by the name of the superclass. If no superclass is defined, the Java compiler assumes that you are deriving a class using Java's top-level superclass named **Object**. Here is an example:

```
public class Element extends Object {
    public static void main() {
        Atom_ant ATOMOBJ = new Atom_ant();
        Molecule MOLEOBJ = new Molecule();
        System.out.println(ATOMOBJ.proton);
```

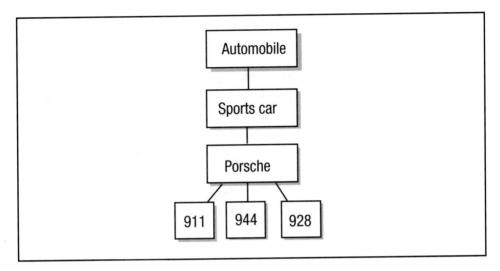

Figure 5.2

A sample class hierarchy.

```
    }
}

class Molecule extends Element {
    static String neutron = "molecule";
}

class Atom_ant extends Molecule {
    static String proton = "atom_ant";
}
```

In this class declaration section, the top-level class defined is **Element**. Notice that it is derived or "extended" from **Object**—the built-in Java class. The first line of the declaration of **Element** could have also been written as

```
public class Element {
...
```

since the Java compiler will assume that a class is automatically derived from the **Object** class if the **extends** clause is omitted. The second class, **Molecule**, is derived from **Element** and the third class, **Atom_ant**, is derived from **Molecule**. As Figure 5.3 shows, both **Molecule** and **Atom_ant** inherit the components of the **Element** class.

Using the implements Clause to Create Class Interfaces

When classes are used to derive other classes, the derived classes can access the data and methods of the classes higher up in the hierarchy chain. Fortunately, Java provides a mechanism called *interfaces* so that classes that are not part of a hierarchy can still access components of other classes. An interface is created for a class by using the **implements** clause. A class can implement as many interfaces as it wishes, but all the interfaces introduced must have all their methods defined in the body of the class implementing it. Thus, all the subclasses that follow from that point on will inherit the methods and variables defined.

Let's develop the **Atom_ant** class we introduced in the previous section to see how an interface can be coded:

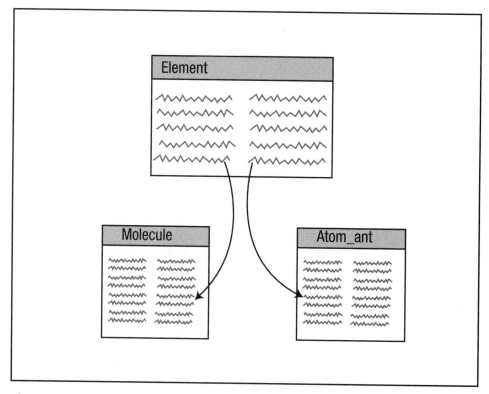

Figure 5.3

Using the **extends** keyword to derive a series of classes.

```
class Atom_ant extends Molecule implements Protons, Neutrons, Electrons {
    static int proton = 45378444;
    void Proton_function() {
        ... // definition of the Proton_function()
    }

    void Neutron_function() {
        ... // definition of the Neutron_function()
    }

    void Electron_function() {
        ... // definition of the Electron_function()
    }
}
```

Here we are making the assumption that the interfaces **Protons**, **Neutrons**, and **Electrons** only have one method declared in each of the interfaces. For example, **Protons** may be set up as follows:

```
Public interface Protons {

    void Proton_function(); // declares the method that will be used
}
```

As you can see, setting up the interface is a two step process. The class where the methods are defined uses the **implements** clause to indicate which interfaces can have access to the methods. Then, **interface** statements are used to declare the method that will be used.

If you recall from Chapter 2, the **TickerTape** class implemented the interface **Runnable** from the package java.lang. The **Runnable** interface has only one method declared in it, which is **run()**. This method is then defined in the class that is implementing it. In this case, the applet TickerTape has defined **run()** to instruct the thread to sleep, call the **setcoord()** method, and rerun the **paint()** method every time the applet calls the **run()** method. This happens in situations where the screen is resized or, in this case, where the applet is instructed to move the text across the screen and the **run()** method is called.

```
// TickerTape Applet

import java.applet.*;
import java.awt.*;
```

```
// TickerTape Class
public class TickerTape extends Applet implements Runnable {
    ...
    public void run() {
        while(ttapeThread != null){ // verifies the thread is still active
            try {Thread.sleep(50);} catch (InterruptedException e){}
            setcoord();   // changes the placement of the text
            repaint();    // repaints the screen by activating the paint()
                          // method
        }
    }
    ...

} // End TickerTape
```

This allows the ability to effectively encapsulate(hide) the classes and all its methods that actually support the **run**() method. Interfaces allow for distinct behaviors, defined by the programmer, to be used without exposing the class(es) to everyone. We'll discuss these techniques in more detail in Chapter 6.

Class Body

The class body contains the code that implements the class. This is where you provide the detail for the actions the class needs to perform (methods) and the data it needs to use (variables). The body can also contain constructors (special methods) and initializers. The basic format for a class body is:

```
{
    Variable-declarations;
    Method-declarations;
}
```

The variable declarations can be any standard Java declaration (see Chapter 3 and the material presented at the end of this chapter if you need a review). Later in this chapter we'll discuss how methods are declared and used. Here's an example of a class with a body:

```
public class TickerTape extends Applet implements Runnable {
// Beginning of class body
    String inputText;
    String animSpeedString;
    Color color = new Color(255, 255, 255);
```

```
    int xpos;
    ...
    // Methods
    public void paint(Graphics g) {
        paintText(osGraphics);
        g.drawImage(im, 0, 0, null);
    }
    ...
// End of Class Body

}
```

NAME SPACE

Every method and variable defined in a class is recorded into an area called a *name space*. This name space is then inherited by the other classes in a class hierarchy which are derived from the class. If a variable or method has been previously defined elsewhere in the structure with the same name, a *shadowing* effect occurs for that level. To access the value of a variable that supersedes the current value, you need to put the prefix clause **super** in front of the variable name. This clause instructs the expression to take the value of the superclass. To access the value of the current variable, you use the prefix **this**. Let's look at an example:

```
public class House extends Object {   static int tvamount = 8;  // Variable
    void main() {
        Room();
    }
}

public class Room extends House {    static int tvamount = 5;   // Variable
    int Child = this.tvamount;  // Child equals 5—same as saying tvamount
    int Parent = super.tvamount;     // Parent equals 8
}
```

In this example the **House** class is derived from the standard **Object** class. Then, the **Room** class is derived from **House**. Now notice that each class defines a variable named **tvamount** and assigns it a value. In the second assignment statement in **Room**, the variable **Child** is assigned the value 5 because **this** is used to access the class's local copy of the **tvamount** variable. In the next assignment statement, notice how **super** is used to access the value **tvamount** was assigned in **House**—the superclass.

Methods

As we've seen, the mechanisms used to implement operations in classes are called *methods*. This terminology is borrowed directly from object-oriented languages like Smalltalk and C++. Methods define the behavior of a class and the objects created from the class. A method can send, receive, and alter information to perform a task in an application. Java requires that every method be defined within a class or interface, unlike C++ where methods (functions) can be implemented outside of classes.

Let's refer to the car class hierarchy we presented earlier in this chapter to get a better understanding of the role methods play. All of the cars we introduced have doors and we could define two methods to operate on these doors: open and close. These same methods could be designed to perform operations on other car components such as windows, trunks, hoods, and so on. A component like a door can be viewed as an object. Of course, a car would be made up of many objects and many methods would be required to process all of the objects. As a programmer, it would be up to you to decide how to arrange the objects you need and what methods must be implemented.

Declaring a Method

If you recall from Chapter 2, our TickerTape applet included a number of methods. The first one defined was the **init**() method, which was responsible for initializing the applet upon loading. Let's take a step back and look at the full declaration used to define a Java method:

```
[Modifier] ReturnType Identifier([ParameterList]) [Throws]
{
    MethodBody;
}
```

The *Modifier* and *Throws* clauses are optional. They are used to specify how the method needs to be accessed and which exceptions should be checked for. (For more information on exceptions and how to catch errors, refer to Chapter 7.)

Components of a Method Declaration

If you were to break down the method declaration, you would find it performs three main tasks:

- It determines who may call the method
- It determines what the method can receive (the parameters)
- It determines how the method returns information

Method Modifiers

Earlier in this chapter, you learned that a set of modifiers are available for defining how classes can be accessed. Methods also can be defined using modifiers, although the method modifiers only affect how methods are used, not the class they are defined in. Java provides eight modifiers for defining methods, but only one modifier from each of the groups listed next may be used in a method declaration. For example, you cannot use a **public** and **private** modifier in the same declaration. Here is the complete set of method modifiers:

- **public, protected, private**
- **static**
- **abstract, final, native, synchronized**

Keep in mind that it doesn't make sense to use some modifiers in one group with modifiers from another group. For example, a method that is defined using the **private** and **abstract** modifiers contradicts itself. An abstract method is one that requires its actual code to be defined in the subclasses that follow, whereas a private method is one that can only be accessed in the class it is defined in. The rule of thumb when choosing and combining modifiers is that you need to make sure that they are complementary rather than contradictory. If a modifier is not used, the method may be accessed only by the classes that are in the current package.

PUBLIC METHOD

A method declared as public can be accessed by *any* class in the same package. It can also be accessed by other classes from other packages. This modifier gives a method the most freedom.

PROTECTED METHOD

A method declared as protected can only be used by other classes within the same package. All the subclasses beneath the class the method is defined in may access the method unless shadowing occurs. Shadowing involves naming a method using a name that already exists in a superclass above the class the method is defined in.

Private Method

A method declared as private is one that can only be accessed by the class it is defined in. This modifier gives a method the least amount of freedom.

Static Method

A method declared as static is one that cannot be changed. This type of method is also referred to as a *class method,* because it belongs explicitly to a particular class. When an *instance* of the class that defines the method is created, the static method cannot be altered. For this reason, a static method can refer to any other static methods or variables by name. Limitations of static methods to keep in mind are that they cannot be declared as final, and they cannot be overridden.

Abstract Method

A method declared as abstract is one that must be defined in a subclass of the current class. However, an abstract method must be declared in the current class with a (;) semicolon in place of the method's block of code. Methods that are declared abstract are not required to be implemented in every subclass.

Final Method

A method declared as final is one that ends the hierarchical tree. No methods having the same name can be defined in subclasses that exist below the class that declares the method as final.

Native Method

A method declared as native is one that will be implemented using outside code—code that is written in another language, to be used in conjunction with your current program. This limits you to a specific platform and restricts you from creating Java applets. Native methods are declared by leaving out the method body and placing a semicolon at the end of the method declaration.

Synchronized Method

A method declared as synchronized limits it from being executed by multiple objects at the same time. This is useful when you are creating Java applets and you could have more than one thread running at the same time accessing one central piece of data. If the method is static (e.g., a class method), the whole class would be locked. If you just declare a particular method as synchronized, the object containing the method would only be locked until the method finishes executing.

Return Type of a Method

Any information that is returned from a method is declared as the *return type*. This assures that the information that is returned from a method call will be of the correct type; otherwise, a compile-time error will be generated. If no information will be returned by a method, the **void** keyword should be placed in front of the method name. The different data types that may be returned by methods are covered in Chapter 4.

Parameter Lists for a Method

The parameter list consists of the ordered set of data elements passed to a method. You can pass zero, one, or multiple parameters by listing them between the parentheses, with each type and variable name being separated by a comma. If no parameters are passed, the parentheses should be empty. All variables that are passed become local for that instance of the method. Here's an example of how methods can be declared with and without parameters:

```
public static void MyFirstMethod(String Name, int Number) {
   ...
   // the String variable Name is assigned whatever is passed to it
   // the integer variable Number is assigned whatever is passed to it
   ...
}

public static void MyFirstMethod() {
   ...
   // Nothing is passed  to it.
   ...
}
```

Method Throws

The **throws** clause is used to specify the type of error(s) that will be handled within a method. In effect, it is used to help you set up an automatic error-handler. In the event of an error, the error must be assignable to one of the exceptions in either the **Error**, **RunTimeException**, or **Exception** classes. (These are special classes that Java provides for catching compile-time and run-time errors. We'll cover them in more detail in Chapter 7.) Each method you declare does not need to use the **throws** clause in its declaration, but in the event of an error, the omission of this clause will leave the error handling up to the Java compiler or the Java interpreter. Let's look at an example of how the **throws** clause is used.

In the following method declaration, the Java exception named **ArrayOutOfBoundsException** is specified so that in the event an array range error occurs, the method will know how to handle the error:

```java
public class Array_check() {
   String arr[5];

   public static void main(void) throws ArrayOutOfBoundsException {
      int i=0;
      char ch;

      // Specify which code should be tested
      try {
        while (i <= 5) ch = arr[i++];
      }
      // An error has occurred—display a message
      catch {
        System.out.println("Array out of bounds");
      }
   }
}
```

At some point **main()** will try to access a location outside the legal range of the array **arr[]**. When this happens, an exception will be "thrown" and the **catch** clause will handle it. Also notice the use of the **try** clause which is needed to specify which code in the method should be tested. In our case, we want to check each iteration of the **while** loop.

Method Body

All executable code for Java classes is contained in the body of the methods. Unless a method is declared as abstract, native, or is declared in the body of an interface, the code for the method is placed between a pair of curly braces. This code can be any valid Java statements including variable declarations, assignment statements, method calls, control statements, and so on.

Here's an example of how a basic method is defined:

```java
public int SimpleMethod(int Number) {

   // The integer variable Number is assigned whatever is passed to it

   int lowrange = 1;  // Local declarations for the method
```

```
    int highrange = 10;

    if (Number <= lowrange) return -1;
    if (Number >= highrange) return 100
        else return 50;
}
```

In this case, the method's name is **SimpleMethod**(). Because it is declared as public, it can be used by any class in the package in which the method is defined. The return type for the method is **int** and it accepts one **int** parameter. The method body contains a few local declarations and a set of if-then decision-making statements.

For a method declared as abstract, native, or one that is declared in an interface, the body is left blank and the declaration is terminated with a semicolon. The bodies are then defined elsewhere depending on how they are declared. Here's an example:

```
abstract class Aparticles extends Quark {

    abstract int abstract_method();  // Defined in the subclasses of the class

    native void native_method ();  // Defined in an external process

    public String normal_method() {
        ... // Definition of the method
    }
}
```

Using the this and super Keywords

To access class variables and methods from within an object, you can reference them by using the keywords **this** and **super**. When the Java compiler encounters the **this** keyword in the body of a method, it knows that you are accessing other methods and variables defined within the scope of the class the method is defined in. On the other hand, variables and methods that are available for accessing in the parent class (superclass) to the current class are referenced using the **super** keyword. Here's an example of how each of these keywords can be used:

```
class Atom_ant extends Molecule {
    int Number;
    ...
}
```

```
class Quark extends Atom_ant {
    int Proton;
    int Neutron;
    String Electon = "Negative attraction";
    ...
    void Count() {
        System.out.println(this.Proton + " is the number of Protons"); // Correct
        System.out.println(Neutron + " is the number of Neutrons"); // Correct
        System.out.println(super.Number + " is the number of Atoms"); // Correct
        System.out.println(Atom_ant.Number + " is the number of Atoms");
          // Correct
        ...
    }
}
```

In this example, this.Proton references the local variable Proton defined in the class Quark. But take a look at the second method call in the Count() method. Here, the variable Neutron, which is also declared in Quark, is referenced without the use of the **this** keyword. What gives? Actually, since both of these variables are defined within Quark, the **this** keyword is not really needed.

As for the two following lines of code, they each reference the **Number** variable declared in the **Atom_ant** class, which serves as the parent to the **Quark** class. Notice that the keyword **super** is placed in front of the variable **Number** to allow it to be accessed. This is the same as using the superclass name in the statement **Atom_ant.Number** to reference the value of **Number**. Superclass names can be referenced further up the hierarchical tree but the **super** keyword can only be used to access class members that reside one level above the current class. If the **Molecule** class contained a variable named **M1**, and we wanted to reference it from the **Quark** class, a statement like this would be required:

```
Proton = Molecule.M1;
```

Here the superclass named **Molecule** is included in the assignment statement. If it was omitted or the **super** keyword was used instead,

```
Proton = super.M1;
```

the Java compiler would return an error because it would try to locate the **M1** variable in the class that is directly above the **Quark** class.

Overloading and Overriding Methods

A method may be declared with multiple declarations, each specifying different types and arguments that may be passed to the method. *The context in which the method is called will determine which actual method code is used.* The techniques of using a method's name more than once to define an operation in a class involves overloading and overriding methods. As long as you can define each method having the same name so that it can be distinguished from the others sharing the same name, the Java compiler will not give you an error. The technique for creating overridden methods involves using different parameters (types and numbers) and return types. Methods that are inherited from a superclass may be overridden but the overriding method must provide at least the same access.

Let's look at some examples of how we can override methods:

```java
class Atom_ant extends Molecule {
    int Number;
    protected void Count(String Astring, int Number) {


        ...
    }
}

class Quark extends Atom_ant {
    int Proton;
    int Neutron;
    String Electon = "Negative attraction";
    ...
    public void Count(int Number, String Astring) { // Correct
        ...
    }

    protected void Count() {   // Correct
        ...
    }
}
```

Here we've declared two classes: **Atom_ant** and **Quark**. **Atom_ant** serves as the superclass. The method that is overridden is **Count()**. It is first introduced as a protected method in the **Atom_ant** class. Notice that it is declared here as taking two parameters: **Astring** and **Number**. Because **Atom_ant** is declared as a protected method, it is restricted from being called by other classes outside of the package **Atom_ant** is declared in.

The **Quark** class, which is derived from **Atom_ant**, provides two new variations of the **Count**() method, each one being overridden from the base method defined in **Atom_ant**. Notice that each of the overridden methods uses different parameters and/or return types than the original method.

To see how the different versions of the **Count**() method can be called, let's expand the **Quark** class a little:

```
class Atom_ant extends Molecule {
    int Number;
    protected void Count(String Astring, int Number) {
        ...
    }
}

class Quark extends Atom_ant {
    int Proton;
    ...
    public void Count(int Number, String Astring) { // Correct
    ...
    }

    void check() {
        Atom_ant.Count("Hello", 5); //Correct refer to superclass method
        super.Count("GoodBye", 5);  //Correct same as previous
        Molecule.Count("Hello World"); //Correct as long as it exists
        Count(5, "World");          //Correct same as this.Count
    }
}
```

The first two calls to the **Count**() method result in calling the **Count**() method defined in **Atom_ant**. For the third call, we are making the assumption that the class **Molecule**, which **Atom_ant** is derived from, contains a **Count**() method. If it doesn't, a compiler error will occur. The last call to **Count**() accesses the method of the same name defined in **Quark**.

Constructors—The Special Methods

Although constructors are identified as special methods, it is important to distinguish between the two. Methods define an object's behavior in terms of what operations the object can perform. A constructor, on the other hand, determines how an object is initialized by creating a new instance of a class with specified parameters.

Methods and constructors actually differ in three ways. First, constructors do not have their own unique names; they must be assigned the same name as their class name. Second, constructors do not have a return type—Java assumes that the return type for a constructor is **void**. And third, constructors are not inherited by subclasses, as are methods.

To understand how constructors work conceptually, let's return to the car analogy we introduced earlier in this chapter. Each car in our hierarchy represents an object and the blueprint for each car is a class structure. Also recall that operations such as opening and closing car doors were considered to be our methods.

Now, imagine that we have a subclass, called *BodyShop*, which defines the body style for a car. This class could be inserted under the general *car* class in the class hierarchy. An object could be created from this class called *FrameCreation*, which is responsible for making body frames for cars. The process of building a frame could involve first calling a constructor to do the dirty work of "setting up the shop" for building a particular car frame. The manner in which the different classes are defined in the hierarchy will determine what frame a particular car gets at the *BodyShop* from the *FrameCreation* team. (The *FrameCreation* team is responsible for initializing an "object" depending on the information passed to a constructor.)

Now let's assume we have three choices for making body frames:

- 4 Door(*integer*) Falcon(*String*)
- 3 Door(*integer*) Pinto(*String*)
- 2 Door(*integer*) Mustang(*String*), which is the default.

We could just say 2, 3, or 4 doors, but the *FrameCreation* team insists on a certain format for each. The Falcon requires (*integer* Doors, *String* Name), the Pinto requires (*String* Name, *integer* Doors), and the Mustang doesn't require any values (). When you pass these values, known as **types** to the *FrameCreation* team, they immediately know which frame to create, or *initialize*, by the arrangement of the information passed to them (data types and number of parameters). By passing the information in a distinct pattern *FrameCreation(Doors, Name)*, *FrameCreation(Name, Doors)*, or *FrameCreation()* to create an object, we are using a *constructor*.

A constructor is a special method that determines how an object is initalized when created. The constructor is named the same as the class it follows. The code for our example could be written like this:

```
class FrameCreation extends BodyShop {
   //  ** Initializing the object newcar **
   FrameCreation newcar = FrameCreation(4 , Falcon);

// ** The Beginning of the Constructor **
   FrameCreation {
   // ** An example of Overloading the Constructor **
      FrameCreation(int, String) {
     // Creates the FALCON
   }
// ** An example of Overloading the Constructor **
   FrameCreation(String, int) {
   // Creates the Pinto
   }

   FrameCreation() {   // ** An example of Overloading the Constructor **
   // Creates the Mustang
   }
// ** The End of the Constructor **
}
```

FrameCreation is the constructor, which is declared multiple times—each taking different parameter configurations. When it is called with a configuration (a number, a word), the constructor with the matching configuration is used.

In calling a constructor, you need to disregard the rules for calling methods. Methods are called directly; constructors are called automatically by Java. When you create a new instance of a class, Java will automatically initialize the object's instance variables, and then call the class's constructors and methods. Defining constructors in a class can do several things, including:

- Setting initial values of the instance variables
- Calling methods based on the initial variables
- Calling methods from other objects
- Calculating the initial properties of the object
- Creating an object that has specific properties outlined in the new argument through overloading

Components of a Constructor Declaration

The basic format for declaring a constructor is:

```
[ConstructorModifier] ConstructorIdentifier([ParameterList]) [Throws] {
    ConstructorBody;
}
```

As with the other declarations we've introduced in previous sections, only the identifier and body are necessary. Both the modifier and the throws clause are optional. The identifier is the name of the constructor; however, it is important to remember that the name of the constructor must be the same as the class name it initializes. You may have many constructors (of the same name) in a class, as long as each one takes a different set of parameters. (Because the different constructors in a class must have the same name, the type, number, and order of the parameters being passed are used as the distinguishing factors.) For example, all constructors for a class named **Atom_ant**, must be named **Atom_ant**, and each one must have different set of parameters.

In addition to having a unique declaration from that of a method, a special format is used for calling a constructor:

```
Typename([ParameterList]);
```

The only required element is *Typename*, which names the class containing the constructor declaration. Here's an example of a constructor, with the class **Atom_ant** and a constructor that uses the **new** operator to initialize instance variables:

```
class Atom_ant {
    String  superhero;
    int height;

    Atom_ant(String s, int h) {  // Declare a constructor
        superhero = s;
        height = h;
    }

    void printatom_ant() {
        System.out.print("Up and attam, " + superhero);
        System.out.println("!  The world's only " + height +
            " inch Superhero!");
    }

    public static void main(String args[])  {
        Atom_ant a;
```

```
        a =  new Atom_ant("Atom Ant" , 1); // Call the constructor
        a.printatom_ant();
        System.out.println("------");

        a = new Atom_ant("Grape Ape", 5000);
        a.printatom_ant();
        System.out.println("------");
    }
}
```

The output for this program looks like this:

```
Up and attam,  Atom Ant!  The world's only 1 inch Superhero!
------
Up and attam, Grape Ape!  The world's only 5000 inch Superhero!
------
```

Notice that each constructor call is combined with the **new** operator. This operator is responsible for making sure a new instance of a class is created and assigned to the object variable **a**.

USING JAVA'S DEFAULT CONSTRUCTOR

If you decide not to declare a constructor in a class, Java will automatically provide a default constructor that takes no arguments. The default constructor simply calls the superclass constructor **super**() with no arguments and initializes the instance variable. If the superclass does not have a constructor that takes no arguments, you will encounter a compile-time error. You can also set a class's instance variables or call other methods so that an object can be initialized.

Here is an example of a Java class that does not use a constructor but instead allows Java to initialize the class variables:

```
class Atom_ant2 {
   String  superhero;
   int height;
   Boolean villain;
   void printatom_ant() {
      System.out.print("Up and attam, " + superhero);
      System.out.println("!  The world's only " + height +
        " inch Superhero!");
    }

   public static void main(String args[])  {
      Atom_ant2 a;
```

```
        a =  new Atom_ant2();
        a.printatom_ant();
        System.out.println("------") ;
    }
}
```

Because no constructor is defined for this example program, the Java compiler will initialize the class variables by assigning them default values. The variable **superhero** is set to null, **height** is initialized to zero, and **villain** is set to false. The variable **a**, in the **main**() method, could have been initialized at the time the constructor was called by substituting the code **a = new Atom_ant2();** for **Atom_ant2 a = new Atom_ant2();**. Either statement provides an acceptable means of creating an instance of a class—the object **a**. Once this object is in hand, the method **printatom_ant**() can be called.

The output for this program looks like this:

```
Up and attam, The world's only 0 inch Superhero!
    ------
```

CONSTRUCTOR MODIFIERS

Java provides three modifiers that can be used to define constructors:

*   **public**
*   **protected**
*   **private**

These modifiers have the same restrictions as the modifiers used to declare standard methods. Here is a summary of the guidelines for using modifiers with constructor declarations:

*   A constructor that is declared without the use of one of the modifiers may only be called by one of the classes defined in the same package as the constructor declaration.

*   A constructor that is declared as public may be called from any class that has the ability to access the class containing the constructor declaration.

*   A constructor that is declared as protected may only be called by the subclasses of the class that contains the constructor declaration.

*   A constructor that is declared as private may only be called from within the class it is declared in.

Let's look at an example of how each of these modifiers can be used:

```
class Atom_ant2 {
    String  superhero;
    int height;
    String  villain;
    int numberofsuperheros;

    Atom_ant2() {
        this("Dudley Do Right", 60);
    }

    public Atom_ant2(String s, int h) {
        superhero = s;
        height = h;
    }

    protected Atom_ant2(int s, int h) {
        numberofsuperheros = s;
        height = h;
    }

    private Atom_ant2(String s, int h, String v) {
        superhero = s;
        height = h;
        villain = v;
        }

    void printatom_ant() {
        System.out.print("Up and attam, " + superhero);
        System.out.println("!  The world's only " + height +
          " inch Superhero!");
    }
    public static void main(String args[]) {
        Atom_ant2 a;

        a =  new Atom_ant2();
        a.printatom_ant();

        a = new Atom_ant2("Grape Ape", 5000);
        a.printatom_ant();
    }
}

class Molecule_mole extends Atom_ant2 {
    String  superhero;
    int height;
```

```
    public static void main(String args[]) {
        Atom_ant2 a;

        a = new Atom_ant2(); // Compile-time Error
        a.printatom_ant();

        a = new Atom_ant2("Atom Ant", 1);  // Correct
        a.printatom_ant();

        a = new Atom_ant2(5, 5); // Correct
        a.printatom_ant();

// Compile-time Error
        a = new Atom_ant2("Atom Ant", 1 , "Dudley Do Right");
        a.printatom_ant();
    }
}
```

In this example, the **Atom_ant2** class uses constructors with all three of the modifiers: **public, protected,** and **private.** In addition, a constructor is declared that does not use a modifier. Notice how the constructors are called from the **Molecule_mole** class. Each constructor type is both defined and called using a different parameter configuration. (This is how the Java compiler knows which constructor to use.)

The first constructor call, **Atom_ant2(),** produces a compiler error because of Java's scoping rules—the declaration of this constructor is outside of the range of the **Molecule_mole** class, and the constructor was not declared as public or protected. Also notice that the call to the fourth constructor produces a compiler error. In this case, the constructor was declared in the **Atom_ant** class as private, which limits the constructor from being called by the class it is declared in.

As this example illustrates, you need to make sure you understand the restrictions that modifiers can place on method declarations. For example, here is an example of a compile-time error you will encounter if you try to access a constructor from another class when its modifier has been declared as private:

```
Compiling...
E:\java\jm\Molecule_mole.java
E:\java\jm\Molecule_mole.java:8: No constructor matching _
  Atom_ant2(java.lang.String, int, java.lang.String) found in class Atom_ant2.
                a = new Atom_ant2("Atom ant",5,"Dudley");
^1 error
Compile Ended.
```

Parameter List and Throws Clause

Both the parameter list and throws clause follow the same rules used for declaring and calling methods; after all, a constructor is just a special method. When calling a constructor, different parameter configurations (type of parameters and quantity) can be used as long as you have a matching declaration that uses the same parameter configuration.

Constructor Body

The body of the constructor is essentially the same as the body of a method. The only difference occurs in the first statement. If the constructor is going to call "itself" (an alternate constructor for the same class having the same name) or call the constructor of its superclass, it must do this in the first statement. To access its own class, the **this**() statement is used as a placeholder for the class's identifier. To refer to the class's superclass, the **super**() statement is used. Following each of the clauses are parentheses containing the parameter list to be passed to the constructor, identified by the keyword. Here is an example of how both the **this**() and **super**() statements are used within the constructors defined for **Atom_ant2**:

```
class Atom_ant2 extends Quark {
    String  superhero;
    int height;
    String  villain;
    int numberofsuperheros;

    Atom_ant2() {
      this("Atom Ant", 1);    // Call another Atom_ant2() constructor
    }

    public Atom_ant2(String s, int h) {
        superhero = s;
        height = h;
    }

    Atom_ant2(String s, int h, String v) {
      super(s, h);    // Call the superclass's constructor
    }

    protected Atom_ant2(int s, int h) {
        numberofsuperheros = s;
        height = h;
    }
```

```
    synchronized void printatom_ant() {
        System.out.print("Up and attam, " + superhero);
        System.out.println("!  The world's only " + height +
            " inch Superhero!");
    System.out.print("\n-----\n");
    }

    public static void main (String args[ ])  {
        Atom_ant2 a;

        a =  new Atom_ant2();
        a.printatom_ant();
        System.out.println ("------") ;
    }
}
```

When the program runs, the call to **Atom_ant2**() results in the first constructor defined in the **Atom_ant2** class being called. Then, the first constructor calls the second constructor defined in the class. This process is illustrated in Figure 5.4.

In the first constructor, **this**() is used so that the constructor can directly call one of **Atom_ant2**'s other constructors. How does the compiler know which one to use? It looks for a match between the parameters based on **this**("Atom Ant", 1) and one of the other **Atom_ant2**(...) constructors. Since the **this**() statement passes a string and an integer, the actual constructor that is called is the second one defined in the **Atom_ant2** class.

In the third constructor declaration, the **super**() statement performs a similar operation except this time it searches the immediate superclass's constructor for

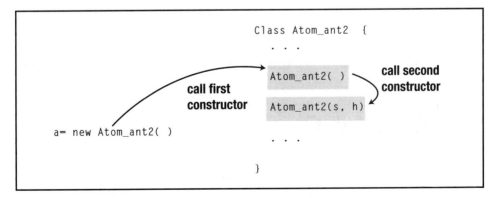

Figure 5.4

The chain of constructor calls in the Atom_ant2 example.

a match. It is important to remember that when using either of these statements, you may not directly call instance variables of the object being created. Furthermore, an instance variable cannot be dependent upon another variable that has not yet been defined, or is defined after it.

Here's an example:

```
class Foo {
   int variableNow = variableLater + 10;
   int variableLater = 20;
}
```

As you can see, **variableNow** is trying to initialize itself before **variableLater** is assigned a value.

Object Creation

There are two ways to create an instance of a class: use a literal, specific to the **String** class or use the **new** operator. The **new** operator is placed in front of the constructor. The parameter list of the constructor determines what constructor is used to create an instance of an object.

```
...
public static void main(String args[])  {
   Atom_ant2 a;

   a =  new Atom_ant2();
   a.printatom_ant() ;
   System.out.println ("------");
}
...
```

Here, the **new** operator initializes **Atom_ant2** with an empty parameter list, initializes the variable to create an instance of the class **Atom_ant2**, and assigns it to **a**.

Variables for Classes

If you've read Chapter 3, you should already be familiar with the basics of declaring variables in Java. Let's refresh your memory: A variable is a named storage location that can hold various values, depending on the data type of the variable. The basic format for declaring a variable is as follows:

```
VariableModifiers Type Indentifier = [VariableInitializer];
```

Only the *Type* and *Identifier* components are necessary. The modifiers are optional.

As with all the identifiers we've used throughout this chapter, the variable identifier simply names the variable. However, you can name any number of variables in the declaration by naming them in the identifier position and separating them with commas. If you decide to declare multiple variables, also realize that the modifiers and *Type* apply to all the variables that are named. For example, in these declarations

```
int paul, david, kelly;
static String henry, diana;
```

the variables **paul**, **david**, and **kelly** are declared as integers, and the variables **henry** and **diana** are declared as static strings.

VARIABLE MODIFIERS

Java provides seven different modifiers for declaring variables within classes. However, you can only use two of them—one from each group—in a declaration. Also, you can't use two modifiers that contradict each other in the same declaration. The two groups of modifiers are:

- **public, protected, private**
- **static, final, transient, volatile**

The **public**, **protected**, and **private** modifiers are discussed under the modifiers sections of class, method, and constructors.

STATIC MODIFIERS

A static variable is also known as a class variable. This is because there is only one variable of that name, no matter how many instances of the class are created. Here's an example of how the **static** modifier can be used:

```
Atom_ant2() {
   static int Doug = 9;
   this("Atom Ant", 1);
}
```

```
...
public static void main(String args[])  {
   Atom_ant2 a, b, c, d;

   a =  new Atom_ant2();
   b =  new Atom_ant2();
   c =  new Atom_ant2();
   d =  new Atom_ant2();
   a.printatom_ant() ;
   System.out.println("------") ;
}
...
```

Here, no matter how many objects we create, there is exactly one variable **Doug** for every instance of **Atom_ant()**.

FINAL MODIFIER

When a variable is assigned final, it acts as a constant throughout the instance of the class. They must be declared at time of initialization of the class or method.

TRANSIENT MODIFIER

This is a modifier that has been reserved by Java virtual machine language for low level segments that do not pertain to the persistent state of an object. Other implementations will follow for this modifier in future versions.

VOLATILE MODIFIER

These are modifiers that are processed through the multi-processor in an asynchronous manner. The variables are reloaded from and stored to memory every time the variables are used.

The Art of Casting with Classes

When we introduced the fundamental data types in Chapter 3, we showed you how to use casting techniques to convert the values assigned to variables of predefined data types to other data types. For example, in a set of statements like this

```
int i;
short s;
```

```
s = 10;
i = (int) s;
```

the contents of the variable **s**—originally defined to be of the **short** type—is converted to an **int** type by using a cast in the assignment statement. When casting variable types from one to another, no information will be lost as long as the receiver is larger than the provider. Java also allows you to cast instances of a class, known as objects, to instances of other classes. The declaration for an explicit cast to a class is as follows:

```
(Classname)reference
```

The *Classname* is the name of the class you wish to cast to the receiving object. The reference specifies the object that is to receive the cast. When applying a narrowing effect to a class, as you will read about later, this type of cast is required by the Java compiler. Figure 5.5 illustrates this concept.

If a superclass attempts to cast an instance of itself to a subclass beneath it, a runtime error will occur even though this type of cast will be accepted by the Java compiler. The technique of passing object references down a class hierarchy is referred to as *widening*. As a class is located at lower levels in a hierarchy it becomes more specific and thus it contains more information than the classes above it in the hierarchy. Superclasses, on the other hand, are usually more general than the classes beneath them. Conversions that occur when you pass the references up the hierarchy are thus referred to a narrowing because not all the information is passed along to the receiving object. Furthermore, all instance variables of the same name in the receiving object are set to the class variables that are being casted.

Java Note

Casting an Object vs. Creating an Object

When casting between instances of a class, an object only assumes reference of the class. A new instance of the class is not created; the object merely points to the methods and variables of the casting class. It is important *not* to confuse the process of casting a object with the process of creating an object. Just as you pass the value of a variable through different types (e.g, **int**, **float**, **double**, and so on), you can pass an object through different classes, as long as the class is in the current hierarchy.

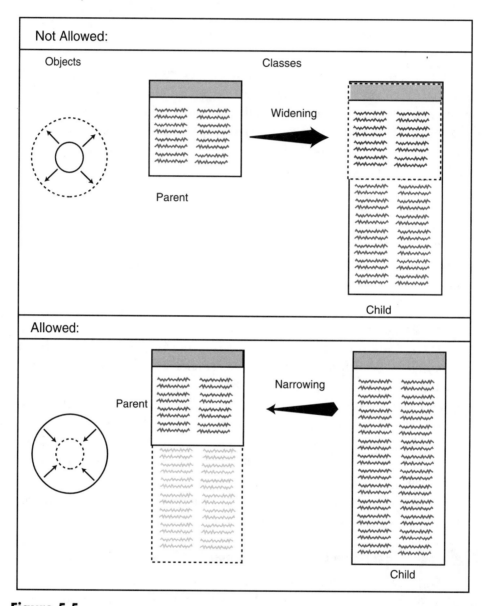

Figure 5.5

Widening and narrowing an instance of a class by using casts.

Here is an example of how you can cast references to objects between class types:

```
public class atom_ant {
    String  superhero = "Atom Ant";
    int height = 10;
```

```java
    atom_ant() {
    }

    void print() {
        System.out.print (superhero + " is " + height + "\n");
    }

    public static void main(String arg[]) {

        atom_ant a1;
        a1 = new atom_ant();
        a1.print();

        proton_pal p1, p2;
        p1 = (proton_pal) a1; // Runtime error due to casting error
        p1.print();   // Unable to execute because of the previous line

        electron_enemy e1;
        e1 = (electron_enemy) p2; // Compile-time error due to casting to a
                                  // sibling class
        e1.print();   // Unable to execute because of the previous line

        atom_ant a2;
        a2 = (atom_ant) p2;
        a2.print();
    }
}

class proton_pal extends atom_ant {

    String  superhero = "Proton Pal";
    int height = 1;

    proton_pal() {
    }

    void print() {
        System.out.print (superhero + " is " + height + "\n");
    }
}

class electron_enemy extends atom_ant{

    String  superhero = "Electron Enemy";
    int height = -1;
```

```
electron_enemy() {
}

void print() {
    System.out.print (superhero + " is " + height + "\n");
}
}
```

Here we've modified our previous **atom_ant** class to illustrate the basics of casting. Notice that two of the casts used will produce a runtime and compile-time error, respectively. (Thus, don't try to compile the code unless you remove the two illegal casts.) The first cast used in the **main()** method, **p1 = (proton_pal) a1**, produces a *widening* effect. Although this statement will compile, it produces a runtime error because the object **a1** cannot be expected to *grow* to accommodate the new variables and methods it references in **proton_pal**. The second casting statement used is a sibling cast: **e1 = (electron_enemy) p2**. It generates a compile-time error because an illegal reference to a *sibling* class, **electron_enemy** is used. This is due to the fact that the classes can have completely different variables and methods not related to each other. The last form of casting that is addressed in the **atom_ant** class produces a *narrowing* effect. In the statement, **(a2 = (atom_ant) p2)**, the object **p2** references variables that are defined in the class, **atom_ant**, that is being casted. The reference is then past to the variable **a2**.

6

Interfaces and Packages

Interfaces and Packages

6

If you're ready to move beyond the stages of writing applets and simple standalone applications and applets, you'll find that Java's flexible interfaces and packages provide a welcome relief.

After writing a few applets and applications, you'll probably notice that the directory your classes are written to will start to become obscenely large. This is the downside of the way Java processes classes; but the good news is that Java provides two key features called *interfaces* and *packages* to help you organize your code. We put these two topics in a chapter by themselves instead of covering in detail in the previous chapter to emphasize how important they are. (Many Java books simply lump interfaces and packages in with classes, or they just skim over them—shameful!) As you start to work more with interfaces and packages, you'll discover a myriad of important program design issues that come into play which you'll need to master to use interfaces and packages effectively.

In this chapter you'll learn about:

- The basics of interfaces
- Techniques for implementing interfaces
- The hierarchical structure related to interfaces themselves
- Techniques for using casts with interfaces
- The basics of packages
- Techniques for creating packages
- Techniques for using Java's predefined packages

The underlying goal of this chapter is to help you transition from writing small standalone Java applications and applets to creating classes that can be used over and over. As you start to adopt this style of programming, you'll need the flexibility that interfaces and packages provide.

Understanding Interfaces

An *interface* is a collection of methods and variables that are declared as a unit but they are not implemented until a later stage. Basically this means that the code declarations placed in an interface serve as a shell so that you can create a truly *abstract class*. The goal behind an abstract class is to provide a mechanism so that you can define the *protocols* for a class—how a class should essentially communicate with other classes—early on in the development cycle. The upshot is that when you create your interfaces or abstract classes, you don't have to specify all of the details of how they will be implemented. This is saved for a later stage.

Before we jump in and start writing Java code for declaring interfaces, let's explore a few conceptual examples. The concept of abstract classes and interfaces is tricky to grasp at first. In fact, many experienced object-oriented programmers will tell you that they didn't quite master the concepts until they had written a number of programs. Fortunately, we can help you understand and use the techniques much quicker by providing the background information and conceptual models you'll need to apply them.

The simplest form of an interface involves adding methods and/or variables that are necessary to a particular class, but would disrupt the hierarchy of the class structure you are currently building for an application. If you chose to actually implement these elements in your class, they could limit how you planned to use the class to derive other classes. To make your classes more flexible, you can add interfaces to your classes in your hierarchy early on, so that the interfaces can be used in multiple ways to help construct the "behavior" of other classes that appear elsewhere in your class hierarchy. (If this discussion sounds like we are talking in circles—welcome to the world of interfaces! Hopefully these fine points will start to make sense to you in a moment when we look at a specific example.)

Let's assume that we need to develop an application that processes information about different forms of transportation. Figure 6.1 shows the hierarchy that could be used along with the list of components that could be implemented as interfaces.

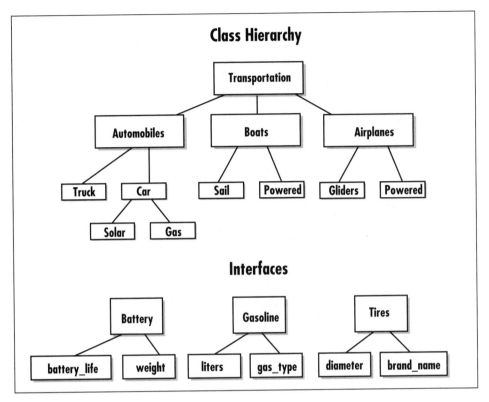

Figure 6.1

The hierarchy of classes for the transportation example.

As with typical class hierarchies, the classes shown in Figure 6.1 become more specific as they appear further down in the hierarchy tree. The interface components are advantageous when you have operations that are to be performed in one section of the hierarchy and not in the other areas. For example, the class *Car* has two subclasses: *Solar* and *Gas*. Let's assume you need to calculate the liters of gas that a gas car will use. You could include the methods and variables for performing this operation in the *Car* superclass, or even better, up two levels in the *Transportation* class, so that the *Powered\Boats* and *Powered\Airplanes* classes could use this code also.

Unfortunately, when you consider the scope of the application and all of the subclasses that inherit this useless information, you'd probably agree that this design approach is flawed. After all, the *Solar\Car* class would never calculate the liters of gas used and neither would the *Sail\Boats* or *Gliders\Airplanes* classes. A class that handles the gas calculating operation would be an incredible pain to incorporate at the *Transportation* level so that it could be designed into the hierarchy, and thus forcing all the subclasses to inherit all of its methods. If we were creating a small application that only required a few classes, this approach could be used. But if you are building an application that uses lots of classes from the beginning or you are expecting to expand the application in the future, this approach could quickly become a programmer's nightmare because limitations could arise from placing such restrictions early on.

In applications that have class hierarchies like our transportation example, interfaces become priceless because they allow us to "mix-in" classes into the application, adding them only where they become absolutely necessary. Another feature that enhances the interface's capabilities is the use of multiple implementations of interfaces per class. For example, in our transportation application, theoretically the *Car* class would be interested in the *Gasoline* interface, but the *Tire* interface could also be of use. An abstract class could incorporate both of these interfaces (the methods and variables that define them) at the *Transportation* level, but the *Boat* class would also be forced to inherit them. The *Boat* class never would have any use for the *Tire's* methods or variables.

Design Issues with Interfaces

Interfaces will usually fall into a class hierarchy without any problems when you are creating small scale applications. They also help separate the design process from the implementation process because they keep you from having to combine the more abstract design issues with implementation details in one component. They also allow you to derive classes without relying on the more limited technique of *single inheritance*. If you recall from Chapter 5, a single inheritance model requires you to create class hierarchy trees by deriving one class from a single parent or superclass. Each class in the tree is created by using only data and operations that were defined in the levels above the current class.

Interfaces help you build class hierarchies that use more powerful object-oriented techniques like *multiple inheritance*. With interfaces, you can define classes that have multiple parents. You can incorporate interfaces into a hierarchical class tree to include new methods and variables without having to worry about disrupting your current implementation tree.

Declaring an Interface

Let's look at the basic declaration for an interface and then we'll show you the syntax for implementing an interface. After that, we'll introduce some code to illustrate how the transportation example we presented in the previous section could be set up. The basic syntax for declaring an interface looks similar to the syntax used for defining a Java class:

```
public interface InterfaceName {
    StaticVariables;
    AbstractMethods;
}
```

In this case, however, the **class** keyword is not used; the keyword **interface** takes its place. The *InterfaceName* serves as the interface indentifier name and the rules for specifying this name are the same as those used to name classes. The body of the interface declaration simply consists of the declaration of static variables and the names of one or more methods. Here's an example of an interface declaration:

```
public interface Gasoline {
// This variable is  defined as a constant
    public static final int Feet_in_Miles = 7245;

// A Method that is to be defined in a class
    void gas_type(String Name);
// Another method to be defined later
    void liters(int Amount);
}
```

Note that the variable **Feet_in_Miles** is declared as both static and final. This is required because all variables in interfaces *cannot* be changed. This type of declaration essentially turns the variable into a constant. If you leave out the **static** and **final** keywords, Java will force the variable to be declared as a constant. The two methods listed include both the method name and the method's parameter list. The actual code for the method will come when the interface is implemented.

Implementing an Interface

Declaring an interface is only half of the work. At some point, the interface must be implemented. This is accomplished by using the interface definition (or abstract class) to create a class. In a sense, a class can be "derived" using the interface shell. The syntax for implementing an interface is:

```
modifier class Identifier extends Superclass
implements InterfaceName [, InterfaceList ] {
   ClassBody;
}
```

In implementing an interface, you are essentially defining a special type of class. First, the class *modifier* is needed, followed by the **class** keyword. Then, the name of the class is provided. Next, the **extends** keyword is used followed by a superclass name to indicate that the class being defined is derived from a parent class. The **implements** keyword followed by the name of one or more interfaces, tells the Java compiler which interfaces will be used to implement the class. It is important to keep in mind that a class can implement more than one interface.

The class body consists of all of the variables and method definitions for the class. This is where all of the code must be placed for the methods that are listed in the interface declarations that are used. Using the **Gasoline** interface we declared earlier, here is a class called **Gas** that "implements" the **Gasoline** interface:

```
public class Gas extends Car implements Gasoline {
   int Miles;    // Variable declarations
   ...
   void gas_type(String Name) {
   ... // Add code  for this method
   }

   void liters(int Amount) {
   ... // Add code for this method
   }
}
```

Notice that this class is derived from a superclass named **Car**.

Now that we've covered the basics of declaring and implementing an interface, let's return to the transportation example we presented earlier. The first thing we need to do is declare the interfaces for the ones listed in Figure 6.1—**Gasoline**, **Batteries**, and **Tire**:

```
public interface Gasoline {
// This variable is  now a constant
   public static final int Feet_in_Miles = 7245;

// A Method that is to be defined in a calling class
   void gas_type(String Name);
```

```
// Another method to be defined later
   void liters(int Amount);
}

public interface Batteries {
// A Method that is to be defined in a calling class
   void battery_life(int Time);
// Another method to be defined later
   void weight(int Amount);
}

public interface Tires {
// A Method that is to be defined in a calling class
   void diameter(int Distance);
// Another method to be defined later
   void brand_name(int Name);
}
```

With these interfaces in hand, we're ready to create the two classes—**Gas** and **Powered**—each one will implement some of the interfaces in different ways. They will also show you how multiple interfaces can be used in a class definition:

```
public class Gas extends Car implements Gasoline, Batteries, Tires {

    int Feet_Traveled;
    int Miles_Traveled = 20;

    Feet_Traveled = Miles_Traveled * Feet_in_Miles;

    public static gas_type(String Name) {
       ... // Any functions that are to be performed with gas_type
       if(Name.equals("Diesel"))
         System.out.println("Ah, good power");
       if(Name.equals("Unleaded"))
         System.out.println("ok power");
       if(Name.equals("Leaded"))
         System.out.println("eh, clogged injectors");
    }

    public static liters(int Amount) {
       ... // Any functions that are to be performed with liters
    }

    public static battery_life(int Time) {
       ... // Any functions that are to be performed with battery_life
    }
```

```
    public static weight(int Amount) {
       ... // Any functions that are to be performed with weight
    }

    public static diameter(int Distance) {
       ... // Any functions that are to be performed with diameter
    }

    public static brand_name(int Name) {
       ... // Any functions that are to be performed with brand_name
    }
}

public class Powered extends Boat implements Gasoline, Batteries {

    int Feet_Traveled;
    int Miles_Traveled = 20;

    Feet_Traveled = Miles_Traveled * Feet_in_Miles;

    public static gas_type(String Name) {
       ... // Any functions that are to be performed with gas_type
       if(Name.equals("Diesel"))
          System.out.println("Required");
       if(Name.equals("Unleaded"))
          System.out.println("Not applicable");
       if(Name.equals("Leaded"))
          System.out.println("Not applicable");
    }

    public static liters(int Amount) {
       ... // Any functions that are to be performed with liters
    }

    public static battery_life(int Time) {
       ... // Any functions that are to be performed with battery_life
    }

    public static weight(int Amount) {
       ... // Any functions that are to be preformed with weight
    }
}
```

Notice that the **Gas** class is extended from the superclass **Car** and implements the interfaces **Gasoline**, **Batteries**, and **Tires**. In the class body of **Gas**, the methods declared for these interfaces are coded as well as other variables that the class needs, such as **Feet_Traveled** and **Miles_Traveled**. The **Boat** class, on the other hand, only implements two interfaces: **Gasoline** and **Batteries**. Notice that the **Boat** class implementation for the **gas_type**() method (declared in the **Gasoline** interface) differs from the version implemented in the **Gas** class.

Tips on Using Interfaces

The implements clause lists all of the interfaces that are to be included in the class definition. By referencing the interface, the class implementing it must restate the methods and their definitions in the body of the class. Constructors—the special methods that initialize new objects—may not be included in the interface declaration because interfaces can not instantiate new objects. Interfaces reference an object that is an instance of a class. By doing this they state that the object being referenced includes all the methods in the class that created the object.

The Art of Casting with Interfaces

If you recall from Chapter 5, where we covered casting between class types, we discussed how a cast can be used to change a reference to an object and not the actual object itself. We also showed you how instance variables are created and initialized to reflect the current reference to an object. This occurs when the names of the variable are the same in two classes—the one casting the object and the object the variable references. (If this is beginning to sound Greek to you, refer back to Chapter 5 for a refresher.) When we first introduced casting techniques for classes, this may have seemed to be a negative because a cast can relate to different instances of the same variable name, but actually a cast works to our advantage when used with interfaces.

Let's return to our **Gas** class example to see how we can use casts with interfaces. This time around **Gas** will reference the interfaces **Gasoline**, **Tires**, and **Batteries**; and **Gas** will create objects that reference the interfaces in different ways. Some of the references are correct and some of them will produce compile-time errors. We've included line numbers at the start of each line of code so that you can easily refer to the example in the discussion that follows:

```
1 public class Gas extends Car implements Gasoline, Tires, Batteries {
2
```

```
3  Gas       aCar    = makeGasCar();
4  Gasoline  aGasCar = (Gasoline) makeGasCar();     // Use cast
5  Tires     aTireCar = (Tires) makeGasCar();       // Use cast
6
7     aGasCar.gas_type(Diesel);              // Valid
8     aGasCar.liters(5.8);                   // Valid
9
10    aTireCar.diameter(6.9);                // Valid
11    aTireCar.gas_type(Unleaded);           // Not Valid
12
13    aCar.gas_type(Diesel);                 // Valid
14    aCar.weight(12.7);                     // Valid
15    aCar.diameter(6.9);                    // Valid
16    aCar.brand_name(Bridgestone);          // Valid
17
18 . . .    // Any functions that you would perform on the Cars created
19}
```

Let's break down what is going on here so that you can better understand some of the important and subtle Java programming techniques that are being used. Our example is only missing one thing that is not shown in the code—a method named **makeGasCar()** that creates and returns an object. Line 3 shows that an object is returned from the **makeGasCar()** method and is named **aCar** of type **Gas**. By assigning the returned value of **makeGasCar()** to an object variable of the type **Gas**, the object inheirits all the methods pertaining to the **Gas** class. This means it acquires all the methods relating to the class, its superclass, and *the interfaces the class implements.* In line 4, we acquire an object from the **makeGasCar()** method, but this time we cast it as type **Gasoline** from the interface **Gasoline**. This means that the object, **aGasCar**, inheirits all the methods that relate to the **Gas** class, its superclass, and *only the methods and variables declared in the interface Gasoline.* As we'll see in a second, this means no methods or variables from the other interfaces are available for the object to reference. The next line does the same as the previous line, but the **Tires** interface is used in place of **Gasoline**.

Lines 7 and 8 both have the object **aGasCar** call the methods **gas_type()** and **liters()**, which were originally declared in the **Gasoline** interface. These method calls are valid because the correct parameters are used and the object **aGasCar** has access to both of these methods because of the cast that was used. In line 10, the **aTireCar** object references the **diameter()** method which is also valid because this object was created using the (**Tires**) cast and the **diameter**() method is declared within the **Tires** interface. But in line 11, the **aTireCar** object tries to call a method that is declared in the **Gasoline** interface. This produces a compile-time error because the object does not implement the interface **Gasoline**. Only the methods declared in the **Tires** interface are available from the object.

In the last section of the **Gas** class, lines 13 through 16, the object **aCar** may call any of the methods available to the interfaces because this object is an instance of the class **Gas** and is not casted to any particular class. This shows you the versatility possible in creating objects using interfaces.

Tips on Implementing Interfaces

If you refer back to our ticker tape applet in Chapter 2, you'll notice that it implements an interface named **Runnable** for the explicit function of moving (actually redrawing) text across the screen. When the applet is loaded into a browser, the browser checks to see if the object **ttapeThread**, which is an instance of the class **Thread** from a package that is imported into our class **TickerTape**, implements the **Runnable** interface. In this case, the browser detects the interface and uses the **run**() method declared in the class **Thread** during the operation of the applet:

```
// TickerTape Class
public class TickerTape extends Applet implements Runnable{
    ...
    // Change coordinates and repaint
    public void run(){
        while(ttapeThread != null){
            try {Thread.sleep(50);} catch (InterruptedException e){}
            setcoord();
            repaint();
        }
    }
    ...
}
```

This is a powerful feature for creating methods and variables in classes that can be set up with interfaces for future use, as long as the interface explains how information will be transferred to and from it. You don't need to allow others access to your original classes.

Java Note

Using the instanceof Operator

To detect if an object implements an interface, you can use the **instanceof** operator. This operator allows you to look at a group of objects to pick out which ones can perform certain operations. Here's an example:

```
if (ttapeThread iinstanceof Runnable) {
((Runnable)ttapeThread).run(); // performs this function only
                              // if the object ttape implements
                              //  the Runnable interface
}
```

In this case the **if** statement checks to see if the object **ttapeThread** is an instance of the **Runnable** interface. If it is, the **run**() method defined in the **Runnable** interface is called.

Creating and Using Packages

As you begin to design and code Java applications and applets that use multiple classes and interfaces, you'll need a way to organize your code so that you can easily update and reuse your growing library of classes and interfaces. Because the Java language is specifically designed to allow you to use classes and interfaces over and over, it's likely that you'll end up getting some of your class and interface names mixed up.

Furthermore, another programmer may design an excellent class that performs operations that you may want to use. Incorporating this class into one of your applications that already uses a number of classes could become difficult, especially if the class name conflicts with the name of a class you are already using. For example, you may have a custom print class named *Print* that performs certain functions for printing to the screen. After you've developed the class, another programmer might provide you with a class having the same name that prints a certain format to a printer that you need to support. You could actually use both of these classes even if they shared the name "Print"; however, they must be packaged in different groups so that the Java compiler can easily determine which one you want to use.

To help us combine classes into unique groups, Java supports the concept of *packages*. A package is essentially a device for grouping classes that you want to be labeled as a unit. You can actually combine any classes that you want into a single group. Usually, classes that share a common goal are combined in a class. For example, if you were creating a set of classes to handle drawing-related functions for a design application, you might create a package called *Draw* and place all of the related classes in this package.

You might have noticed back in Chapter 2 that some of the methods we implemented in the ticker tape applet were borrowed from classes or interfaces belonging to other packages. For example, one of the packages used was the **Applet** package—a package that Java provides, which contains all the necessary classes for creating an applet. A package is introduced to a class by using the **import** keyword in the beginning of a source code file. This will be covered in more detail later in the chapter. As you will see, classes and packages are segregated according to the functions they perform. This reduces the risk of having methods that share the same name interfere with each other. Here is a simple example of how you can implement methods that belong to different packages into a common class:

```
// TickerTape Applet

import java.applet.*;
import java.awt.*;

// TickerTape Class
public class TickerTape extends Applet implements Runnable {
    ...
    public void init(){
        ...
    }
    public void start(){
        ...
    }
    public void run(){
    ...
    }
    public void graphics() {
    ...
    }
    public void stop(){
        ...
    }
    ...
} // End TickerTape
```

This is the same applet that was used in Chapter 2. All of the methods declared in this example come from somewhere other than the current class. They have been *overridden* to perform a certain function specific to the operation of this applet. For example, the methods **init()**, **start()**, and **stop()** are defined in the **Applet** class that is contained in the java.applet package. The **run()** method is defined in the **Runnable** interface contained in the package java.lang.

Naming and Referencing Packages

Besides the fact that you may want to repeat a simple class name over and over, you'll want to create packages so that you can distribute your classes to other Java programmers. As with files on your computer, you list the directories in which they are contained to reference them. This creates a "path" for the Java compiler to follow so that it can locate designated classes and interfaces in your packages. Figure 6.2 shows an example of the directory hierarchy used to reference the package java.awt.image.

By convention, the first level of the hierarchy has been reserved for the name of the company that develops it. An example of this is **sun**.audio.AudioData—a

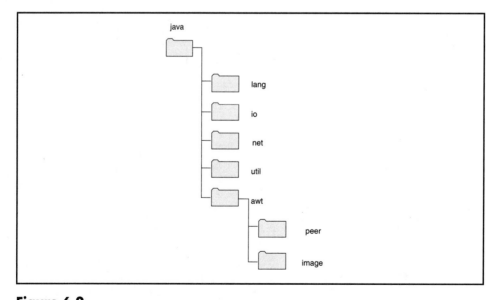

Figure 6.2

A graphical image of the hierarchy of java.awt.image and a call to the (import) java.awt.image on the other side.

package developed by Sun Microsystems. (Of course, as with every programming language, Java provides certain exceptions—one being the guideline for naming and referencing packages. For example, **java**.io.File was developed by Sun Microsystems, but this package is intended to be implemented by other companies as a foundation for building additional I/O packages.) The sections listed beneath the company name reference subdirectories that further specify where the class is located. For example java.**io**.File is a subdirectory that contains classes that relate to the input/output functions of Java. The extension **.class** has been omitted from the reference to the **File** class because interfaces and classes are the only format contained in a package and both end in the **.class** extension.

Uppercase vs. Lowercase Package Names

Java Note

A specific format should be followed for naming packages and the classes that are contained within them. All package names and the directories that follow them should be specified using lowercase letters. On the other hand, the class and interface names you wish to reference within a package should be specified using an uppercase letter as the first character. This allows other programmers who use your packages to easily determine which components are directory names and which ones are class and interface names.

Declaration for Creating Packages

To create a package, the following statement should be placed at the beginning of a source file that contains a set of class definitions:

```
package PackageName;
```

Each class defined in the source file will automatically be added to the package having the name specified by *PackageName*. The *PackageName* will be created under the subdirectory you have defined in the CLASSPATH variable set in your environment. (The instructions for setting this environment variable are presented in the sidebar, *Setting Your CLASSPATH Environment Variable*.) As an example, assume that you have a source file that contains a set of classes that implement different types of airplanes. These classes could be combined into a single package named **airplanes** by placing the package statement at the beginning of each source file that defines a public class:

```
package airplanes;  // This statement must come first

// Provide source code for Glider class

public class Glider {
    ...   // Class definition
}
// The end of this source file


package airplanes;  // This statement must come first

// Provide source code for Single_engine class

public class Single_engine {
    ...   // Class definition
}
// The end of this source file


package airplanes;  // This statement must come first

// Provide source code for Twin_engine class

public class Twin_engine {
    ...   // Class definition
}
// The end of this source file
```

The actual *PackageName* is extended by the Java compiler by preceding it with the *CLASSPATH*. (Each subdirectory included in the path name is separated by a period.) The nice part is that you don't need to create the path for the package you define yourself; it is generated by the compiler at compile-time automatically.

Java Note

Interfaces and Public Classes

If you recall from Chapter 5, only one public class may be declared in any one source file. Only classes defined as public may be referenced from outside the current package. Otherwise, the classes not defined as public are used to support the public classes in the package.

In another example, if the package **coriolis.books.programming.java** is declared, the directory structure will turn out like this:

```
c:\java\lib\coriolis\books\programming\java
```

Essentially, what the Java compiler does when it encounters a statement like **package coriolis.books.programming.java** is create a new directory structure for *coriolis.books.programming.java* using the directory path specified by the CLASSPATH environment variable. It then places all of the compiled class code defined in the source file in the *java* directory. As the example above illustrates, the *CLASSPATH* would be:

```
c:\java\lib;
```

When the package is later referenced by a Java application, the compiler will know exactly where to look for each class that is referenced in the package.

Java Note

Saving Java Source Code Files

It is wise to save your Java source code in the directories containing your compiled class. This will allow you to later edit your source code if you wish, but more importantly, you won't have to worry about your class definitions being overwritten with identical names in the default directory where you create and save your source code (.java extension). You'll want to save the different versions of your source files because as you create more and more classes, the chance for repeating a class name becomes more common. For example, assume you have a *Spreadsheet* class that contains two classes; one that prints a graph and the other that prints a data sheet. Both classes perform very different operations, but both of them could be assigned the name *Print.class*. In doing so, you must take two steps in generating source code with identical class names because the classes will share the same working directory in most instances. If you placed a statement like this in the beginning of your source code

```
package acme.spreadsheet.graph;
```

the Java compiler would automatically place the *Print.class* in the directory graph but the original source file (Print.java) would still be paced in the working directory. The next step would be to place the source file in the same directory. This is because the next Print.java source file created (for example, the class responsible for printing the data sheet) will be saved in the working directory, causing the old file to be overwritten. If you later need to modify the class file, you will still have the original source code. The next source file should provide the statement

```
package acme.spreadsheet.datasheet;
```

at the beginning. Remember, you are required to manually move the source file to the appropriate directory.

Setting Your CLASSPATH Environment Variable

When your source code is compiled, the CLASSPATH environment variable specifies the default base directory for the packages you create. It also tells the compiler which directory path to search for the classes that are predefined. The order of directories defined by CLASSPATH determines the order in which the Java compiler will search for your classes. When a class is found that meets the requirements of the calling class, the compiler stops searching for a match. You should define the path of the default package that accompanies the Java Development Kit (JDK) and the temporary directory that you work from in this order. Here's an example:

```
CLASSPATH = c:\java\lib;.
```

The period sets the current directory you are compiling from. The first directory listed in the *CLASSPATH* also specifies where *your* package structure will begin.

Using Packages

The one feature that makes the Java language very powerful is that it lets you use the same code (classes) over and over countless times. This is accomplished by referencing classes that are contained in packages. To use classes that have already been created by you or other Java programmers, you need to reference the package(s) the classes are grouped in. You can do this in one of three ways:

- Specify the full package reference each time a class is used that is defined in an outside package. This approach is the most cumbersome and least often used. Here's an example:

```
airplanes.Twin_engine twin = new airplanes.Twin_engine("Beach", 1100);
```

In this case, the object variable **twin** is declared and initialized as an instance of a **Twin_engine** class which is included in the **airplanes** package. With this approach, each time a *Twin_engine* class is accessed, its corresponding package name must also be included.

- Import the actual class needed from the package it is defined in. As an example, we could rewrite the previous example by using this code:

```
import airplanes.Twin_engine;
...
Twin_engine twin = new Twin_engine("Beach", 1100);
```

Notice that once the desired class is imported, the name of the **airplanes** package is not needed to reference the **Twin_engine** class.

- Import all of the classes defined in a package. The syntax for doing this is illustrated with this statement:

```
import airplanes.*;
```

In this case, all of the public classes combined in the airplanes class, such as **Glider**, **Single_engine**, and **Twin_engine**, would be included.

Importing Packages Is Like Including C/C++ Header Files

If you are an experienced C / C++ programmer, you can think of the technique of importing a package as you would the technique of using an include file. Typically, you would use an include file to specify the names of function prototypes you wish to call that are defined in external files.

Every class defined in an external package that you want to reference by a class in your Java application or applet must be called directly or with a wild card (*) in the immediate directory. For example, if you refer back to our ticker tape applet presented in Chapter 2, we called an instance of the class **FontMetrics** that is contained in the java.awt package (directory). The **Applet** class imports the java.awt package with a wild card in the beginning of the code (e.g., **import java.awt.*;**). The wild card tells the Java compiler to import *all* of the public classes in the java.awt directory into the **TickerTape** class. The compiler won't, however, import any of the classes that are contained in the peer or image directories beneath java.awt. To include the classes in those directories, you must reference the directories directly (e.g., **import java.awt.peer.*;** or **import java.awt.image.*;**).

```
// TickerTape Applet

import java.applet.*;
import java.awt.*;

// TickerTape Class
public class TickerTape extends Applet implements Runnable {

    // Draw background and text on buffer image
    public void paintText(Graphics g){
        ...
        FontMetrics fmetrics = g.getFontMetrics();
        ...
    }
}
```

Declaration for Importing Packages

When importing a package into a class, the declaration must appear before any class declarations. The format for declaring a package is as follows:

```
import PackageName;
```

The *PackageName* represents the hierarchy tree separating the directories of the package with decimals. The java.lang package is automatically imported into every class that is created. If you look at the ticker tape applet presented in Chapter 2, you will notice that it does not import the java.lang package but uses many of the classes that are contained in the package. The classes **String, Integer**, and **Thread** are just a few of the classes that are called from this package.

```
// TickerTape Class
public class TickerTape extends Applet implements Runnable {
   // Declare Variable
   String inputText;
   String animSpeedString;
   int xpos;
   int fontLength;
   int fontHeight;
   int animSpeed;
   boolean suspended = false;
     . . .
}
```

Standard Java Packages

Since we created our first applet in Chapter 2, we have been using packages already defined by other developers including Sun Microsystems. These packages have been arranged by their category of usage. Table 6.1 shows the packages currently being distributed with the JDK.

Hiding Classes Using the Wild Card

We mentioned before that the Java wild card (*) will only allow you to bring in the public classes from an imported package. The benefit of this feature is that you can hide the bulk of your classes that perform support operations for your public classes. Users who use the public classes won't be able to look at the code or directly access the internal support classes.

Table 6.1 Packages Distributed with the Java Development Kit	
Package	**Description**
java.lang	Contains essential Java classes for performing basic functions. This package is automatically imported into every class that is created in Java.
java.io	Contains classes used to perform input/output functions to different sources.
java.util	Contains utility classes for items such as tables and vectors.
java.net	Contains classes that aid in connecting over networks. These classes can be used in conjunction with java.io to read/write information to files over a network.
java.awt	Contains classes that let you write platform-independent graphics applications. It includes classes for creating buttons, panels, text boxes, and so on.
java.applet	Contains classes that let you create Java applets that will run within Java-enabled browsers.

7

Java Exceptions

Java
Exceptions

Are you tired of writing applications that mysteriously crash, leaving the user to give up in frustration? If so, you'll be glad to learn that Java provides a powerful feature called exceptions that automates the work of catching and handling compile-time and runtime errors.

One of the most difficult and time-consuming tasks of developing software involves finding and fixing bugs. Fortunately, Java provides some built-in features that lend a hand in the debugging process. As errors occur in a Java program, and we all know they will, you can use Java exceptions to provide special code for handling them.

Java programs can detect certain errors on their own and instruct the Java runtime system to take some predefined action. If you don't like the default operations that Java performs when it encounters certain errors, you can write your own custom error handling routines.

In this chapter we'll start by explaining the basics of exceptions. Then, we'll show you

- Why exceptions are important
- How to use **try** clauses to setup exceptions
- How to use **catch** clauses to trap exceptions
- When and how to use your own exceptions

Understanding Exceptions

Exceptions catch your errors and handle them gracefully so that your programs can continue to operate. In Java, this process is called *throwing an error*. This type of error handling can greatly benefit both you and the user of your application. After all, nobody likes an application that just crashes out of the blue. Unlike other languages, such as C, C++, and Pascal, where error detection and reporting can often double and even triple the size of an application, Java provides the means to detect and handle errors and at the same time reduce the overall size of your applications. The best part is that error handling in Java replaces the multiple "**if** this occurs **then** do this" statements so often found in programs written in languages like C.

Java's exceptions allow you to effectively code the main sections of your applications without you having to spend too much time writing code to detect and handle potential errors. As you'll learn in this chapter, exceptions create an object when an error occurs. The exception, which is a subclass of the *Throwable* class, *throws* an object, which is passed up through the hierarchy of the calling classes. The object will continue up through the classes until an *exception handler*—a method that deals with the exception—*catches* the object. This process is illustrated in Figure 7.1. If no exception handler is defined, a default exception handler is used to handle the error. This causes the error to be printed to the command line and the program will cease running.

Using Java's Throwable Class

For a class to throw an error or catch one, it must be declared as a subclass of the Java **Throwable** class. All of the classes in the java package have incorporated the **Throwable** class in the package. This is why you don't see the **Throwable** class imported at the beginning of Java source code files. Although if you wish to refer to this class, you can directly import it into an application by including the statement:

```
import java.lang.Throwable;
```

Having error checking and error handling features in Java is important because Java programs, especially applets, run in multitasking environments. Often when an applet is executed in a Web browser like Netscape 2, other applets will be running at the same time. Each applet will have its own *thread* that the system

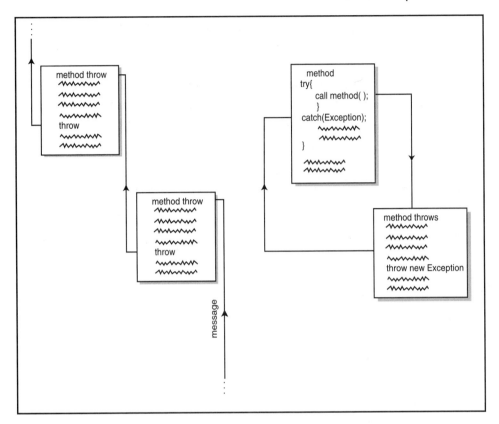

Figure 7.1

The process of throwing and catching an error in Java.

will control. If one applet causes a fatal error, the system could crash. With exceptions, on the other hand, critical errors are caught; and the Java runtime environment will know how to handle each thread that it must manage.

Do You Really Need Exceptions?

Even the smallest program can quickly evolve into a programmer's nightmare when you are trying to locate and fix a troublesome error. Why should you waste your time handling the possible errors that can occur? The fact is, you should only handle errors that you can do something useful with. Grabbing every little error in a program is useless if you do nothing intelligent with them. The best reason to declare exceptions is to provide a means for you and others that follow to understand where your code is having problems during critical operations.

For example, assume you have created a class to write data to a disk file. As your program is running, a number of errors could occur such as your hard disk being full, a file being corrupted, and so on. If you didn't have a way to catch errors like these at some point, the program might crash, leaving the user with nothing except a cryptic error message. Here's a Java program that performs a critical file operation but doesn't provide any error handling:

```
// This program will not compile because an IOException handler is
// expected by the Java compiler
import java.io.*;

public class WriteAFile extends Object {

    WriteAFile(String s) {
        write(s);
    }

    // Writes to a file
    public void write(String s) {          // I/O errors could occur here
        FileOutputStream writeOut = null;
        DataOutputStream dataWrite = null;

        // Begin to Write file out
        writeOut = new FileOutputStream(s);
        dataWrite = new DataOutputStream(writeOut);
        dataWrite.writeChars("This is a Test");
        dataWrite.close();
    }

    // Where execution begins in a stand-alone executable
    public static void main(String args[]) {
        new WriteAFile(args[0]);
    }
}
```

(Actually, this program won't compile just yet because the Java compiler expects to find an exception named *IOException*. We'll explain this in a moment.) The part of the code that could get you into trouble is the **write**() method. This method creates a new file output stream and attempts to write a character string to the stream. If the operation fails for one reason or another, a runtime error would occur, although an exception has not been setup to handle such an error.

To catch potential I/O problems, Java provides a built-in exception called *IOException*. This exception gets "thrown" whenever an I/O error occurs during a transfer to a device, such as a printer, disk drive, and so on. In our sample program, the Java compiler knows you must declare the exception because the **write**() method calls other methods that have declared an *IOException* to be *thrown* to calling methods. To remedy this, we could alter the **write**() method as shown here:

```
// Begin to Write file out
try {
   writeOut = new FileOutputStream(s);
   dataWrite = new DataOutputStream(writeOut);
   dataWrite.writeChars("This is a Test");
   dataWrite.close();
}
   catch(IOException e) {
}
```

Notice that two changes have been made. First, the entire block of code has been placed in a **try** { } clause. Essentially, this tells the Java environment to be on the "lookout" for errors that might occur as each method call is executed. The second change is the addition of the **catch**() method. This block of code performs the job of handling an I/O error that could occur with any of the calls contained in the **try** section. In our example, we are letting Java handle the work of processing an I/O error on its own by using the built-in *IOException,* and that's why no other code is provided with the **catch** statement.

These changes allow the code to compile and run. Unfortunately, they do not address any problems that could arise from actually writing a file to disk. In a perfect world, this code would be sufficient for our needs, but we don't live in a perfect world. For example, what if an error occurred while we were opening the file to be written because the disk is full or not even present? And even if the file could be opened, what would happen if an error occurred while we were writing the data to the file. All of these conditions are valid *exceptions* to writing a file to a disk. Unfortunately, you or others who use your classes might not detect them until it is too late. Remember, the advantage of using a language like Java or other flexible object-oriented languages is the ability to create robust code that can be reused by others.

Now, let's change the **WriteAFile** class once more to make it more robust. Don't worry about the syntax right now, we will discuss the details of implementing exceptions in the sections to follow.

```
// Writes to a file
public void write(String s) {
   FileOutputStream writeOut = null;
   DataOutputStream dataWrite = null;

   try {
      writeOut = new FileOutputStream(s);
      dataWrite = new DataOutputStream(writeOut);
   }
   catch (Throwable e) {
      System.out.println("Error in opening file");
      return;
   }
   try {
      dataWrite.writeChars("This is a Test");
      dataWrite.close();
   }
    catch(IOException e)  {
      System.out.println("Error in writing to file");
    }
}
```

This time around, we've included two **try** clauses. The first one checks the methods used to open the file, and the second one tests the methods used to write to the file and close the file. Notice how each of the **catch** statements specifies the type of object that it will *catch* or the exception that is thrown. We'll show you how to create custom error-handling routines later when we discuss the topic of *catching*. For now it is important to realize that we have separated the possible errors we want to *catch* into two separate cases, opening and writing. By catching these errors, we have prevented the program from crashing as a result of not being able to open or write to a file. If errors like these are found, we could possibly ask the user to change disks or try again instead of having the user loose his or her data. In our case, we have simply written a message to the command-line telling the user where the operation has failed if an error occurs.

Defining a Try Clause

The **try** statement is responsible for indicating which section of code in a Java applet or application will most likely throw an exception. The syntax for using this statement is as follows:

```
try {
  statement;
```

```
     statement;
   }
catch (Throwable-subclass e) {
   statement;
   statement;
}
```

For every **try** section, you must include at least one **catch** block that follows the **try** section. If an exception is thrown in the **try** section during the execution of the code, control flow is transferred to the matching section defined in the **catch** statement. If no match is found, the exception is passed up through the hierarchy of method calls. This allows each level to either handle the exception or pass it on. We'll cover this more when we present exception *throws*.

Using the catch Statement

If an exception is thrown during the execution of a **try** section, the flow of the program is immediately transferred to the corresponding **catch** block. The object, which is a reference to an instance of the exception class being thrown, is compared to the **catch**'s parameter type, also known as an *Exception Handler*. Here is the declaration for the **catch** block:

```
catch (ExceptionType ExceptionObject) {
   statement;
   statement;
}
```

The *ExceptionObject* reference parameter is a subclasses of the *Throwable class*. In most code, this reference is declared as **e** to distinguish it as a reference to an exception. In the event of an error, a subclass of the *Throwable* class is thrown, which is triggered by a violation of one of the procedures. This violation creates an object of the class type that the error originated from and is compared to the *Exception Handler* listed in each of the **catch** blocks that immediately follow the **try** section. The following code example illustrates how this process works:

```
import java.io.*;

// Reads from a file
public class  ReadAFile extends Object {
```

```
ReadAFile(String s) {
    String line;
    FileInputStream fileName  = null;
    BufferedInputStream bufferedInput = null;
    DataInputStream dataIn = null;

    try {
        fileName = new FileInputStream(s);
        bufferedInput = new BufferedInputStream(fileName);
        dataIn = new DataInputStream(bufferedInput);
    }

    catch(FileNotFoundException e) {
        System.out.println("File Not Found");
        return;
    }
    catch(Throwable e) {
        System.out.println("Error in opening file");
        return;
    }

    try {
        while ((line = dataIn.readLine()) != null) {
            System.out.println(line + "\n");
        }
        fileName.close();
    }
    catch(IOException e) {
        System.out.println("Error in reading file");
    }
}

// Where execution begins in a stand-alone executable
public static void main(String args[]) {
    new ReadAFile(args[0]);
}
}
```

Here, the **try** block instructs the code to watch for an exception to be thrown from one of the methods contained in the block. The initializer that creates an instance of the class type **FileInputStream** named **fileName** is capable of throwing an exception in the event of an error. More specifically, the method contained in the class **FileInputStream** declares that an exception is to be thrown to the calling method. The topic of *throwing* exceptions will be covered later in the chapter, but for now you just need to know that you are required to address all exceptions thrown by handling them or passing them on. You *handle* the exception being thrown by placing *exception handlers*, declared in **catch** statements that the errors are then compared to. In the event of an error, the code will break from the normal flow of the code and immediately jump to the first *exception handler* that matches the class type defined in the **catch**. In the **ReadAFile()** method, the first **catch** identifies the **FileNotFoundException** class as a type that may be thrown upon instance of an error. This is followed by another **catch** identifying the **Throwable** class, which will act as a "catch all" for the exceptions being thrown. This match occurs because all exception classes are derived from the **Throwable** parent class.

When to Use the finally Statement

When an exception is "thrown," the compiler does not necessarily return to the exact spot it left off. The developers of Java realized that some procedures need to perform additional routines after an exception is handled, so they defined a **finally** statement. This statement instructs the Java Virtual Machine to return and finish any code after handling the exception before moving on. Here is the syntax required for using the **finally** statement:

```
try {
  statement;
  statement;
 }
 catch (Exception Handler) {
  statement;
  statement;
 }
 finally {
  statement;
  statement;
 }
```

The **finally** statement is not necessary to handle an exception, but it can be useful when you wish to handle an operation specific to a class. To see how it is used, let's expand our **WriteAFile** class to incorporate a **finally** statement that will create a backup file whether or not an exception occurs:

```
import java.io.*;

public class WriteAFile {
```

```
WriteAFile(String s) {
   write(s);
}

// Writes to a file
public void write(String s) {
   FileOutputStream writeOut = null;
   DataOutputStream dataWrite = null;

   try {
      writeOut = new FileOutputStream(s);
      dataWrite = new DataOutputStream(writeOut);
      dataWrite.writeChars("This is a Test");
      dataWrite.close();
   }
   catch(IOException e)  {
      System.out.println("Error in writing to file");
    }
   catch(Throwable e)  {
      System.out.println("Error in writing to file");
    }
   finally {
      System.out.println("\n\n.....creating a backup file.");
      try {
         writeOut = new FileOutputStream("MyBackup.sav");
         dataWrite = new DataOutputStream(writeOut);
         dataWrite.writeChars("This is a Test");
         dataWrite.close();
      }
      catch (IOException e) {
         System.out.println("Error in writing backup file");
      }
   }
}
   // Where execution begins in a stand-alone executable
   public static void main(String args[]) {
       new WriteAFile(args[0]);
   }
}
```

The Hierarchy of Exceptions

Like any other built-in Java classes you use in your applications, the standard exceptions are designed around a class hierarchy. Every exception is derived from the superclass **Throwable** as shown in Figure 7.2. The first subdivision is where the class splits into two categories: *Errors* and *Exceptions*. The *Exceptions* cat-

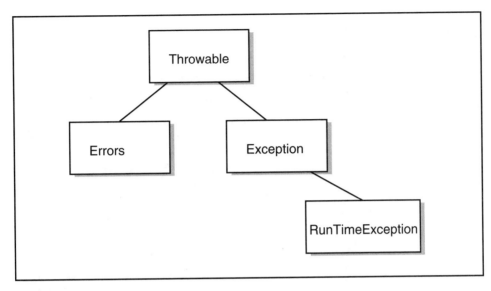

Figure 7.2

The Hierarchy of the *Throwable* class.

egory consists of the more common exceptions that you will want to "catch." The *Errors* category, on the other hand, consists of the low level exceptions that most programmers won't need to deal with.

The next major split occurs with the *Run-Time Exception* category, which is a subclass of *Exception*. Sun has arranged the hierarchy like this because they realized that by separating commonly used exceptions from specific exceptions, programmers would not be forced to include tons of handlers in their code.

Error Class

The exceptions included in the **Error** class are problems such as Linkage Error, ThreadDeaths, and other catastrophes that result in fatal errors. For the most part, these exceptions will not be handled by most applications. They are reserved for lower level programming tasks that require you to get into the internal workings of the language. For that reason, it is not a good idea to derive your own exception classes from **Error** unless you have a good working knowledge of Java. Table 7.1 provides a list of the key exceptions that are provided. All of the exceptions are defined in the Java Language Package java.lang, expect for **AWTError**, which is defined in the Advanced Windowing Toolkit Package, java.awt.

Table 7.1 Exceptions Included in the Error Class

Exception	Description
AbstractMethodError	This exception is thrown when your code attempts to call an abstract method.
AWTError	This exception is thrown when an error occurs in the Advanced Windowing Toolkit.
ClassCircularityError	This exception is thrown when a class hierarchy tries to establish a circle by linking itself to a parent class and the parent links itself to the child class or one of the children classes beneath it.
ClassFormatError	This exception is thrown as a result of an invalid file format being implemented.
IllegalAccessError	This exception occurs when an illegal access has been triggered.
IncompatibleClassChangeError	This exception is thrown when a class of incompatible types is changed.
InstantiationError	This exception occurs when a program attempts to instaniate an object from an abstract class or interface.
InternalError	This exception is thrown when an internal error occurs in the Java Virtual Machine.
LinkageError	This exception is thrown when the current class is dependant on another class, but the other class is not compatible with the current class.
NoClassDefFoundError	This exception is thrown when a class cannot be found by checking the path specified by the CLASSPATH environment variable or the current directory.
NoSuchFieldError	This exception is thrown when a specific field cannot be found.
NoSuchMethodError	This exception is thrown when a particular method cannot be found in the current class or one of its superclasses.
OutOfMemoryError	This exception is thrown in the event that no more memory can be allocated.
StackOverflowError	This exception signals that the stack has overflowed.
ThreadDeath	This exception is thrown in the thread that is being terminated. It should be handled when additional procedures are needed to be carried out before the **stop()** method has finished executing. If the exception is caught, it must be "rethrown" to actually finish killing off the thread. Because the exception is not required to be caught, it will not produce a command line message when it cycles up to the base class.
UnknownError	Bearing a close relation to mystery meat, this exception is triggered when a seriously unknown error occurs.
UnsatisfiedLinkError	This exception is thrown when a link to a library is unsuccessful.
VerifyError	This exception is thrown when the Java compiler is unable to verify if a linkage between classes is valid.
VirtualMachineError	This exception is thrown when the Virtual Machine has depleted its resources.

EXCEPTION CLASS

The exceptions included in the **Exception** class represent the most common errors that a programmer will want to deal with. For the most part, these excep-

Table 7.2 Exceptions Included in the Exception Class

Defined in the Language Package (java.lang)	
Exception	**Description**
ClassNotFoundException	This exception is thrown when the compiler is unable to locate a class in the current directory or the directory path specified by the environment variable CLASSPATH.
CloneNotSupportedException	This exception is thrown when an object attempts to clone an object that does not want to be cloned.
IllegalAccessException	This exception is thrown when a method is called from a class that does not have permission to do so. The access is determined by the modifiers used for the class and methods, resulting in the compiler being able to see or not see the calling method.
IllegalMonitorStateException	This exception is thrown in the event that a monitor is accessed that you do not own.
InstantiationException	This exception is thrown because of an attempt to create an instance of an abstract class or interface.
InterruptedException	This exception is thrown when a thread has interrupted the currently running thread.
NoSuchMethodException	This exception is thrown when a method can't be found in the calling class.
Defined in the Utility Package (java.util)	
Exception	**Description**
EmptyStackException	This exception is thrown in the event of an empty stack.
NoSuchElementException	This exception is thrown in the event that an enumeration is empty.
Defined in the Input/Output Package (java.io)	
Exception	**Description**
EOFException	This exception is thrown when an EOF is reached unexpectedly during input.
FileNotFoundException	This exception is thrown when a file is not found.
IOException	This exception is thrown in the event of an I/O error.
InterruptedIOException	This exception is thrown when an I/O operation has been interrupted.
UTFDataFormatException	This exception is thrown when a malformed UTF-8 string has been read in a DataInput stream.

continued

Table 7.2 Exceptions Included in the Exception Class (Continued)	
Defined in the Networking Package (java.net)	
Exception	**Description**
MalformedURLException	This exception is thrown in the event of a bad URL.
ProtocolException	This exception is thrown when connect receives an EPROTO. This exception is specifically caught in the Socket class.
SocketException	This exception is thrown when an error occurs during the use of a socket.
UnknownHostException	This exception is thrown when there is an error in the connection to server from the client.
UnknownServiceException	This exception is thrown when a service is not identified.
Defined in the Advanced Windowing Toolkit Package (java.awt)	
Exception	**Description**
AWTException	This exception is thrown in the event of an error with the Advanced Windowing Toolkit.

tions can effectively be handled in the average program, to address problems between the user and the program. This class makes an obvious choice to derive your own personal classes from. Table 7.2 provides a list of the key exceptions that are provided in the **Exception** class.

RUNTIME CLASS

The exceptions included in the **Runtime** class are thrown during the execution of Java code. All of these exceptions are exempt from the restrictions of handling the exception at compile time. These exceptions are optional because of the need to keep Java code compact and easy to read. Table 7.3 provides a list of the key exceptions that are provided in the **Runtime** class. These exceptions are defined in the Language Package (java.lang).

Declaring a Method Capable of Throwing Exceptions

All methods capable of throwing an exception to a calling method must declare the exception in the method declaration. The type of exception being thrown to the calling method must be declared so that it understands how to handle the object it is receiving. The format for a method capable of throwing an exception is as follows:

Table 7.3 Exceptions Included in the Runtime Class

Exception	Description
ArithmeticException	This exception is thrown when an integer is divided by zero.
ArrayIndexOutOfBoundsException	This exception is thrown when an array is referenced outside the legal range.
ArrayStoreException	This exception is thrown when you attempt to store an incompatible class or type in an array.
ClassCastException	This exception occurs when you attempt to cast an instance of a class to a subclass or a sibling class.
IllegalArgumentException	This exception is thrown when an invalid parameter is passed to a method that is outside the legal range or value.
IllegalThreadStateException	This exception occurs when a thread state is changed to an invalid state or one that the thread is currently in.
IndexOutOfBoundsException	This exception is thrown when an index to an array is outside the legal range.
NegativeArraySizeException	This exception occurs when an array of negative size is to allocated.
NullPointerException	This exception is thrown in the event that an object contains a null reference.
NumberFormatException	This exception is thrown when an invalid string to a number or a number to a string is encountered.
SecurityException	This exception is thrown when an applet attempts to breach the security defined by the browser.
StringIndexOutOfBoundsException	This exception occurs when a string is accessed outside the legal length of a string.

```
[Modifier] Return-type Identifier ([Parameter List]) [throws
  ExceptionName]
{
    Body;
}
```

The **throws** clause may list as many exceptions as will be thrown to it by separating each of them with a comma. For an example, let's take our **ReadAFileAFile** class to the next level and introduce a **throws** method:

```
import java.io.*;

public class wordProcessor extends Object {
```

```
    String fileName;

    void save(String fileName) {
       System.out.print ("Saving File Procedure\n");
       try {
               System.out.print ("Saving File " + fileName + "\n");
               ReadAFile aFile = new ReadAFile(fileName );

       }
       catch(FileNotFoundException e) {
          System.out.print ("Procedure to get another name and try again\n");
          // Procedure to get another name and try again
       }
       catch(IOException e) {
          System.out.print ("Procedure to try again\n");
          // Procedure to try again
       }
       finally {
          System.out.print ("Perform any cleanup\n" );
          // Perform any cleanup
       }
     }

   // Where execution begins in a stand-alone executable
   public static void main(String args[]) {
       wordProcessor myProgram = new wordProcessor();
       myProgram.save(args[0]);
   }
}

// Reads from a file
class  ReadAFile extends wordProcessor {

   ReadAFile(String s) throws  FileNotFoundException, IOException {
      String line;
      FileInputStream fileName  = null;
      BufferedInputStream bufferedInput = null;
      DataInputStream dataIn = null;

      try {
         fileName = new FileInputStream(s);
         bufferedInput = new BufferedInputStream(fileName);
         dataIn = new DataInputStream(bufferedInput);
      }
      catch(FileNotFoundException e) {
         System.out.println("File Not Found");
         throw e;
      }
```

```
     catch(Throwable e) {
        System.out.println("Error in opening file");
     }

     try {
        while ((line = dataIn.readLine()) != null) {
           System.out.println(line + "\n");
        }
   fileName .close();
     }
     catch(IOException e) {
        System.out.println("Error in reading file");
        throw e;
     }
   }
}
```

Notice that we didn't need to make many changes to the **ReadAFile** class used in this application. This class can quickly be made to pass exceptions as well as handle the ones that apply specifically to the class. The object **myProgram**, which is an instance of the class **wordProcessor**, calls the method **save()**. This method then calls the **ReadAFile()** method which declares that it will pass an exception to the calling method in the event of an error. Because the **ReadAFile()** method declares that it throws an exception, **save()** is required to address the exception that is being passed to it. If the method will not handle the exception, it must declare that it passes the particular exception on to the method that derived it:

```
ReadAFile(String s) throws  FileNotFoundException, IOException {
...
```

In our example, this line of code tells the method, **ReaAFile()**, that two exceptions, **FileNotFoundException** and **IOException**, can be thrown from the **try** block. This requires the **save()** method to handle them or declare the exceptions to be passed on to the method **main()** to deal with them.

Throwing Exceptions

The **throw** operator declares a particular exception may be thrown from the current method on to the calling method. This effectively passes the exception to the next method for it to deal with. In our previous example, the **ReadAFile** class declared that the method **save()** would pass two exceptions. In the code that follows, the example identifies which exceptions will be thrown.

```
try {
        fileName = new FileInputStream(s);
        bufferedInput = new BufferedInputStream(fileName);
        dataIn = new DataInputStream(bufferedInput);
    }
    catch(FileNotFoundException e) {
        System.out.println("File Not Found");
        throw e;
    }
    catch(Throwable e) {
        System.out.println("Error in opening file");
    }

    try {
        while ((line = dataIn.readLine()) != null) {
            System.out.println(line + "\n");
        }
    fileName .close();
    }
    catch(IOException e) {
        System.out.println("Error in reading file");
        throw e;
    }
```

The statement **throw e** specifies that the exception will be passed on for the calling method to deal with. Furthermore, much like error codes in other languages, messages can be passed along with the object to identify particular details to help process the exception. The following line of code shows how to throw an exception with a message attached:

```
throw new FileNotFoundException("MyFile.txt");
```

To reference the message in the calling method, you could simply call a **getMessage**() method to read the message attached to the file. The following code presents an example of this method:

```
catch(FileNotFoundException e) {
    System.out.println("The file " + e.getMessage +
      " was unable to be located.");
}
```

When to Catch and When to Throw

The issue of knowing when to catch an exception versus when to throw it to the calling method is typically a factor of what the exception does. If you refer back to our WriteAFile example, you'll see that we deal with a couple of exceptions. One of them caught an error that occurs in the event of an **IOException** by printing a message to the command line. This notifies the user of an error when writing to a file; but suppose **WriteAFile** class was a subclass in the hierarchy of the class **wordProcessor**. Here is a new version of our example that has been expanded to handle this:

```java
import java.io.*;

public class WriteAFile extends wordProcessor{

WriteAFile(String s) throws IOException {
   write(s);
}

// Writes to a file
public void write(String s) throws IOException {
   FileOutputStream writeOut = null;
   DataOutputStream dataWrite = null;

   try {
      writeOut = new FileOutputStream(s);
      dataWrite = new DataOutputStream(writeOut);
   }
   catch (Throwable e) {
      System.out.println("Error in opening file");
      return;
   }
   try {
      dataWrite.writeChars("This is a Test");
      dataWrite.close();
   }
    catch(IOException e)  {
      System.out.println("Error in writing to file");
      throw e;
    }
}

}

import java.io.*;

public class wordProcessor extends Object {
   wordProcessor(String s) {
      new WriteAFile(s);
   }
```

```
wordProcessor() {
    System.out.println("Create a backup file");
}

// Where execution begins in a stand-alone executable
public static void main(String args[])  throws IOException {
    new wordProcessor(args[0]);
}
}
```

Now, lets suppose we pass a filename to the **write**() method and it triggers the **IOException**. The **IOException** again writes a message to the command line, but notice it re-throws the exception to the calling method **wordProcessor**(). This method then allows for an additional message to be printed, in this case "Create a backup file." In place of the message, we could write an additional file to another location or do some other operation specific to the class **wordProcessor**. In addition, any other class could call the method and use it to fit its needs without being forced to perform an operation specific to **wordProcessor**.

Knowing When to Create Your Own Exceptions

The process of creating your own exceptions in Java is similar to creating other types of classes. Knowing when to create an exception is sometimes trickier than writing the exception itself. Here are some guidelines to help you create your own exceptions:

- Make sure you derive your new exception from the correct class. For example, if you create an exception that detects the corruption of a file, you'd want to subclass it beneath an **IOException**. Deriving the new exception from an exception like **ArrayOutOfBoundsException** would be pointless.

- If your code generates an error condition, you should handle it unless there is an obvious exception already created. For example, in the **ReadAFile** class we coded in this chapter, we used an exception to detect if a file cannot be found. On the other hand, if you created a class that determines whether a file has a virus or not, an **IOException** wouldn't necessarily be a wise choice. This would be a good place to subclass, however.

- Exceptions created in most applications should be derived from the **Exceptions** class. Only specific (lower-level) situations should require exceptions that need to be derived from the **Errors** or **RunTime** classes.

To create and use your exception classes, follow the same rules as standard classes. If you need a refresher, refer to Chapter 5. Here is a basic example of an exception:

```
public class AVirusDetectedException extends Exception {

   AVirusDetectedException(String fileName) {
   //perform some actions like read in libraries of virus types
      while(viruslibrary != null) {
         if (virus(fileName)) {
            throw new AVirusDetected(NameofVirus);
            //code after the throw operator is never executed.
         }
      }
   //this code is only executed if no virus is found
   }

   int virus(String fileName) {

   //perform some actions like read in libraries of virus types
   //test the byte code against patterns associated to viruses
      if (fileName = viruspattern) {
         return 1;
      }
   return 0;
   }
}
```

Trying to compile the source code will only result in an error. We subclassed the **AVirusDetectedException** from the **Exception** class because it will be triggered in the event of an I/O operation, but it does not fall under one of the predefined exceptions. This is used to demonstrate how an exception would look if it were created by you. To call this exception in your code, place the following code in your program:

```
try {
   if (file is questioned) {
      throw new AVirusDetectedException(fileName);
   }
} catch (AVirusDetectedException e) {
   System.out.println(e.getMessage + " has been found in " + fileName);
}
```

This tests whether a file was read from a disk drive, downloaded, and so on. An exception is then thrown in the event of a virus, as declared in the exception code above.

8

Threads

Threads

To create Java applets and applications that won't turn into system resource hogs, you'll need to arrange your programs into separate processes, which are called threads.

Imagine what our lives would be like if we could only do one thing at a time. You wouldn't be able to listen to music and program at the same time; and you definitely couldn't cook dinner, watch TV, and carry on a conversation with a friend. Although programming languages don't need to perform tasks like these, newer operating systems and environments like the Web are placing greater demands on programs, requiring them to handle multiple processes at the same time.

Java offers an advantage over most other languages because it was designed from the ground up to support multiple processes. When a Java applet runs in an environment like a Web browser, the browser can determine which parts of the program are separate processes and manage them to keep the program from draining the available system resources. As you gain more experience writing Java programs, you'll learn how to structure your programs to take advantage of the flexibility that multiple processes provide.

In this chapter we'll examine how threads are used to create multiple processes in Java programs. You'll learn how to create threads using either the pre-defined **Thread** class or the **Runnable** interface.

What Is a Thread?

One of the key jobs performed by the Java runtime system is to be able to handle programs that contain multiple processes called *threads*. If you've done any programming for an operating system such as Windows 95 or Windows NT, you've probably come across the concept called *multithreading*. The idea is to create applications that can handle different tasks at the same time, or at least be able to convince the user that multiple tasks are being performed. For example, a multithreaded version of an application that monitors the stock market would be able to download data from a central computer network, perform calculations in the background, and accept input from the user. Although only one thread can be executed at a time, the operating system that runs the program expertly divides up the different processes or threads, runs pieces of them, and jumps from thread to thread.

If you have ever loaded a Web page that contains multiple applets, you can see the process of multithreading at work. Assuming each applet is coded properly, your Web browser will make it look like each one is running at the same time. Of course, since most computers have only a single processor, the Web browser must be able to juggle each process so that each one gets its share of processing time.

To better understand how threads are coded, let's start with a simple example that contains a single process. Then we'll add to it so that you can see the effect that using threads has on the execution of the program. In the following **Hi3Person** class, the code executes in a linear fashion until the last line is reached, and the process ends:

```
public class Hi3Person {

    public static void main(String args[]) {
        Hi3Person people = new Hi3Person();

        people.hi("Person");
        people.hi("Person 2");
        people.hi("Person 3");

        System.out.println("Hello Everyone");
    }

    void hi(String who) {
        System.out.println("Hi " + who);
    }
}
```

Code execution begins by creating an instance of the class **Hi3Person.** Next, the three **hi()** methods are called. Each of these is executed one at a time, returning control back to the main body of the code. The final statement in **main()** writes the text "Hello Everyone" before the program ends.

As we introduce the concept of threads to **Hi3Person**, the linear path of execution will be disrupted. The program will be split into multiple processes, each responsible for writing to the screen. Let's look at the new version of our code to see what is going on behind the scenes:

```
public class Hi3People implements Runnable {

    public static void main(String args[]) throws InterruptedException {

        int i = 0;

        Hi3People person = new Hi3People();
        // Create thread #1
        Thread aThread = new Thread(person, "Person 1");
        // Create thread #2
        Thread anotherThread = new Thread(person, "Person 2");

        aThread.start();                // Start the first thread
        anotherThread.start();          // Start the second thread

        // Body of main program
        while ((aThread.isAlive()) || (anotherThread.isAlive())) {
            i++;
        }

        // Executes after both threads have finished
        System.out.println(i + "\n");
        System.out.println("Hello Everyone");

        aThread.stop();                 // Stop the first thread
        anotherThread.stop();           // Stop the second thread
    }

    public void run() {
        System.out.println("Hi " + Thread.currentThread().getName());
    }
}
```

(For now, don't worry about the syntax used to create the threads that are used. We'll explain the techniques for implementing threads a little later in this chapter.) Notice that the **Hi3People** class initiates two threads that run concurrently as our application continues on. After each thread has been created, the **start()**

method of the thread is called, which tells the Java interpreter to begin processing this thread. The **main**() method is responsible for setting up each thread and determining when the threads are finished. This is necessary because our program needs to know when it is safe to execute the code starting with the line:

```
System.out.println(i + "\n");
```

Otherwise, the program will end before the threads have finished and it will hang. In this case, we have placed a **while** loop to count continuously during the execution of the threads:

```
while ((aThread.isAlive()) || (anotherThread.isAlive())) {
    i++;
}
```

If you compile and run this example, you will notice that the value stored in the variable **i** will change after each execution of the code. This variable stores the number of times the **while** loop repeats during the life of *both* threads. The fact that this value changes illustrates the control that Java can have as it executes programs that are divided up into separate processes. Running a single- or multi-threaded program is not the only task that the Java runtime system must perform. Java also has its own internal threads that it must perform to manage tasks such as garbage collection.

Java Note

To Thread or Not to Thread

The trick to programming with threads is knowing when you need to use them. Threads have the ability to hinder as well as help the execution of programs. You should only use threads when two or more processes need to exist at the same time. For example, in a windows environment, multiple windows can be opened at once *to give the impression* that two operations are occurring at the same time. These are examples of threads being implemented into real world application. Most Java programmers implement threads for building interface components by using the AWT package, which we'll explore in Chapter 9.

Keep in mind that when an application runs, multiple processes don't actually run at the same time. It's the operating system's job to give the user the impression that everything happens at once. Even in a multithreading environment like Unix, processes do not occur at the same time. As Figure 8.1 shows, the illusion of processes running concurrently is created by carefully and quickly cycling instructions through a channel. The Java Virtual Machine handles its own type of processor management by determining what executions will occur and in what order.

When you add multiple threads to your program, you effectively set up an events manager. You must manage how the instructions from your application are handled. You determine what process receives more or less time and when to change the focus of the program. As you will see later in this chapter, you can make your application appear transparent or painfully slow just by the way you schedule your threads.

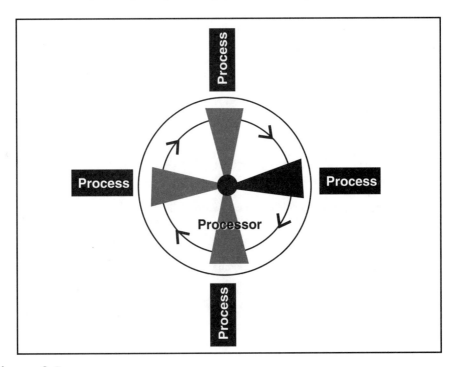

Figure 8.1

The technique of managing multiple processes.

Creating a Thread

Before you can create a thread, you must set up a class to handle the thread. This is done in either of two ways: extending a class (subclassing the **Thread** class) or implementing an interface. As you'll see in the next two sections, the approach you use will depend on your own needs.

Subclassing the Thread Class

The most obvious way to create a thread is to subclass the **Thread** class that Java provides. This approach allows you to override the methods in the **Thread** class to perform the functions you define for your program. Here is the syntax for creating a class using the **Thread** class.

```
[Modifier] class ClassName extends Thread {
    ClassBody;
}
```

Here's an example Java application that utilizes the **Thread** class as a superclass:

```
public class Hiagain extends Thread {

    public static void main(String args[]) {

        int i =0;

        Hiagain tony = new Hiagain();  // Create a new object
        Thread t1 = new Thread(tony);  // Create each thread of the object type
        Thread t2 = new Thread(tony);

        t1.start();     // Start each thread
        t2.start();

      while ((t1.isAlive()) || (t2.isAlive())) {
         i++;
      }

        System.out.println("Hello Everyone");
        t1.stop();      // End the threads
        t2.stop();
    }

    public void run() {
        System.out.println("Hi");
    }
}
```

The class **Hiagain** subclasses the **Thread** class and overrides the **run**() method defined by the **Thread** class. Because **Hiagain** is derived from **Thread**, it inherits all of the methods defined in **Thread** including **start**(), **run**(), and **stop**(). The original versions of these methods defined in **Thread** are used except in the case of the **run**() method, which has been overridden. Because this method tells the thread which operations to perform after the thread has been started, it typically needs to be overridden. The key methods that are defined in the **Thread** class will be presented later in this chapter.

Implementing the Runnable Interface

When designing class hierarchies for your Java applications or applets, situations arise where subclassing from the **Threads** class is just not possible. In such cases, you can implement the **Runnable** interface to avoid a conflict. To declare a class **Runnable**, follow the template shown here:

```
[Modifier] class ClassName extends SuperClass implements Runnable {
    ClassBody;
}
```

The advantage of this approach is that you can create a new class that is both derived from another class and uses the methods defined by the **Runnable** interface. Of course, you will then be required to go along with the implementation created by the designers of this interface. Let's revisit our ticker tape applet introduced in Chapter 2 because it provides a good example of an implementation of the **Runnable** interface:

```
// TickerTape Class
public class TickerTape extends Applet implements Runnable{

    ....

    // Initialize Applet
    public void init(){
    ....
    }

    ....
// Start Applet as thread
    public void start(){
        if(ttapeThread == null){
            ttapeThread = new Thread(this);
```

```
            ttapeThread.start();
        }
    }
    ...
    // Change coordinates and repaint
    public void run(){
        while(ttapeThread != null){
            try {Thread.sleep(50);} catch (InterruptedException e){}
            setcoord();
            repaint();
        }
    }
....
// Stop thread then clean up before close
    public void stop(){
        if(ttapeThread != null)
            ttapeThread.stop();
        ttapeThread = null;
    }

} // End TickerTape
```

As with all applets, you must use the **Runnable** interface to implement threads. (You are forced to subclass the **Applet** class to perform the basic operations of initializing and starting your applet.) The reason you would want to implement threads in an applet is to reduce the processor load for performing operations that occur over and over. One example would be the graphics routine in our ticker tape applet that updates the screen to make the text appear as if it floats across the screen. The **run**() method is coded to redraw the screen and then set the thread to sleep for a specified amount of time:

```
// Change coordinates and repaint
public void run() {
    while(ttapeThread != null) {
        try { Thread.sleep(50); } catch (InterruptedException e) {}
        setcoord();
        repaint();
    }
}
```

The reason for putting the thread to sleep is covered in more detail later in the chapter. The two methods responsible for moving the text are **setcoord**() and **repaint**(). They are executed as long as the thread exists.

Initializing a Thread

Before you can use a thread, you must initialize it by creating an instance of the **Thread** class. The best way to do this is to use the constructor for the **Thread** class. The simple form of this constructor is:

```
Thread Identifier = new Thread();
```

A few other variations of this constructor are also supported:

```
Thread(ObjectReference);
Thread(StringName);
Thread(ObjectReference, StringName);
```

In the first example, a parameter that references the object to be used to create the thread for is provided. We actually used this type of constructor in the **Hiagain** class example presented earlier:

```
Hiagain tony = new Hiagain();    // Create a new object
Thread t1 = new Thread(tony);    // Create a thread of the object type
```

The next two constructors allow you to pass a string to create references to individual threads, which can then be used as symbolic references. We'll show you how to use this feature later in this chapter to keep track of multiple threads created from the same class instance.

If you return to the ticker tape applet outlined above, you'll see that the thread is created in the **start()** method for the applet:

```
// Start Applet as thread
public void start() {
    if(ttapeThread == null) {
        ttapeThread = new Thread(this);
        ttapeThread.start();
    }
}
```

In this case, notice the **Thread()** constructor is passed the **this** parameter. Using **this** allows us to tell the constructor the name of the class that implements the **Runnable** interface. The new thread object that is created is assigned to the variable ttapeThread. Once the thread has been initialized, the **start**() method for the thread can be called by using the statement **ttapeThread.start**().

Who Goes First; Who Finishes Last?

Although only one thread can be started at a time, don't expect the first one called to always be the one that finishes first. In fact, the order in which threads are called won't necessarily determine the order in which they finish. In most cases, it is impossible to determine which thread will finish first. Let's return to our simple **Hi3People** class introduced in the beginning of this chapter, to see how the execution of threads can be hard to predict:

```
public class Hi3People implements Runnable {
  public static void main(String args[]) throws InterruptedException {

    int i1 = 0;
    int i2 = 0;

    Hi3People person = new Hi3People();
    Thread aThread = new Thread(person, "Person 1");
    Thread anotherThread = new Thread(person, "Person 2");
    aThread.start();
    anotherThread.start();
    while ((aThread.isAlive()) || (anotherThread.isAlive())) {
       if (aThread.isAlive()) { ++i1;}  // Counter for the first thread
       if (anotherThread.isAlive()) { ++i2;} // Counter for the second thread
    }

    System.out.println("The time for Person1 is " + i1 + "\n");
    System.out.println("The time for Person2 is " + i2 + "\n");

    aThread.stop();
    anotherThread.stop();
    }

    public void run() {
       System.out.println("Hi " + Thread.currentThread().getName());
    }
}
```

First, notice the types of constructors that are used:

```
Hi3People person = new Hi3People();
Thread aThread = new Thread(person, "Person 1");
Thread anotherThread = new Thread(person, "Person 2");
```

Both the object name (**person**) and a unique string is passed to each call to **Thread**(). Since both threads are created using the same object, the string is passed to assign each thread its own unique name. In the **run**() method of the program, the **getName**() method is used to display the name of the current thread. A companion method named **setName**() is provided in the **Thread** class for setting the name of a thread.

Next, by changing a few lines of code, we converted our while loop to count the time it takes to process *each* thread instead of counting the time it takes to process the two together. You would need to run this code about 10 to 15 times before running across an instance where the first person beats the second one. This is due to the fact that Java's scheduler is still in a beta version. (Hopefully, Sun will consider implementing a method for determining the order in which threads are processed.) The scheduler is responsible for determining what threads may run and which ones must wait in the queue. This process is determined in either one of two methods: priority or first in first out (FIFO).

Priority versus FIFO Scheduling

When a thread is processed, it is automatically thrown into a queue. Then, the thread must wait until its turn is up. This process of waiting is called *blocking*. The implementation of the thread that is ahead of the one waiting will determine if a thread will wait until the current thread has completed. This method of waiting is referred to as *First in First Out* (*FIFO*). Like everything in this world, there are exceptions to the rules. If a thread has priority over another thread, it switches places with the thread. This process continues up the queue until a thread reaches an equal or greater priority or it is executed. The threads that were pushed aside may not continue their operation until all the higher priority threads either step aside or finish. The most common case of this is the Garbage Collector, the thread that runs in the background and has the lowest priority.

To control how the priority is set for a thread, the **Thread** class provides the following three variables:

- MAX_PRIORITY
- NORM_PRIORITY
- MIN_PRIORITY

Each of these variables holds integer values that specify a thread's priority level. For example, **MAX_PRIORITY** stores a number that indicates the maximum allowable value for a thread's priority. To set or retrieve the current priority setting of a thread, the **Thread** class provides the **setPriority()** and **getPriority()** methods. In setting priorities, you can use one of the three priority instance variables. For example, the following method call would set a thread's priority to the value contained in the NORM_PRIORITY variable:

```
Thread aThread = new Thread(person, "Person 1");
aThread.setPriority(aThread.NORM_PRIORITY);
```

Controlling the Life of a Thread

A thread is like a human or plant life form; it has a beginning, middle, and an ending. During these stages, a thread will take many different paths depending on the objective to be reached. Figure 8.2, shows the cycle of life that a thread can *possibly* take.

The stages of life of a thread are determined by a set of pre-defined methods that can be overridden to perform certain tasks.

The start() Method

This method starts the "birthing" process for a thread. By default, it sets up a few initializations and calls the **start()** method. You can override it to initialize your own variables and then call the **start()** method:

```
// Start Applet as a thread
   public void start() {
      if(ttapeThread == null) {
         ttapeThread = new Thread(this);
         ttapeThread.start();
      }
   }
```

In this example the **start()** method checks to see if the thread **ttapeThread** exists. If it doesn't, it creates an instance of the **Thread** class and assigns the variable **ttapeThread** to it.

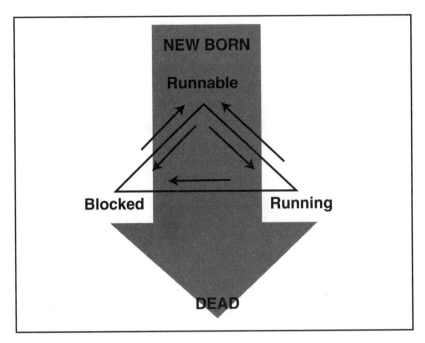

Figure 8.2
The cycle of life pertaining to a thread.

The run() Method

This method defines the actions to take place during the life of a thread. Here's an example:

```
// Change coordinates and repaint
   public void run() {
      while(ttapeThread != null) {
         try {Thread.sleep(50);} catch (InterruptedException e) {}
         setcoord();
         repaint();
      }
   }
```

In this example, the **run**() method makes the process sleep for 50 milliseconds while the instance of the class named **ttapeThread** is not equal to null. Then, the **setcoord**() method is called followed by the **repaint**() method.

The sleep() Method

This method releases control of a thread from the processor for a specified amount of time. The syntax for calling this method is:

```
Thread.sleep(Miliseconds);
```

In the **run**() method we just presented, the **sleep**() method is called to allow other threads to be processed while the **ttapeThread** is put on hold. This allows the browser to accept other input and not redraw the screen every instance of the thread.

The suspend() Method

This method suspends execution of a thread. As the following example shows, it requires no parameters:

```
// Handle mouse clicks
   public boolean handleEvent(Event evt) {
      if (evt.id == Event.MOUSE_DOWN) {
         if (suspended) {
            ttapeThread.resume();
         } else {
            ttapeThread.suspend();
         }
      suspended = !suspended;
      }
      return true;
   }
```

This line of code states that in the event of a mouse click and the thread is running, the thread will be suspended from operation. This allows other threads in the queue to be processed; but as soon as the thread is reactivated, it will resume its place in the queue as long as a higher priority thread is not executing.

The resume() Method

This method resumes a suspended thread. Here's an example of how it is used:

```
// Handle mouse clicks
   public boolean handleEvent(Event evt) {
      if (evt.id == Event.MOUSE_DOWN) {
         if (suspended) {
            ttapeThread.resume();
         } else {
            ttapeThread.suspend();
```

```
        }
    suspended = !suspended;
    }
    return true;
}
```

The **resume()** method is responsible for reactivating a method that is asleep. This allows for the thread to re-enter the queue.

The yield() Method

This method causes the current thread to move to the end of the queue and lets the next thread take control of the processor. Here's an example of how it can be used:

```
// Change coordinates and repaint
    public void run() {
        while(ttapeThread != null) {
            setcoord();
            repaint();
            yield();
        }
    }
```

If the thread exists, the **setcoord()** method is executed followed by the **repaint()** method. Then the **yield()** method is called to permit the next thread in line to execute. Unfortunately, this is not wise if we are to depend on a scheduled **repaint()**. We could fall victim to the mercy of the threads that will be placed before the current thread that is moved to the end of the queue.

The stop() Method

This method ceases the life of a thread and performs the required cleanup operations:

```
// Stop thread then clean up before close
    public void stop(){
        if(ttapeThread != null)
            ttapeThread.stop();
        ttapeThread = null;
    }
```

In the event that the end of the process is reached, this method is called to clean up after the thread and perform any final procedures before closing out.

The destroy() Method

This method causes a thread to die without any cleanup operations being performed:

```
// Stop thread then clean up before close
   public void stop(){
      if(ttapeThread != null)
         ttapeThread.destroy();
      ttapeThread = null;
   }
```

In the event that the **stop**() method of the applet is called, the thread **ttapeThread** will be destroyed and no further lines of code for that object will be executed.

Multiple Objects Interacting with One Source

When you have multiple threads in your application running all at once, the need for limiting access to devices that write data and perform other critical tasks becomes absolutely necessary. After all, there is no way of telling when objects may try to update a storage device like a file at the same time. As a result, data may become corrupt or false information may be extracted from a device.

Synchronizing Revisited

If you recall from Chapter 5, we showed you how to declare a **synchronized** method. If you don't remember, here is the syntax.

```
synchronized ReturnType Identifier([ParameterList]) [Throws]
{
   MethodBody;
}
```

The **synchronized** modifier is used to declare a method of which only one object can execute at any one time. This is accomplished by the Java Virtual Machine setting up an object monitor for every portion of code that declares itself as synchronized. In order for the code to run, the object must attain this monitor. In the event that a thread wants to run a synchronized section of code, it is blocked until the thread ahead of it finishes executing the particular section of code. Let's look at an example of how the synchronized techniques works:

```java
import java.awt.*;
import java.lang.*;

public class MyApp2 extends Frame implements Runnable {

    static TextArea t1;
    static TextArea t2;

    MyApp2() {
        // Calls the parent constructor Frame(string title)
        // Same as setTitle("Duck Duck Goose");
        super("Counting example");

        // A new panel to the south that 4 buttons and 1 choice
        t1 = new TextArea();
        t2 = new TextArea();
        add("East", t1);
        add("West", t2);

        pack();
        show();
    }

    public static void main(String args[]) {

        int i = 0;

        MyApp2 game = new MyApp2();
        Thread person1 = new Thread(game, "duck");
        Thread person2= new Thread(game, "goose");

        person1.start();
        person2.start();

        while ((person1.isAlive()) || (person2.isAlive())) {
            ++i;
            t2.setText(Integer.toString(i));
        }

        t2.appendText("\n Time through the loop \n\nYour It");
        person1.stop();
        person2.stop();

    }
```

```
public synchronized void run() {
    int d = 0;
    int change = 0;

  while(d < 100) {
      t1.appendText("\n  " + Thread.currentThread().getName() +
        "  " + d );
      ++d;
    }
 }


  public boolean handleEvent(Event evt) {

    switch(evt.id) {
      case Event.WINDOW_DESTROY: {
          System.exit(0);
          return true;
      }
    default:
        return false;
      }
   }
}
```

The above code initiates two threads that cycle through the synchronized **run()** method. When you compile this program, you will see the first thread, **person1**, count up to 99, followed by the next thread, **person2**, count up to 99 and end. The thread **person2** must wait until the monitor is released by the previous thread before executing. While this process is occurring, notice that the counter timing the execution of the synchronized threading event is running alongside.

Wait() a Second... Notify() Me When...

Running a thread through a synchronized method is perfectly fine if you don't need any additional information from the outside. But let's suppose you wish to execute a thread within a synchronized method, and half way through you need to collect information from an additional thread. The first thread establishes a foundation, perhaps opening a file. Then, the following thread will enter the method and write the information and leave. Finally, the original thread will perform the cleanup necessary for closing the file. Well, this is all great, but remember we synchronized the method to permit only one thread to execute at any one time. This is easily remedied by using the **wait()** method, which causes the currently executing method to release the monitor to the next thread. The thread that released the monitor can then reacquire the monitor when the **notify()** method is called from within the same method. The thread waiting then picks up right from the point where it began waiting. Let's modify our previous example **MyApp2** to utilize the **wait()** and **notify()** methods:

```
public synchronized void run() {
    int d = 0;
    int change = 0;


    while(d < 100) {
        t1.appendText("\n  " + Thread.currentThread().getName() + "  " +
          Integer.toString(d) );
        ++d;
        if( d == 50) {
            try {
                    if (Thread.currentThread().getName().equals("duck")) {
                        this.wait();
                    }
                }
            catch(InterruptedException e) {
            }
        }
    }
    if (Thread.currentThread().getName().equals("goose")) {
        this.notify();
    }
}
```

After compiling the class again and running it, you will notice that the first thread counts to 50. The thread **person1** then releases the monitor to the next thread, **person2**. The thread then counts up to 99 and notifies the previous thread to begin executing from where it left off.

Grouping Your Threads

Once you have created your threads, they are like children who run loose in the mall. No matter how often you call them, they will go off into their own little world. Just like children, threads themselves can have parents. These parents are established by assigning them to a **ThreadGroup**. The **ThreadGroup** is actually a class just like the one the threads are derived from. You can create a **ThreadGroup** the same way you initialize any class in Java:

```
ThreadGroup parentAuthor = new ThreadGroup( " The Potts ");
```

This statement sets up a **ThreadGroup** named " The Potts " with a reference to the object **parentAuthor**. From here we can assign threads to this group by passing the name of the **ThreadGoup** with the initialization of the thread. For example, if we wish to add to threads to the **ThreadGroup parentAuthor**, we would enter the following:

```
Thread child1 = new Thread( parentAuthor, "Angela");
Thread child2 = new Thread( parentAuthor, "Anthony");
```

Creating hierarchies of these groups is just as easy as assigning threads to the group. For example, let's suppose that the **parentAuthor ThreadGroup** also wants to have a subgroup underneath it named **petsAuthor**. To accomplish this we would simply use the following code:

```
ThreadGroup petsAuthor = new ThreadGroup( parentAuthor, "Our Pets");
```

This allows for quick subgrouping of like threads. There are three main advantages to subgrouping threads:

- Controlling the states of all the threads contained within the group without having to individually set each one.
- Retrieving all the threads in the group easily so that you can identify a thread quickly.
- Setting the priority of all the threads within the group with one command to the group.

   Note: Setting the priority of the ThreadGroup only effects the threads of less priority than the calling method. If a thread is currently set at a high priority, it will continue at this level until it dies.

The Java AWT

The Java AWT

If you're wondering where to look for information on creating interface components for Java programs, you've come to the right place. The AWT provides a treasure chest of powerful interface classes.

No one would use a programming language these days if it did not have built-in support for common user interface objects like windows, menus, dialogs, and buttons. Fortunately, the designers of Java did not overlook this. They created a package called the *Abstract Window Toolkit* or *AWT,* which allows Java programmers to build GUIs very easily. Although AWT is very flexible and powerful, its shear size will overwhelm you until you understand how it is organized and the basics for using it.

To help you get more out of the AWT, we'll look at how the AWT is arranged. Then we'll present each of the key AWT classes. We'll show you how to use the layout manager, and we'll present the basics for creating interface components such as menus. If we tried to cover the AWT in a lot of detail, we could easily turn this chapter into an entire book. However, since Java is still a very young language and much of the AWT is still being solidified, we will only cover enough of this library to get you started with the AWT so that you can use it effectively. You'll want to keep your browser tuned to Sun's Java site for the latest information on this powerful package.

Introducing the AWT

When you first start to work with the AWT, you may notice that it lacks many of the features that you would find in other graphical user interface (GUI) li-

227

braries. This is because Java is a cross-platform language, and the tools provided with any Java library must be designed so that they can work with all systems.

As you build more complex applets and applications, you will find it difficult to *not* use the AWT because of its extreme flexibility. If a component such as a window or menu doesn't do what you need, you can simply subclass it and add your own custom features.

To use the AWT in a Java applet or program, you must first import the AWT package by using the **import** statement as shown here:

```
import java.awt.*;   // Include the AWT
```

The asterisk (*) is used with the **import** statement to tell the Java compiler to include *all* classes in the *immediate* subdirectory. Once you include this package, you can use any of the AWT controls or packages to derive your own. With just a little bit of programming effort, you'll be amazed at the types of interface components you can create for your Java applications—everything from scrollable windows to fully functional pop-up menus.

Here's an example of a simple Java program that displays a window that contains a text message:

```
import java.awt.*;   // Include the AWT

public class testWin extends Frame {   // Use the Frame class

    public testWin(){}   // Constructor

    public static void main(String args[]) {
        testWin Test = new testWin();
        // Display a line of text
        Test.setText("This text will be displayed in the window");
        // Add a second line
        Test.appendText(" Add this text to the next line in the window");
        Test.show();   // Display the frame
    }
}
```

Introducing the Layout Manager

Creating applications with a visual programming language like Visual Basic and Delphi can simply involve choosing from a selection of custom components written by other programmers and then dragging a component onto a form. Visual programmers like to refer to this practice as "drop-and-drag" programming. Unfortunately, Java programming is not quite this easy (although Java development is headed in this direction). When you place controls on forms to build applications with visual languages, you usually specify absolute positions. In other words, you tell your development environment exactly where you want to place a control—right down to the pixel. The problem with this approach is that different operating systems use different methods to display graphical components. So, a form that looks good on a PC may not look right on a Mac screen.

If you have only programmed for an environment like Windows, many of these problems are not as apparent because Windows takes care of specific system and interface related details for you. To provide this type of flexibility, Java provides a development tool called the layout manager, which works in conjunction with the AWT.

Java's layout manager helps you control where items will appear on the screen. The layout manager is actually an abstract class itself that you can use to create custom layouts. There are several custom layout methods that come with the Java Development Kit. As we present the AWT in this chapter, you'll learn more about the layout manager.

What About Menus?

You can't create a good user interface without implementing some form of menus. The Macintosh and Windows environments are filled with menus. Computer users expect your applications to present them with some sort of menuing system so that they can access the available features. When creating applets, menus are not as important and can be confusing because your Web browser already has its own menu system. But when you are creating Java applications, you'll more than likely want to add menus to your programs—and that's where the AWT comes in. The AWT can help you create menus very easily. However, it's up to you to make them functional and intuitive.

The AWT Hierarchy

The AWT package consists of many classes and subclasses. Most of the controls, like buttons and text fields, are derived from the **Component** class. Since all of the

AWT controls are descendants from the **Component** class, they all share some of the same key methods such as **createImage()**, **disable()**, and **hide()**. Figure 9.1 presents a tree that illustrates the class hierarchy for the controls of the AWT and Table 9.1 lists the complete set of classes.

If you have done any graphics or interface programming before, some of these class names should be somewhat familiar to you. Instead of reinventing the wheel, the developers of Java used traditional user interface components—windows, dialogs, scrollbars, and so on—to build up the AWT. Of course, you'll find that the AWT heavily embraces object-oriented programming techniques.

- Component
    - Button
    - Canvas
    - Checkbox
    - Choice
    - Container
        - Panel
        - Window
            - Dialog
            - Frame
    - Label
    - List
    - Scrollbar
    - TextComponent
        - TextArea
        - TextField

Figure 9.1

The class hierarchy of the AWT.

The Component Class

Since all of the controls and GUI elements that we'll be using are subclassed from the **Component** class, let's start with it. The **Component** class is rarely (if ever) used as is. It is almost always subclassed to create new objects that inherit all its functionality. **Component** has a tremendous number of methods built into it that all of the classes that subclass it share. You will be using these methods quite often to perform tasks such as making the control visible, enabling or disabling it, or resizing it.

Key Component Class Methods

The declarations and descriptions for the **Component** class would fill up a hundred pages. Fortunately, they are available online at Sun's Java site. You can download the API reference and load up the **Component** class to examine the methods

Table 9.1   The Complete List of Classes in AWT

BorderLayout	FlowLayout	MenuComponent
Button	Font	MenuItem
Canvas	FontMetrics	Panel
CardLayout	Frame	Point
Checkbox	Graphics	Polygon
CheckboxGroup	GridBagConstraints	Rectangle
CheckboxMenuItem	GridBagLayout	Scrollbar
Choice	GridLayout	TextArea
Color	Image	TextComponent
Component	Insets	TextField
Container	Label	Toolkit
Dialog	List	Window
Dimension	MediaTracker	
Event	Menu	
FileDialog	MenuBar	

available in this class. However, there are a few methods that are important, and you will probably use them for all the controls that subclass the **Component** class. We'll introduce these methods next, and we'll examine some of the key event handling methods in Chapter 10.

BOUNDS()

This method returns the current rectangular bounds of the component.

DISABLE()

This method disables a component.

ENABLE([BOOLEAN])

This method enables a component. You can pass zero arguments, or a Boolean argument to enable or disable a control. Here's a few examples of how this method can be called:

```
myComponent.enable();
myComponent.enable(x==1);
```

GETFONTMETRICS()

This method gets the font metrics for the component. It returns null if the component is currently not on the screen.

GETGRAPHICS()

This method gets a graphics context for the component. This method returns null if the component is currently not on the screen. This method is an absolute necessity for working with graphics.

GETPARENT()

This method gets the parent of the component.

HANDLEEVENT(EVENT EVT)

This method handles all window events. It returns true if the event is handled and should not be passed to the parent of the component. The default event handler calls some helper methods to make life easier on the programmer. This method is used to handle messages from the operating system.

HIDE()

This method hides the component. It performs the opposite operation of **show**().

INSIDE(INT X, INT Y)

This method checks to see if a specified x,y location is "inside" the component. By default, x and y are inside a component if they fall within the bounding box of that component.

ISENABLED()

This method checks to see if the component is enabled. Components are initially enabled.

ISSHOWING()

This method checks to see if the component is showing on screen. This means that the component must be visible, and it must be in a container that is visible and showing.

ISVISIBLE()

This method checks to see if the component is visible. Components are initially visible (with the exception of top level components such as Frame).

LOCATE(INT X, INT Y)

This method returns the component or subcomponent that contains the x,y location. It is very useful for checking for mouse movement or mouse clicks.

LOCATION()

This method returns the current location of the component. The location will be specified in the parent's coordinate space.

MOVE(INT X, INT Y)

This method moves the component to a new location. The x and y coordinates are in the parent's coordinate space.

REPAINT([TIME])

This method repaints the component. This will result in a call to the **update**() method as soon as possible. You can specify a time argument so that Java knows that you want the component repainted within a specified number of milliseconds. You can also update just a certain portion of a control by sending the x and y coordinates that specify where you want to start the update and a width and height that specify how much to update. Here are some examples:

```
// Regular update
myComponent.update();

// Update within 250 milliseconds
myComponent.update(250);

// Update rectangle
myComponent.update(50, 50, 200, 200);

// Update same rectangle within 250 milliseconds
myComponent.update(250, 50, 50, 200, 200);
```

RESIZE(INT WIDTH, INT HEIGHT)

This method resizes the component to the specified width and height. You could also pass it a dimension object instead of the two integers. Here are a few examples:

```
myComponent.resize(300, 200);

myComponent.show(new dim(300, 200));
```

SETFONT(FONT)

This method sets the font of the component. The argument passed is a **Font** object. For example, this method call

```
myComponent.setFont(new Font("Helvetica", Font.PLAIN, 12);
```

would change the font of **myComponent** to a Helvetica type face with no bolding or italics or underline and a point size of 12.

SHOW([BOOLEAN])

This method "shows" the component. By calling this method you make a control visible or not. It can also be passed a conditional statement. Here are a few examples:

```
myComponent.show();
myComponent.show(x==1);
```

SIZE()

This method returns the current size of the component. The size is returned in dimensions of width and height.

The Frame Class

The **Frame** class is used to create standard application windows. It is a direct descendant of the **Window** class and is used to create windows that automatically include the menu bar, title bar, control elements, and so on. **Frame** looks like a standard window that you would expect to see running under most operating systems like Windows or Macintosh OS.

You will probably use the **Frame** class to create window interface components for the majority of your applications. However, when you need to create custom windows for special situations, you may need to use the **Window** class instead.

Hierarchy for Frame

```
java.lang.Object
   java.awt.Component
      java.awt.Container
         java.awt.Window
            java.awt.Frame
```

Declaration for Frame

To create a frame, you need to use a constructor to initialize your class. The constructor method does not even need to have any code in it; the method just needs to be provided so that you can instantiate your object. The following listing shows a complete Java application that uses a frame:

```java
import java.awt.*;   // Include the AWT

public class testWin extends Frame {   // Use the Frame class

   public testWin(){}   // Constructor

   public static void main(String args[]) {
      testWin Test = new testWin();
      Test.show();   // Display a window
   }
}
```

Figure 9.2

A simple windowed Java application.

In the **main**() method we use our class's constructor to create our object named **Test**. Then we call the object's **show**() method to make the window frame visible (frames are invisible by default). If you were running this Java program in Windows 95, you'd see a window that looks like the one shown in Figure 9.2.

As you can see, the window is quite simple. You need to use several of the **Frame** class's methods to make the frame useful. The other thing you may notice is that when you try and close the window and terminate the program, nothing happens! That's because you have not told Java to do it. You need to add an event handling method to catch windows messages. In this case, we are looking for the **WINDOW_DESTROY** call from the operating system. Here is the extended code that sets the sizes of the frame, gives it a title, and catches messages:

```
import java.awt.*;

public class winTest1 extends Frame {

    public winTest1() {}

    public synchronized boolean handleEvent(Event e) {
        if (e.id == Event.WINDOW_DESTROY) {     // Has window been destroyed?
            System.exit(0);
            return true;
        }
        return super.handleEvent(e);
    }

    public static void main(String args[]) {
        winTest Test = new winTest();
        Test.setTitle("Test Window");
        Test.resize(300 ,200);
        Test.show();
    }
}
```

Figure 9.3 shows what the new application looks like.

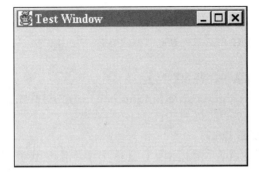

Figure 9.3

A fully functioning application using a frame.

We are gong to discuss event handling in more detail in the next chapter, so don't get worried if you do not understand that part of the above code.

What you should notice is the two new calls to two of the frames methods: **setTitle**() and **resize**(). These methods perform the function they are named after; they set the title of our application and resize it respectively.

Let's look at the methods that are specific to the **Frame** class.

Methods for the Frame Class

DISPOSE()

This method removes the frame. It must be called to release the resources that are used to create the frame. This method should be called when you exit a window in an applet. In an application, you would usually use the **System.exit**() method to terminate the program and release all memory used by the application. This method overrides the **dispose**() method from the **Window** class.

GETICONIMAGE()

This method returns the icon image for the frame.

GETMENUBAR()

This method gets the menu bar for the frame.

GETTITLE()

This method gets the title of the frame.

isRESIZABLE()

This method returns true if the user can resize the frame.

REMOVE(MENUCOMPONENT M)

This method removes the specified menu bar from the frame.

setCURSOR(IMAGE IMG)

This method sets the current cursor image that will be used while the cursor is within the frame.

setICONIMAGE(IMAGE IMG)

This method sets the image to display when the frame is iconized. Note that not all platforms support the concept of iconizing a window. The icon will also be displayed in the title window in Windows 95.

setMENUBAR(MENUBAR MB)

This method sets the menu bar for the frame to the specified **MenuBar**.

setRESIZABLE(BOOLEAN BOOL)

This method sets the resizable flag.

setTITLE(STRING TITLE)

This method sets the title for the frame to the specified **title**.

The Panel Class

Panels are probably one of the most useful components that no one will ever see. Most of the time, panels are just used as storage containers for other components. You could also use a panel for drawing or to hold images, but panels are not usually used for these tasks.

Panels are important because they offer you a way to gain very strict control over the layout of the other interface controls in your program. Unless you have a very simple application, you will need multiple controls on the screen at once. Usually these controls will not all fit where you want them using one layout class or another. Panels provide a mechanism so that you can mix and match.

Let's look at an example. Assume you have a frame that you want to fill with a text field in the upper part of the frame, and three buttons lined up along the bottom. If you only used a single layout class for the entire form, you would not have enough control to do this. Figure 9.4 illustrates what we want the frame to look like. Figure 9.5 and 9.6 shows the best you can achieve using a single layout class. This is not bad, but if you resize the frame the layout gets pretty ugly.

What we need to be able to do is use one type of layout class for the upper part of the frame, and another for the bottom. We can do this by using a pair of panels, one for the top using a border style layout and another panel for the bottom using a flow style layout. Now, when we add our controls, we add them to their respective panels instead of the frame, and everything is taken care of for

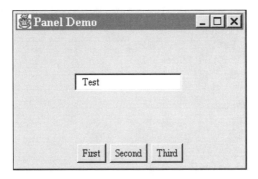

Figure 9.4

Creating a window using the Panel class.

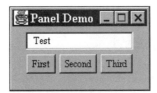

Figure 9.5

A close approximation with a single layout class.

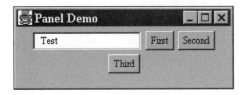

Figure 9.6

Resizing the Panel.

us. The user can resize the control all they want and our controls will stay where we placed them originally. Here is the code that performs this new configuration. The output is shown in Figure 9.7.

```
import java.awt.*;

public class mixLayout extends Frame {

    public mixLayout() {
        super("Mixed Layout Demo");
        setLayout(new BorderLayout());
        Panel top = new Panel();
        Panel bottom = new Panel();
        top.setLayout(new BorderLayout());
        top.add("Center", new TextArea("HelloWorld", 15, 5));
        bottom.setLayout(new FlowLayout());
        bottom.add(new Button("Load"));
        bottom.add(new Button("Save"));
        bottom.add(new Button("Quit"));
        add("Center", top);
        add("South", bottom);
        resize(300, 200);
        show();
    }
    public static void main(String args[]) {
        mixLayout test = new mixLayout();
    }

}
```

Hierarchy for Panel

```
java.lang.Object
   java.awt.Component
      java.awt.Container
         java.awt.Panel
```

Declaration for Panel

Panels have a very straight-forward declaration because they cannot accept any arguments whatsoever.

```
Panel myPanel = new Panel();
```

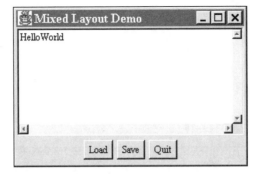

Figure 9.7
The new two-panel program with different layout methods.

Methods for Panel

Panels have very few new methods ouside of the ones inherited from the **Container** class. The key new method that is introduced is **setlayout**().

SETLAYOUT(LAYOUTMANAGER)

As you have already seen, the **setlayout**() method is used to define which layout manager will be used to place controls on the panel. If you do not set a layout manager, the panel control defaults to **flowLayout**().

The Label Class

The **Label** class defines a very simple control that is simply used to display a text string. This text string is usually used to indicate what tasks are controlled by another user interface control. For example, if you had a group of radio buttons, a label control might be used to tell the user what the group is about.

Hierarchy for Label

```
java.lang.Object
   java.awt.Component
      java.awt.Label
```

Declaration for Label

The most common declaration for a label is to assign the text string as the control is being declared. Here's an example:

```
new Label("Fruits of the world:");
```

We can also assign the text string to an object variable like this:

```
Label fruitLabel = new Label("Fruits of the world:");
```

Table 9.2 shows the three ways you can declare a **Label** class.

Methods for Label

Labels have very little functionality of their own—they can't even process mouse clicks. They are not intended to do much more than sit there and display their string. There are, however, a few methods you should know about.

GETALIGNMENT()

This method returns the current alignment of the label.

GETTEXT()

This method does what it sounds like—it returns the text the label is displaying.

SETALIGNMENT(INT)

This method changes the alignment of the label. The argument is the same as the one used with **Label.LEFT**, **Label. CENTER**, and **Label.RIGHT** (see Table 9.2 for more information).

Figure 9.8 shows a few labels with different alignments. Here is the code used to produce them:

```
add(new Label("Left")); // no need to specify alignment because it
                        // defaults to left
add(new Label("Center", Label.CENTER));
add(new Label("Right", Label.RIGHT));
```

Table 9.2 Options for Declaring a Label Class

Declaration	Description
Label()	This constructor will create an empty label.
Label(String)	This constructor will create a label with the given string.
Label(String, int)	This constructor will create a label with the given string as well as define the alignment of the string. The **int** part of the declaration is represented by setting it to **Label.LEFT**, **Label.CENTER**, or **Label.RIGHT**. (These labels should be pretty self-explanatory.) Remember though, that if you do not assign an alignment, the label control will default to left-justified.

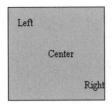

Figure 9.8

The Label component.

SET TEXT(STRING)

This method sets or changes the displayed text.

Button Class

The **Button** class is one of the most often used classes, for obvious reasons. How often do you see Windows or Mac programs without some sort of button somewhere?

Buttons are UI components that trigger actions when they are pressed. They have multiple states to provide feedback to the user. The neat thing about buttons (and all the UI elements for that matter) is that a button you create for a Java program will change its appearance depending on the operating system. That's one of the benefits of cross-platform. A button on your application or applet will look like a standard Windows button on a PC. Or, it will look like a standard Mac button on a Mac. The disadvantage here is that if you create other elements that are dependent on the size and/or shape of the graphics for your button, then you will run into trouble.

Figure 9.9 illustrates a few different buttons. Notice that the size of the buttons depends on the length of the caption.

Hierarchy for Button

```
java.lang.Object
   java.awt.Component
      java.awt.Button
```

Declaration for Button

Buttons have two different constructor options. The first one simply creates a blank button. The second option creates a button that you assign a string to display.

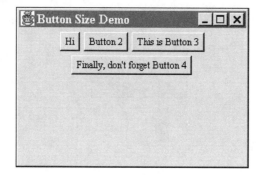

Figure 9.9
A few Button components.

```
new Button(); // Empty button
new Button(String); // Button with "String" as the caption
```

Methods for Button

There are only two methods specific to the button component.

GETLABEL()

This method returns the current caption of the button.

SETLABEL()

This method changes the caption of the button.

The real power behind buttons is realized when you handle the events a button triggers. This is usually handled in the **handleEvent**() method that we will be showing you how to use in the next chapter.

The Canvas Class

The **Canvas** class is a very simple component. It is designed to be subclassed and used as a container for graphics methods, much like an artist's canvas.

Hierarchy for Canvas

```
java.lang.Object
    java.awt.Component
        java.awt.Canvas
```

Declaration for Canvas

The **Canvas** component has only a single constructor:

```
new Canvas();
```

Methods for Canvas

The only method that is used with the **Canvas** component is the **paint**() method which is called to update the contents. If you do not override this method, the **Canvas** component is pretty much worthless because it has very little functionality of its own.

When you subclass a **Canvas** component, you can really have some fun. Override the **paint**() method and add in calls to painting and geometric methods. Or, you can create a Canvas object and make up your own calls to it that react to button clicks, mouse movements, and so on.

The Checkbox Class

The **Checkbox** class is actually two controls in one. Along with checkboxes you also can implement the functionality of radio buttons by grouping multiple checkbox controls. Checkboxes are great for giving yes/no options. Radio buttons are good for multiple choice questions.

Figure 9.10 shows a couple of individual checkboxes on the left and a single group of checkboxes on the right. Here is the code that produced them:

```
import java.awt.*;

public class testMe extends Frame {

    public testMe() {
        super("Checkbox Demo");
        Panel P1 = new Panel();
        Panel P2 = new Panel();
        CheckboxGroup G1 = new CheckboxGroup();
        setLayout(new GridLayout(1,2));
        add(P1);
        add(P2);
        P1.setLayout(new FlowLayout());
        P1.add(new Checkbox("E-Mail Tom"));
        P1.add(new Checkbox("E-Mail Jack"));
        P2.setLayout(new FlowLayout());
```

```
      P2.add(new Checkbox("Me", G1, true));
      P2.add(new Checkbox("You", G1, false));
      P2.add(new Checkbox("Them", G1, false));
      resize(300, 200);
      show();
   }

   public static void main(String args[]) {
      testMe test = new testMe();
   }
}
```

Hierarchy for Checkbox

```
java.lang.Object
   java.awt.Component
      java.awt.Checkbox
```

DECLARATION FOR CHECKBOX

A number of options are available for calling a **Checkbox** constructor. Here is each option with a summary description:

```
new Checkbox();
```

Constructs a checkbox with no label, no checkbox group, and initializes it to a false state.

```
new Checkbox(String);
```

Constructs a checkbox with the specified label, no checkbox group, and initializes it to a false state.

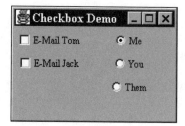

Figure 9.10

A few iterations of the Checkbox component.

```
new Checkbox(String, boolean);
```

Constructs a checkbox with the specified label, no checkbox group, and initializes it to a specified boolean state.

```
new Checkbox(String, CheckboxGroup, boolean);
```

Constructs a checkbox with the specified label, specified checkbox group, and initializes it to a specified boolean state.

Methods for Checkbox

Although checkboxes are simple UI components, they offer us a lot of options and therefore provide a few custom methods we can use to control them.

GETCHECKBOXGROUP()

This method returns the checkbox group that this checkbox belongs to.

GETLABEL()

This method gets the label of the button.

GETSTATE()

This method returns the boolean state of the checkbox.

SETCHECKBOXGROUP(CHECKBOXGROUP)

This method sets the **CheckboxGroup** of the check box.

SETLABEL(STRING)

This method changes the label of the checkbox.

SETSTATE(BOOLEAN)

This method sets the checkbox to the specified boolean state.

The Choice Class

The **Choice** class implements a pop-up menu that shows the currently chosen option normally; but when it has the focus, it opens up and displays all the options a user can select from. Figure 9.11 shows a **Choice** component at rest and Figure 9.12 shows the same component in action.

Here is the code that creates the **Choice** component shown in Figures 9.11 and 9.12:

```java
import java.awt.*;

public class testMe extends Frame {

    public testMe() {
        super("Choice Demo");
        Choice C1 = new Choice();
        setLayout(new FlowLayout());
        add(C1);
        C1.addItem("You");
        C1.addItem("Me");
        C1.addItem("Them");
        C1.addItem("Us");
        C1.addItem("Everyone");
        resize(300, 200);
        show();
    }

    public static void main(String args[]) {
        testMe test = new testMe();
    }
}
```

Hierarchy for Choice

```
java.lang.Object
   java.awt.Component
      java.awt.Choice
```

Declaration for Choice

When you are creating a **Choice** component, you cannot set any options. All the options must be set after the object is created. The call for initializing **Choice** is simply:

```
new Choice();
```

Methods for Choice

The set of special methods available for the **Choice** class include:

Figure 9.11

The Choice component without the focus.

Figure 9.12

The Choice component with the focus.

ADDITEM(STRING)

This method adds an item to the list of choices.

COUNTITEMS()

This method returns the number of items.

GETITEM(INT)

This method returns the item at the specified index.

GETSELECTEDINDEX()

This method returns the index of the currently selected item.

GETSELECTEDITEM()

This method returns a string representation of the current choice.

SELECT(INT)

This method selects the item with the specified index position.

SELECT(STRING)
This method selects the item with the specified **String** if present.

The List Class

The **List** class is actually very similar to **Choice** except that it allows you to display multiple items and scroll through the ones not displayed. It also gives you the ability to select multiple items.

Figure 9.13 shows a form that contains a simple list with multiple elements. Here is the code that created these lists:

```
import java.awt.*;

public class testMe extends Frame {

    public testMe() {
        super("List Demo");
        List L1 = new List();
        setLayout(new FlowLayout());
        add(L1);
        L1.addItem("You");
        L1.addItem("Me");
        L1.addItem("Them");
        L1.addItem("Us");
        L1.addItem("Everyone");
        resize(300, 200);
        show();
    }

    public static void main(String args[]) {
        testMe test = new testMe();
    }
}
```

Hierarchy for List

```
java.lang.Object
  java.awt.Component
    java.awt.List
```

Figure 9.13
Create lists with the List class.

Declaration for List

Here are the two constructors you can call to initialize a **List** class:

```
new List();
```

Creates a scrolling list initialized with no visible lines and multiple selections disabled.

```
new List(int, boolean);
```

Creates a new scrolling list initialized with the specified number of visible lines and a boolean stating if multiple selections are allowed or not.

Methods for List

You'll find a number of methods for this class because of all the different options it offers.

ADDITEM(STRING)

This method adds the specified item to the end of list.

ALLOWSMULTIPLESELECTIONS()

This method returns true if the list allows multiple selections.

CLEAR()

This method clears the list.

COUNTITEMS()

This method returns the number of items in the list.

DELITEM(INT)

This method deletes an item from the list at the specified index.

DELITEMS(INT, INT)

This method deletes multiple items from the list. Items are deleted from the index position specified by the first parameter to the index position specified by the second parameter.

DESELECT(INT)

This method deselects the item at the specified index.

GETITEM(INT)

This method gets the item associated with the specified index.

GETROWS()

This method returns the number of visible lines in the list.

GETSELECTEDINDEX()

This method returns the selected item in the list or -1 if no item is selected.

GETSELECTEDINDEXES()

This method returns the selected indexes in the list in the form of an array.

GETSELECTEDITEM()

This method returns the selected item in the list or null if no item is selected, or it returns the first selected item if multiple items are selected.

GETSELECTEDITEMS()

This method returns the selected items in the list into an array of strings.

GETVISIBLEINDEX()

This method gets the index of the item that was last made visible by the method makeVisible().

ISSELECTED(INT)

This method returns true if the item at the specified index has been selected; false otherwise.

MAKEVISIBLE(INT)

This method forces the item at the specified index to be visible. The method automatically scrolls the list to display the specified index.

MINIMUMSIZE()

This method returns the minimum dimensions needed for the list.

MINIMUMSIZE(INT)

This method returns the minimum dimensions needed for the number of rows in the list.

PREFERREDSIZE()

This method returns the preferred dimensions needed for the list.

PREFERREDSIZE(INT)

This method returns the preferred dimensions needed for the list with the specified amount of rows.

SELECT(INT)

This method selects the item at the specified index.

SETMULTIPLESELECTIONS(BOOLEAN)

This method sets up a list to allow for multiple selections or not.

TextField and TextArea Classes

The **TextField** and **TextArea** classes implement other controls that you will use often. They are often accompanied with **Label** controls that tell the user what a text entry box is used for. Text fields can only have a single line of text, while text areas can have multiple lines like a word processor. One of the nice things about the **TextField** and **TextArea** components is that they interact with both the keyboard and the mouse. You can enter text by typing it on the keyboard. Then, you can use the mouse to place the cursor within that text. If you are a Windows

95 user, the components even support the right mouse button. If you right-click within a text field or text area, a pop-up menu will be displayed like the one shown in Figure 9.14.

Hierarchy for TextField and TextArea

```
java.lang.Object
   java.awt.Component
      java.awt.TextComponent
         java.awt.TextField
         java.awt.TextArea
```

Declaration for TextField and TextArea

A number of constructors are available for initializing **TextField** and **TextArea** classes:

```
new TextField();
```

Constructs a new **TextField**.

```
new TextField(int);
```

Creates a new **TextField** initialized with the specified number of columns (1 column = 1 character).

```
TextField(String)
```

Creates a new **TextField** initialized with the specified text.

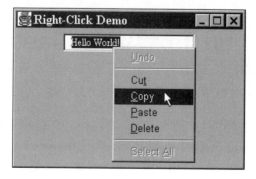

Figure 9.14

Right-clicking on a TextField component to display a pop-up menu.

```
new TextField(String, int);
```

Creates a new **TextField** initialized with the specified text and number of columns.

```
new TextArea();
```

Creates a new **TextArea**.

```
new TextArea(int, int);
```

Creates a new **TextArea** with the specified number of rows and columns.

```
new TextArea(String);
```

Constructs a new **TextArea** with the specified text displayed.

```
new TextArea(String, int, int);
```

Creates a new **TextArea** with the specified text and the specified number of rows and columns.

Methods for TextField and TextArea

Many of the methods used with these two classes are actually methods of the **TextComponent** class which both of these classes subclass. Let's look at these methods first.

GETSELECTIONEND()

This method returns the selected text's end position.

GETSELECTEDTEXT()

This method returns the selected text contained in the text component.

GETSELECTIONSTART()

This method returns the start position of the selected text. If no text is selected, the method returns -1.

GETTEXT()

This method returns the text contained in the text component.

isEditable()

This method returns a boolean value that tells us if the text component is editable or not. Text components are editable by default.

select(int, int)

This method selects the text found between the specified start and end locations.

selectAll()

This method causes all of the text in the text component to be selected.

setEditable(boolean)

This method sets whether or not this text component can be edited.

setText(String)

This method changes the text of the text component to the specified text.

Now, let's look at a few methods that are specific to the **TextField** component:

echoCharIsSet()

This method returns true if the **TextField** has a character set for echoing. Echoing is used for situations where you do not want the text people are typing to be displayed.

getColumns()

This method returns the number of columns in the **TextField**.

getEchoChar()

This method returns the character to be used for echoing. The character is not returned in a **String** format, just a simple **char**.

minimumSize()

This method returns the minimum size dimensions needed for the **TextField** in columns.

minimumSize(int)

This method is used to request a minimum size for the text box. The parameter specifies the number of columns for the text box. The method returns the minimum size dimensions needed for the **TextField** with the specified amount of columns.

PREFERREDSIZE()

This method returns the preferred size dimensions needed for the **TextField** class.

PREFERREDSIZE(INT)

This method returns the preferred size dimensions needed for the **TextField** with the specified amount of columns being passed to it.

SETECHOCHARACTER(CHAR)

This method sets the echo character for the **TextField**. Most often you'll want to set this character to the asterisk symbol, especially if you are working with password boxes.

Now, we need to look at the methods specific to the **TextArea** class:

GETCOLUMNS()

This method returns the number of columns in the **TextArea**.

GETROWS()

This method returns the number of rows in the **TextArea**.

INSERTTEXT(STRING, INT)

This method inserts the specified text at the specified position. The position tells Java the number of characters it needs to move over before it inserts the string.

PREFERREDSIZE()

This method returns the preferred size dimensions of the **TextArea**.

PREFERREDSIZE(INT, INT)

This method returns the row and column dimensions of the **TextArea**.

MINIMUMSIZE()

This method returns the minimum size dimensions of the **TextArea**.

MINIMUMSIZE(INT, INT)

This method returns the specified minimum size dimensions of the **TextArea**.

REPLACETEXT(STRING, INT, INT)

This method replaces text from the indicated start to end positions with the specified new text.

The Scrollbar Class

Several of the Java components we've been discussing in this chapter automatically use scrollbars when needed. For example, the **TextArea** control we just described will automatically create scrollbars when the text runs off the edge or the bottom. Scrollbars can also be created as standalone components. Scrollbars are useful when you need a user to pick a value. They offer a graphical interface rather than a simple text box where a user would usually have to type in a value.

Scrollbars are implemented using the concepts of a minimum, maximum, and current value. A scrollbar can be moved in three ways: small increments, large increments, or to an absolute position. The small increment occurs when the user clicks on the arrows at the top or bottom of the scrollbar. The large changes occur when the user clicks on the space between the current position and either arrow. Finally, the absolute change occurs when the user drags the current location indicator (sometimes called an *elevator*) and drags it to a specific spot within the scrollbar. Figure 9.15 shows a standard scrollbar and labels each part.

Let's consider a very typical use of a scrollbar. In this case, we have two components, a **Textfield** control and a **Scrollbar** control. We want to display the current value of the **Scrollbar** in the text box. Also, when the user changes the value in the text box, the scrollbar should match the change. Figure 9.16 shows what this simple application looks like.

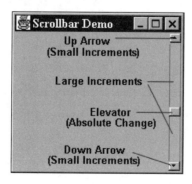

Figure 9.15

A typical Java scrollbar.

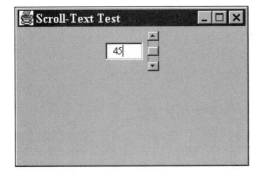

Figure 9.16
A Scrollbar control and a Textfield control with linked values.

And, here is the code for the entire application. Type it in and give it a try:

```
import java.awt.*;

public class ScrollTest extends Frame {
    TextField text;
    Scrollbar scroll;
    public ScrollTest() {
        super("Scroll-Text Test");
        text = new TextField(5);
        scroll = new Scrollbar(Scrollbar.VERTICAL, 0, 10, 0, 100);
        setLayout(new FlowLayout());
        add(text);
        add(scroll);
        resize(300, 200);
        show();
    }
    public boolean handleEvent(Event evt) {
        if (evt.target.equals(scroll)) {
            text.setText("" + scroll.getValue());
            } else if (evt.target.equals(text))
                {scroll.setValue(Integer.parseInt(text.getText()));
            } else if (evt.id == Event.WINDOW_DESTROY) {
            System.exit(0);
            return true;
        }
        return super.handleEvent(evt);
    }
    public static void main(String args[]) {
        ScrollTest test = new ScrollTest();
    }
}
```

Keep in mind that the scrollbar, like all the other controls, will change its appearance to match the operating system. Obviously, you would not want Windows 95 style scrollbars being displayed on a Macintosh. That would sure cause a commotion!

Hierarchy for Scrollbar

```
java.lang.Object
   java.awt.Component
      java.awt.Scrollbar
```

Declaration for Scrollbar

The three constructors provided for initializing scrollbars include:

```
new Scrollbar();
```

Constructs a new vertical **Scrollbar.**

```
new Scrollbar(int);
```

Constructs a new **Scrollbar** with the specified orientation. You can specify **Scrollbar.HORIZONTAL** or **Scrollbar.VERTICAL.** Scrollbars are vertical by default.

```
new Scrollbar(int, int, int, int, int);
```

Creates a new **Scrollbar** with the specified orientation, current value, large change size, minimum value, and maximum value.

Methods for Scrollbar

Here are the set of specialized methods for the **Scrollbar** class:

getMaximum()
This method returns an integer representing the maximum value of the scrollbar.

getMinimum()
This method returns an integer representing the minimum value of the scrollbar.

GETORIENTATION()

This method returns an integer that gives us the orientation for the scrollbar. You can check the returned integer against **Scrollbar.HORIZONTAL** and **Scrollbar.VERTICAL** to determine the scrollbar's orientation.

GETVALUE()

This method returns an integer representing the current value of the scrollbar.

GETVISIBLE()

This method returns the visible amount of the scrollbar.

SETVALUE(INT)

This method sets the value of the scrollbar to the specified value. If you try to set the current value to a number that is greater than the maximum or less than the minimum, the number becomes the new maximum or minimum, respectively.

SETVALUES(INT, INT, INT, INT)

This method changes the values for the scrollbar. The arguments in order of appearance include:

- value - the position in the current window
- large change - the value that will be moved each time the user clicks in the area between the elevator and the arrows. This value is also called the *amount visible per page.*
- minimum - the minimum value of the scrollbar
- maximum - the maximum value of the scrollbar

Building Menus

Menus in Java are as easy to build and manage as the other visual components. Every part of a menu, from the menu bar to individual items is represented as a separate class, each having specialized properties and methods. Let's start our investigation of menus with the main component—the menu bar. Then, we'll work our way down into the other more specialized components, such as a menu itself and menu items.

The MenuBar Class

Each window or frame you create in a Java application or applet can have its own menu bar. The standard menu bar is always displayed along the top of the window. You are not allowed to have multiple menu bars within a single window unless you create the entire system yourself (but why would you want to!).

The **MenuBar** class itself provides little functionality. By itself it looks like a blank bar across the top of your window. To give your menuing system functionality, you need to add **Menu** and **MenuItem** components, which we will discuss later.

Hierarchy for MenuBar

```
java.lang.Object
   java.awt.MenuComponent
      java.awt.MenuBar
```

Declaration for MenuBar

Only a single constructor is provided for initializing a **MenuBar** class. This constructor creates a menu object but does not display it. You must first assign the **MenuBar** to a frame for it to be displayed:

```
new MenuBar();
```

Methods for MenuBar

ADD(MENU)

This method adds the specified menu to the menu bar.

COUNTMENUS()

This menu returns an integer representing the number of menus on the menu bar.

GETHELPMENU()

This method returns the name of the menu component on the current menu bar that has been designated as the "Help" menu. Help menus are discussed in the next section in more detail.

GETMENU(INT)

This menu gets the specified menu. Input is an integer representing the index position of a menu and it returns a **Menu** object.

REMOVE(INT)

This method removes the menu located at the specified index from the menu bar.

REMOVE(MENU)

This method removes the specified menu from the menu bar.

SETHELPMENU(MENU)

This method sets the current help menu to the specified menu on the menu bar.

The Menu Class

The **Menu** class is used to implement the selections for the section headings for each type of menu. Typical **Menu** components will be labeled "File," "Options," and "Help." Figure 9.17 shows a few menus.

Menu classes are always children of a single **MenuBar** class. They usually have **MenuItem** classes as children. However, a **Menu** class does not *need* to have menu items under it; it can react to events on its own. In Figure 9.17, you could click on the **Menu** component labeled "File" to expose its **MenuItem** children. However, if you were to click on the "Help" **Menu** item, it would not display any child **MenuItem** components because it does not have any. It acts on its own.

Hierarchy for Menu

```
java.lang.Object
   java.awt.MenuComponent
      java.awt.MenuItem
         java.awt.Menu
```

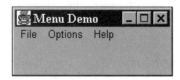

Figure 9.17

Examples of menus created with the Menu class.

Declaration for Menu

Here are the two constructors provided for the **Menu** class:

```
new Menu(String);
```

Constructs a new **Menu** with the specified string as the label. This menu will not be able to be "torn off." Tear-off menus are menus that will still appear on the screen after the mouse button has been released.

```
new Menu(String, boolean);
```

Constructs a new **Menu** with the specified label. The menu will be able to be torn off if the boolean value is set to true.

Methods for Menu

The specialized methods for the **Menu** class include:

ADD(MENUITEM)

This method adds the specified item to the menu.

ADD(STRING)

This method adds an item with the specified label to the menu.

ADDSEPARATOR()

This method adds a separator line to the menu at the current position.

COUNTITEMS()

This method returns the number of elements in the menu as an integer.

GETITEM(INT)

This method returns the menu item located at the specified index of the menu.

ISTEAROFF()

This method returns true if the menu is a tear-off menu.

REMOVE(INT)

This method deletes the item at the specified index from the menu.

REMOVE(MENUITEM)

This method deletes the specified item from the menu.

The MenuItem Class

The **MenuItem** class is the last in the line of children of the three menu classes. We should mention, however, that **Menu** classes can have other **Menu** classes as children. These child **Menu** components look like menu items, but another menu would be under each menu to display more menu items. This is technique is used to create cascading menus as shown in Figure 9.18.

Here is the Java code that implements the menu system shown in Figure 9.18:

```java
import java.awt.*;

public class testMe extends Frame {
    public testMe() {
        super("Menu Demo");
        MenuBar MB = new MenuBar();
        Menu M1 = new Menu("File");
        Menu M2 = new Menu("Options");
        Menu M3 = new Menu("More");
        MB.add(M1);
        MB.add(M2);
        MB.add(new Menu("Help"));
        M1.add(new MenuItem("Open"));
        M1.add(new MenuItem("Close"));
        M1.add(new MenuItem("Save"));
        M2.add(new MenuItem("General"));
        M2.add(M3);
        M3.add(new MenuItem("Screen"));
        M3.add(new MenuItem("Font"));
        setMenuBar(MB);
        resize(300, 200);
        show();
    }
    public static void main(String args[]) {
        testMe test = new testMe();
    }
}
```

The AWT also provides a subclass of the **MenuItem** class called **CheckboxMenuItem**. This class is identical to the standard **MenuItem** class

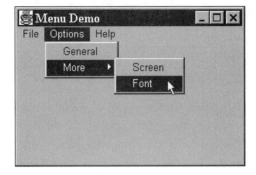

Figure 9.18
Creating cascading menus using Menus as subclasses.

except that it provides the ability to be "checked" or "unchecked" when the user clicks on a menu item. Figure 9.19 shows an example of this component.

Hierarchy for MenuItem

```
java.lang.Object
   java.awt.MenuComponent
      java.awt.MenuItem
```

Declaration for MenuItem

The **MenuItem** class provides a single constructor that takes one argument:

```
new MenuItem(String);
```

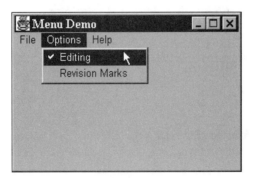

Figure 9.19
Using the CheckboxMenuItem to check and uncheck menu items.

This class constructs a new **MenuItem** with the specified **String** displayed as the menu component's label. Note that the hyphen symbol (-) is reserved to mean a separator between menu items. Separators should do nothing except delineate different sections of a menu.

Methods for MenuItem

The specialized methods for the **MenuItem** class include:

DISABLE()

This method makes the menu item "unselectable" by the user and grays it out.

ENABLE()

This method makes the menu item "selectable" by the user. The user is given a visual cue when the menu is disabled because it is grayed out.

ENABLE(BOOLEAN)

This method conditionally enables a component.

GETLABEL()

This method gets the label for the menu item. The value is returned as a string.

ISENABLED()

This method checks to see if the menu item is enabled. The return value is a boolean value.

SETLABEL()

This method sets the label to be the specified string.

The following two methods are used only with the **CheckboxMenuItem** component.

GETSTATE()

This method returns a boolean value that represents the state of the menu item.

SETSTATE(BOOLEAN)

This method sets the state of the menu item.

Creating a Sample Menu Application

Now that we've introduced you to each of the three key classes for creating menus (**MenuBar**, **Menu**, and **MenuItem**), you're probably anxious to write a Java program that puts them to work. Let's build a sample application that incorporates all of them to create a practical menuing system. The application will not respond to any of the menu items being chosen, but it will show you the basic techniques for constructing a menuing system.

We need to start by planning our menu. Let's use three **Menu** components with the labels "File," "Options," and "Help." Under the File menu we will have seven **MenuItems** including two separators. The "Options" **Menu** component will have two **CheckboxMenuItem** components, and the "Help" menu will not have any menu items associated with it.

Figures 9.20 through 9.22 show several different views of our test program with different menu options being chosen. The code that creates this menuing system is as follows:

```java
import java.awt.*;

class TestFrame extends Frame {
    TestFrame() {
        super("Menu Test");
        MenuBar mb = new MenuBar();
        Menu fileMenu = new Menu("File");
        Menu optionMenu = new Menu("Option");
        Menu helpMenu = new Menu("Help");
        fileMenu.add(new MenuItem("New"));
        fileMenu.add(new MenuItem("-"));
        fileMenu.add(new MenuItem("Open"));
        fileMenu.add(new MenuItem("Close"));
        fileMenu.add(new MenuItem("Save"));
        fileMenu.addSeparator();
        fileMenu.add(new MenuItem("Exit"));
        optionMenu.add(new CheckboxMenuItem("Large Fonts"));
        optionMenu.add(new CheckboxMenuItem("Save Settings on Exit"));
        mb.setHelpMenu(helpMenu);
        mb.add(fileMenu);
        mb.add(optionMenu);
        mb.add(helpMenu);
        setMenuBar(mb);
        resize(300,200);
        show();
    }
```

```java
public boolean action(Event evt, Object obj) {
    String label = (String)obj;
    if (evt.target instanceof MenuItem) {
        if (label.equals("Exit")) {
            System.exit(0);
            return true;
            }
    }
    return true;
}

public boolean handleEvent(Event evt) {
    if (evt.id == Event.WINDOW_DESTROY) {
        System.exit(0);
        return true;
    }
    return super.handleEvent(evt);
}
public static void main(String args[]) {
    TestFrame tf = new TestFrame();
}
}
```

You my notice that we used two different methods for creating the two separators in the "File" menu. The **addSeparator**() method is probably easier. However, if using the standard **add**() method with the hyphen character, you can create a full-fledged menu item that you can then change options for and set up so that it can respond to mouse clicks. Now that you've seen the basics for creating menus and GUI objects, you'll need a way to position them within the frames you build. And that's where the layout manager comes in.

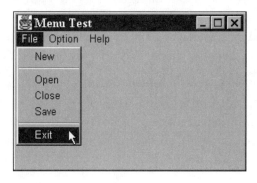

Figure 9.20

Menu test app view #1.

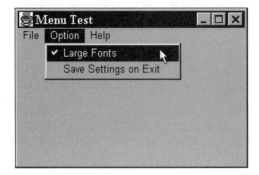

Figure 9.21

Menu test app view #2.

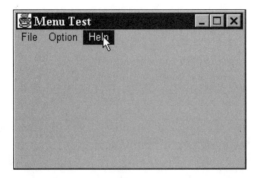

Figure 9.22

Menu test app view #3.

Working with the Layout Manager

To most programmers, the layout manager is a pretty strange concept. Instead of telling Java exactly where you want components to be located within a window, you use the layout manager to actively place interface components depending on the container size, shape, and on a few variables you set.

All controls you create for a Java application must *always* use the layout manager. Even if you do not implicitly tell Java what to do, it defaults to using a particular version of the layout manager. The layout manager comes in different "flavors" for different situations. At this point in the evolution of Java, five different layout managers are provided:

- FlowLayout
- BorderLayout
- GridLayout
- GridBagLayout
- CardLayout

The layout manager is actually just an Interface. You then create classes that implement the **LayoutManager** interface. These classes are used by the AWT and your program to get the look and feel you want for the user. Let's look at each of the layout manager classes in detail.

Any component that is a container in Java can use a different layout. So, you could have a **Frame** that uses one class to lay out two panels which each have their own layouts, and so on.

The FlowLayout Class

The **FlowLayout** class is the default layout for all containers in Java. This class tries to lay out components in a very orderly fashion that is much like a word processor that wraps your words and centers them. The order in which you add components to a container using **FlowLayout** is vital. The first component you add is the first in line and the last will be placed at the end. It is possible to go back and insert and remove components, but it is much easier to do it all correctly at the beginning.

Figure 9.23 shows several buttons on a panel. As you can see, they are centered as a group within the panel. If we resize the panel, the buttons automatically align themselves again to be centered. If we continue to shrink the panel so that all the buttons no longer fit across the panel, the last button will be "wrapped" to the next row as shown in Figure 9.24.

Declaration for FlowLayout

To set the layout for a container, you use the **setLayout**() method. This method has a single argument which is an instance of one of the layout classes. Let's look at an example. The code shown here is used to create the arrangements shown in Figures 9.23 and 9.24:

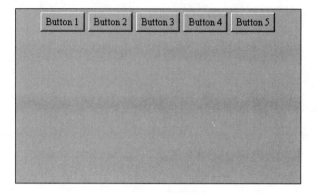

Figure 9.23

Using the FlowLayout class to lay out some buttons.

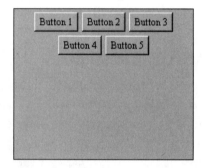

Figure 9.24

The same panel resized so that the buttons wrap to the next row.

```
import java.awt.*;

class LayoutFrame extends Frame {

    LayoutFrame() {
        super("Layout Test");
        setLayout(new FlowLayout());
        add(new Button("Button 1"));
        add(new Button("Button 2"));
        add(new Button("Button 3"));
        add(new Button("Button 4"));
        add(new Button("Button 5"));
        resize(300,200);
        show();
    }
```

```
public static void main(String args[]) {
    LayoutFrame lf = new LayoutFrame();
  }
}
```

Here we call the **setLayout**() method of the **Frame** we have extended, sending it a new instance of the **FlowLayout** class. The frame will then query the **FlowLayout** object where to position each component. This query happens whenever the window needs to be refreshed, such as when it is resized or uncovered.

Methods for FlowLayout

The specialized methods for **FlowLayout** include:

LAYOUTCONTAINER(CONTAINER)

This method lays out the container. It will actually reshape the components in the target container to satisfy the constraints of the **FlowLayout** object.

MINIMUMLAYOUTSIZE (CONTAINER)

This method returns the minimum dimensions needed to lay out the components contained in the specified target container. These dimensions are extremely useful because they can help you ensure that the user will not shrink the container to such a small size that it forces some of the UI components to slip off the visible screen.

PREFERREDLAYOUTSIZE(CONTAINER)

This method returns the preferred dimensions for this layout given the components in the specified target container. The return value is a **Dimension** variable consisting of two values representing the width and height of the layout.

TOSTRING()

This method returns a string representation of this **FlowLayout**'s values, including: (in this order) X position, Y position, container dimensions, layout class being used, whether or not the container can be resized, and the title of the container.

The BorderLayout Class

The **BorderLayout** class creates a unique layout scheme that is useful for working with components that need to maintain their position relative to an edge of your container. Border layouts use a compass analogy to allow you to specify which side of the container to attach your control to.

The controls you use for border layouts are automatically sized to take up as much space as possible. Figure 9.25 shows a sample container with five panels, one in each area of the container that the border layout allows.

To create this sample, we used the same code from the previous figure and made a few very minor changes. In fact, all the changes take place in the constructor for the class, so we will only show you that:

```
LayoutFrame() {
    super("Layout Test");
    setLayout(new BorderLayout());
    add("North", new Button("North"));
    add("East", new Button("East"));
    add("South", new Button("South"));
    add("West", new Button("West"));
    add("Center", new Button("Center"));
    resize(300,200);
    show();
}
```

The first change is obviously the switch to specifying the **BordeLayout**() class as our layout scheme. The other changes occur in the **add**() method. What are

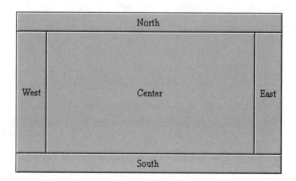

Figure 9.25

The BorderLayout() class in action.

those extra strings doing there? They specify which side of the container to place the new control. In this case, we are using buttons with labels that match the position names (North, East, South, West, and Center). We used buttons here for clarity sake, but you would probably not use them for any real projects. Panel components are probably the best for this type of layout. You would specify a few panels using a border style layout and then use a different layout scheme for the individual panels. Since panels are for design purposes mostly—they do not show up since they default to the same color as the background of the frame—they blend in perfectly and bring the whole thing together.

Declaration for BorderLayout

There are two ways to declare a border layout. You can use the simple constructor we used in the sample application or you can also specify a vertical and horizontal space.

```
new BorderLayout();
```

The simple way. Constructs a new **BorderLayout**.

```
new BorderLayout(int, int);
```

Constructs a **BorderLayout** with the specified gaps. The first integer represents the horizontal gap to be placed between components and the second integer represents the vertical gap to be used.

Methods for BorderLayout

The specialized methods for **BorderLayout** include:

addLayoutComponent(String, component)

This method adds the specified named component to the layout. The **String** argument gives us a name to refer to the component within the layout. The component can be any type of interface component we want to add.

layoutContainer(Container)

This method lays out the specified container. It will actually reshape the components in the specified target container to satisfy the constraints of the **BorderLayout** object.

minimumLayoutSize(Container)

This method returns the minimum dimensions needed to lay out the components contained in the specified target container. The return value is a dimension variable.

preferredLayoutSize(Container)

This method returns the preferred dimensions for the layout given the components in the specified target container. The method also returns a dimension style variable.

removeLayoutComponent(component)

This method removes the specified component from the layout.

toString()

This method returns the string representation of the **BorderLayout**'s values. At this point in the development of Java, this method only returns the size of the horizontal and vertical gaps.

The GridLayout Class

The grid style layout works just like it sounds; it creates a grid pattern for laying out components. You can control the number of rows and columns as well as the space between the components and the space between the components and the edge of the container. Figure 9.26 shows a sample frame using a grid layout.

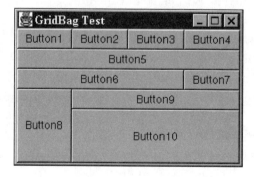

Figure 9.26

Using the GridLayout() class to create a sample frame.

Declaration for GridLayout

Like the **BorderLayout** class, **GridLayout** gives you a few constructor options. If the number of rows or columns is invalid, you will get an error (i.e., no negative numbers). Also, if you specify more columns than you need, the columns will not be used and your grid will appear as if you've specified fewer columns. However, if you specify more rows than you need, they will show up as blank space with enough space that matches the amount of space taken up by a component in this layout. We think this is a bug in Java, so you should experiment with this phenomenon if you plan on using this layout style.

```
new GridLayout(int, int);
```

Creates a grid layout with the specified rows and columns.

```
new GridLayout (int, int, int ,int);
```

Creates a grid layout with the specified rows, columns, horizontal gap, and vertical gap.

Methods for GridLayout

The specialized methods for **GridLayout** include:

ADDLAYOUTCOMPONENT(STRING, COMPONENT)

This method adds the specified named component to the layout. The **String** argument gives us a name to refer to the component within terms of the layout. The component can be any interface component you want to add.

LAYOUTCONTAINER(CONTAINER)

This method lays out the specified container. It will actually reshape the components in the specified target container to satisfy the constraints of the **GridLayout** object.

MINIMUMLAYOUTSIZE(CONTAINER)

This method returns the minimum dimensions needed to lay out the components contained in the specified target container. The return value is a dimension variable.

PREFERREDLAYOUTSIZE(CONTAINER)

This method returns the preferred dimensions for this layout given the components in the specified target container. It also returns a dimension style variable.

REMOVELAYOUTCOMPONENT(COMPONENT)

This method removes the specified component from the layout.

TOSTRING()

This method returns the string representation of the **GridLayout**'s values. At this point in the development of Java, this method only returns the size of the horizontal and vertical gaps.

The GridBagLayout Class

The **GridBagLayout** class is one of the most versatile of all the layout classes. It allows you to create a grid of an arbitrary size and use it to create components within the grid that are of variable size.

You use this layout method to align components vertically and horizontally, without requiring that the components be the same size or without them being sized for you in ways you may not want. Each **GridBagLayout** uses a rectangular grid of cells, with each component occupying one or more cells.

Each component that resides in a container that is using a **GridBagLayout** has an associated **GridBagConstraints** instance that specifies how the component is laid out within the grid. How a **GridBagLayout** places a set of components depends on each component's **GridBagConstraints**, minimum size, and preferred size.

To use a **GridBagLayout** effectively, you must customize one or more of its component's **GridBagConstraints**. Here are some of the variables you need to customize to create a layout:

- **gridx, gridy** Specifies the cell in the grid at the upper left of the component. The upper-left-most cell of a container has address gridx=0, gridy=0.
- **gridwidth, gridheight** Specifies the width and height of our component in grid space terms. You can set either of these to **GridBagConstraints.REMAINDER** to make the component be the last one in its row or column.

- **fill**   Used when the component's display area is larger than the component's requested size to determine whether (and how) to resize the component.

- **ipadx, ipady**   Specifies the internal padding. Padding represents the amount of space to add to the minimum size of the component. The width of the component will be at least its minimum width plus **ipadx*2** pixels (since the padding applies to both sides of the component). Similarly, the height of the component will be at least the minimum height plus **ipady*2** pixels.

- **insets**   Sets the external padding of the component—the minimum amount of space between the component and the edges of its display area.

- **anchor**   Used when the component is smaller than its display area to determine where to place the component. Valid values are:

```
GridBagConstraints.CENTER (the default)
GridBagConstraints.NORTH
GridBagConstraints.NORTHEAST
GridBagConstraints.EAST
GridBagConstraints.SOUTHEAST
GridBagConstraints.SOUTH
GridBagConstraints.SOUTHWEST
GridBagConstraints.WEST
GridBagConstraints.NORTHWEST
```

- **weightx, weighty**   Used to determine how to distribute space; this is important for specifying resizing behavior. Unless you specify a weight for at least one component in a row and column, all the components clump together in the center of their container. This is because when the weight is zero (the default), the GridBagLayout puts any extra space between its grid of cells and the edges of the container.

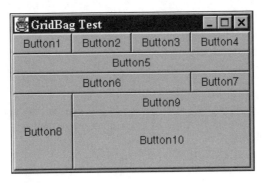

Figure 9.27

Sample program using the GridBagLayout class.

It is probably easiest to give you an example. Figure 9.27 shows the layout we wish to end up with. Following it is the code that we used to create it:

```java
import java.awt.*;
import java.util.*;

public class GridBagTest extends Frame {

    GridBagTest() {
        super("GridBag Test");
        GridBagLayout gridbag = new GridBagLayout();
        GridBagConstraints c = new GridBagConstraints();
        setFont(new Font("Helvetica", Font.PLAIN, 14));
        setLayout(gridbag);
        c.fill = GridBagConstraints.BOTH;
        c.weightx = 1.0;
        makebutton("Button1", gridbag, c);
        makebutton("Button2", gridbag, c);
        makebutton("Button3", gridbag, c);
        c.gridwidth = GridBagConstraints.REMAINDER; //end row
        makebutton("Button4", gridbag, c);
        c.weightx = 0.0;                            //reset to the default
        makebutton("Button5", gridbag, c); //another row
        c.gridwidth = GridBagConstraints.RELATIVE; //next-to-last in row
        makebutton("Button6", gridbag, c);
        c.gridwidth = GridBagConstraints.REMAINDER; //end row
        makebutton("Button7", gridbag, c);
        c.gridwidth = 1;                            //reset to the default
        c.gridheight = 2;
        c.weighty = 1.0;
        makebutton("Button8", gridbag, c);
        c.weighty = 0.0;                            //reset to the default
        c.gridwidth = GridBagConstraints.REMAINDER; //end row
        c.gridheight = 1;                           //reset to the default
        makebutton("Button9", gridbag, c);
        makebutton("Button10", gridbag, c);
        resize(300, 100);
        show();
    }

    protected void makebutton(String name, GridBagLayout gridbag,
                              GridBagConstraints c) {
        Button button = new Button(name);
        gridbag.setConstraints(button, c);
        add(button);
    }
```

```
   public static void main(String args[]) {
      GridBagTest test = new GridBagTest();
   }
}
```

Declaration for GridBagLayout

Since most of the work of setting up a **GridBagLayout** is achieved using a **GridBagConstraints** class, the constructor for **GridBagLayout** is very simple, in fact, it requires no arguments at all:

```
new GridBagLayout();
```

Methods for GridBagLayout

The specialized methods for **GridBagLayout** include:

DumpConstraints(GridBagConstraints)

This method prints the layout constraints to the **System** object. It is useful for debugging.

getConstraints(Component)

This method returns a copy of the **GridBagConstraints** object for the specified component.

layoutContainer(Container)

This method lays out the specified container. This method will actually reshape the components in the specified target container to satisfy the constraints of the **GridBagLayout** object.

lookupConstraints(Component)

This method retrieves the constraints for the specified component. The return value is not a copy, but is the actual constraints class used by the layout mechanism. The object returned by this method can then be altered to affect the looks of the component.

minimumLayoutSize(Container)

This method returns the minimum dimensions needed to lay out the components contained in the specified target container. The return value is a dimension variable.

PREFERREDLAYOUTSIZE(CONTAINER)

This method returns the preferred dimensions for this layout given the components in the specified target container. It also returns a dimension style variable.

SETCONSTRAINTS(COMPONENT, GRIDBAGCONSTRAINTS)

This method sets the constraints for the specified component.

TOSTRING()

This method returns the string representation of the **GridBagLayout**'s values. At this point in the development of Java, this method only returns the size of the horizontal and vertical gaps.

The CardLayout Class

The card layout style is much different than the previous four. Instead of using this class to lay out your controls, you use it like a layering system to specify which layer certain controls appear on. The most common use for this class is to simulate tabbed dialogs. You can create a card layout containing several panels that each use their own layout method and controls. Then, you can make a call to the class to specify which card to display and therefore which panel and respective components to show.

Declaration for CardLayout

Two versions of the **CardLayout**() constructor are available—one requires no parameters. To add extra cards, you simply use the **add**() method and the layout manager automatically handles the extra cards. Optionally, you can specify the horizontal and vertical gaps that surround your cards.

```
new CardLayout();
// Creates a new card layout.
new CardLayout(int, int);
```

Creates a card layout with the specified horizontal and vertical gaps.

Methods for CardLayout

The specialized methods for **CardLayout** include:

ADDLAYOUTCOMPONENT(STRING, COMPONENT)

This method adds the specified named component to the layout. The **String** argument gives us a name to refer to the component within terms of the layout. The component can be any interface component you want to add.

FIRST(CONTAINER)

This method flips to the first card. The argument is the parent container that you assigned the layout style to.

LAST (CONTAINER)

This method flips to the last card of the specified container.

LAYOUTCONTAINER(CONTAINER)

This method lays out the specified container. This method will actually reshape the components in the specified target container to satisfy the constraints of the **CardLayout** object.

MINIMUMLAYOUTSIZE(CONTAINER)

This method returns the minimum dimensions needed to layout the components contained in the specified target container. The return value is a dimension variable.

NEXT(CONTAINER)

This method flips to the next card in the stack.

PREFERREDLAYOUTSIZE(CONTAINER)

This method returns the preferred dimensions for the layout given the components in the specified target container. This also returns a dimension style variable.

PREVIOUS(CONTAINER)

This method flips to the previous card.

REMOVELAYOUTCOMPONENT(COMPONENT)

This method removes the specified component from the layout.

SHOW(CONTAINER, STRING)

This method flips to the specified component name in the specified container. This method is best used when you cannot use any of the previous four methods and/or you want to switch directly to a specified card. The **Container** argument specifies the owner of the card layout and the string is the name of the component you wish to switch to.

TOSTRING()

This method returns the string representation of the **CardLayout**'s values. At this point in the development of Java, this method only returns the size of the horizontal and vertical gaps.

10

Java Applet
Programming
Techniques

Java Applet Programming Techniques

Once you master the basics of using the Java language, you'll want to learn as much as you can about writing powerful applets.

The Java language offers a unique option—to be able to create programs that run as a "stand-alone" applications or as applets that are dependent on a controlling program such as a Web browser. The big difference between applications and applets is that applications contain enough code to work on their own and applets need a controlling program to tell the applet when to do what.

By itself, an applet has no means of starting execution because it does not have a **main()** method. In an application, the **main()** method is the place where execution starts. Any classes that are not accessed directly or indirectly through the **main()** method of an application are ignored.

If you have programmed in a visual environment before, the concept of an applet should be easy to understand. You can think of an applet as you would a type of custom control. When a custom control is used, you don't have to create code to make it go; that is handled for you. All you have to do is respond to events. With applets, you do not have to create the code that makes it go; you only need to write code to respond to events that the parent program calls—usually the browser.

Applet Basics

Let's look closely at some of the key areas you need to be aware of when creating applets. To start, you need to subclass the **Applet** class. By doing this, you inherit quite a bit of applet functionality that is built-in to the **Applet** class.

This listing shows the hierarchy of the Applet class and Table 10.1 provides a detailed look at the components of the **Applet** class that are inherited when you implement it.

Hiererachy of the Applet Class

```
java.lang.Object
    java.awt.Component
        java.awt.Container
            java.awt.Panel
                java.applet.Applet
```

Table 10.1 Methods Available in the Applet Class	
Method	**Description**
destroy()	Cleans up whatever resources are being held. If the applet is active, it is first stopped.
getAppletContext()	Returns a handle to the applet context. The applet context is the parent object—either a browser or applet viewer. By knowing this handle, you can control the environment and perform operations like telling a browser to download a file or jump to another Web page.
getAppletInfo()	Returns a string containing information about the author, version, and copyright of the applet.
getAudioClip(URL)	Returns the data of an audio clip that is located at the given URL. The sound is not played until the **play()** method is called.
getAudioClip(URL, String)	Returns the data of an audio clip that is located at the given location relative to the document's URL. The sound is not played until the **play()** method is called.
getCodeBase()	Returns the URL of the applet itself.
getDocumentBase ()	Gets the URL of the document that the applet is embedded in. If the applet stays active as the browser goes from page to page, this method will still return the URL of the original document the applet was called from.
getImage(URL)	Gets an image at the given URL. This method always returns an image object immediately even if the image does not exist. The actual image details are loaded when the image is first needed and not at the time it is loaded. If no image exists, an exception is thrown.
getImage(URL, String)	Gets an image at a URL relative to the document's URL. This method always returns an image object immediately even if the image does not exist. The actual image details are loaded when the image is first needed and not at the time it is loaded. If no image exists, an exception is thrown.
getParameter(String)	Returns a parameter that matches the value of the argument string.

continued

Table 10.1 Methods Available in the Applet Class (Continued)

Method	Description
getParameterInfo()	Returns an array of strings describing the parameters that are understood by this applet. The array consists of sets of three strings: name, type, and description. Often, the description string will be empty.
init()	Initializes the applet. You never need to call this method directly; it is called automatically by the system once the applet is created. The **init()** method is empty so you need to override it if you need anything initialized at the time your applet is loaded.
isActive()	Returns true if the applet is active. An applet is marked active just before the **start()** method is called.
play(URL)	This method plays an audio clip that can be found at the given URL. Nothing happens if the audio clip cannot be found.
play(URL, String)	This method plays an audio clip that resides at a location relative to the current URL. Nothing happens if the audio clip is not found.
resize(int, int)	Requests that an applet be resized. The first integer is height and the second is width. This method overrides the **resize()** method of the **Component** class that is part of the **Applet** class's hierarchy.
showStatus(String)	Shows a status message in the Applet's context. This method allows you to display a message in the applet context's status bar, usually a browser. This is very useful for displaying URL's when an action the user is about to do will result in a jump to a new Web page.
start()	Starts the applet. You never need to call this method directly; it is called when the applet's document is visited. Once again, this method is empty and you need to override it to make it useful. This is usually where you would put the guts of your code. However, be aware that this method is called *every* time the page that embeds the applet is called. So make sure that the applet is being destroyed if necessary.
stop()	This method is called when the browser leaves the page the applet is embedded in. It is up to you to take this opportunity to use the **destroy()** method to terminate your applet. There may be times, however, when you do not want to destroy it here and instead wait until a "Quit" button is pressed, or until the browser itself closes (then everything is dumped rather ungraciously). **stop()** is guaranteed to be called before the **destroy()** method is called. You never need to call this method directly because the browser will call it for you.

If you return to Chapter 2 and walk through the ticker tape applet we presented, you should get a good overview of the order in which key methods are called and why. As the listing illustrates, the **Applet** class is a descendant of the

Container class; thus, it can hold other objects. You do not need to create a panel first to place objects on because the **Applet** class extends the **Panel** class. Finally, because the **Container** class is derived from the **Component** class, we have the ability to respond to events, grab and display images, and display text among many other things. Table 10.2 presents some of the key methods you have access to because of all the classes that have been extended to get to the **Applet** class.

Table 10.2 Key Methods That the Applet Class Can Use

Derived from the Component class:

Method	Description
getBackground()	Gets the background color. If the component does not have a background color, the background color of its parent is returned.
getFont()	Gets the font of the component. If the component does not have a font, the font of its parent is returned.
getFontMetrics(Font)	Gets the font metrics for this component. It will return null if the component is currently not on the screen. Font metrics tell you things like the height and width of a string using the given font on the current component.
getForeground()	Gets the foreground color. If the component does not have a foreground color, the foreground color of its parent is returned.
getGraphics()	Gets a Graphics context for this component. This method will return null if the component is currently not visible on the screen.
handleEvent(Event)	Handles all events. Returns true if the event is handled and should not be passed to the parent of this component. The default event handler calls some helper methods to make life easier on the programmer.
hide()	Hides the component.
inside(int, int)	Checks if a specified x,y location is inside this component.
locate(int, int)	Returns the component or subcomponent that contains the x,y location.
location()	Returns the current location of this component. The location will be in the parent's coordinate space. The return value is a **point** object which is simply an x and y integer value.
move(int, int)	Moves the component to a new location. The integers are the x and y coordinates and are in the parent's coordinate space.
repaint()	Repaints the component. This will result in a call to update as soon as possible. The screen will also be cleared resulting in a brief flicker.
repaint(long)	Repaints the component. However, the extra argument is a **long** value that instructs Java that it must perform the update within that value in milliseconds.

continued

Table 10.2 Key Methods That the Applet Class Can Use (Continued)	
Method	**Description**
reshape(int, int, int, int)	Reshapes the component to the specified bounding box. The first two integers represent the new x an y coordinates the component should be moved to, and the second set of integers represent the new width and height.
resize(int, int)	Resizes the component to the specified width and height.
setBackground(Color)	Sets the background color.
setFont(Font)	Sets the font of the component.
setForeground(Color)	Sets the foreground color.
show()	Shows the component.
size()	Returns the current size of the component. The return value is a dimension object that has two integer values representing the width and height.
update(graphics)	Updates the component. This method is called in response to a call to **repaint()**. If you override this method and call it instead of the **paint()** method, the screen will not be cleared first.
Derived from the Container class:	
add(Component)	Adds the specified component to this container.
countComponents()	Returns the number of components in this panel.
getComponents()	Gets all the components in this container. The return value is actually an array of **Component** objects.
getLayout()	Returns the layout manager for the container.
remove(Component)	Removes the specified component from the container.
removeAll()	Removes all the components from the container. It is dangerous to use if you are not careful.
setLayout(LayoutManager)	Sets the layout manager for the container.

Applet Drawbacks

Applets can really eat up system resources. If you do not use threads and you create loops in an applet, you may run into serious performance problems with your browser. The browser can get so busy working with the applet that it does not have time to respond to Web page events such as refreshes, scrolls, and mouse clicks.

When some developers first heard about applets and their ability to run on many types of machines, there first response was, "That's dangerous!" Many were concerned that applets would be used for mischievous causes. To prevent applets from causing problems on machines, there are several built-in security measures you can take advantage of.

LIMITED FILE ACCESS

Applets cannot read from or write to files on an end user's hard drive. They can only read files that reside on the machine the applet was called from. Eventually, a user will be able to set up specific directories that an applet can have access to, but that functionality is not very robust yet and may not be implemented on all browsers, so don't count on it.

NATIVE METHODS

The other option or loop-hole (depending on how you look at it) is the use of *native methods*. You can create methods in C++ that can be called directly from Java. This is a very powerful option, especially if you are creating platform-specific programs that need the extra speed that you can get from natively compiled code. However, it can also be a potential gateway for mischievous programs. This feature may or may not be disabled, depending on the browser, so be cautious of how you use it.

FILE EXECUTION

Java applets are not allowed to execute programs on a user's system. So, you can't just run the **Format** program and wipe a hard drive.

NETWORK COMMUNICATION

Applets are only allowed to communicate with the server from which they were downloaded. This is another one of the security features that may or not be in effect depending on the browser. So, once again, do not program for it. This is actually one security option we would like to see go away or at least be able to have the user override it. The ability to talk with multiple servers could be incredibly powerful if implemented well. Just think of a large company with servers all over the world. You could create a little applet that could converse with them all and gather information for the end users.

A DISCLAIMER

Just because Java provides a few security features does not mean that it is completely secure. Java is a language that is still very much in its infancy and someone, somewhere will find a way to hack the system. However, since Java was produced to be an Internet friendly language (one of the first), it is much more secure than other languages. The problem is that it is also getting much more attention than all the others combined. Attention from users, programmers, and *hackers*!

Let's Play

Now that you have seen all the methods that you can use and learned a little about applet security, let's create an applet that uses some of these features. We won't explain every line of code as we did for the ticker tape applet in Chapter 2, but we will show you a few cool things you can do in your applets.

The applet we'll create is a simple navigation applet that will offer the user several buttons with URLs as labels. When the user clicks on a button, the browser will be instructed to go to a particular site. We have also included some sound support just for the fun of it. Lets see the code first:

```java
import java.applet.*;
import java.awt.*;
import java.net.*;

// testNav Class
public class testNav extends Applet {
    AudioClip startClip;
    AudioClip linkClip;
    AudioClip stopClip;

    public testNav() {
        setLayout(new GridLayout(4, 1));
        add(new Button("http://www.coriolis.com"));
        add(new Button("http://www.javasoft.com"));
        add(new Button("http://www.gamelan.com"));
        add(new Button("http://www.microsoft.com"));
    }

    public boolean action(Event evt, Object arg) {
        if (evt.target instanceof Button) {
            linkClip.play();
            fetchLink((String)arg);
            return true;
        }
        return super.handleEvent(evt);
    }
```

```
      void fetchLink(String s) {
      URL tempURL = null;
      try { tempURL  = new URL(s); }
      catch(MalformedURLException e) {
         showStatus("Malformed URL Exception has been thrown!");
      }
      getAppletContext().showDocument(tempURL);
   }

   public void init(){
      startClip = getAudioClip(getCodeBase(),  "start.au");
      linkClip = getAudioClip(getCodeBase(), "link.au");
      stopClip = getAudioClip(getCodeBase(), "stop.au");
   }

   public void start(){
      testNav TN = new testNav();
      startClip.play();
   }

   public void stop(){
      stopClip.play();
   }

} // End testNav
```

Figure 10.1 shows the testNav applet running in the Netscape browser.

Interacting with the Browser

Quite often, you may want your applet to interact with the host browser. That interaction will usually come in the form of asking the browser to go to another Web site, or changing the text displayed in the status bar at the bottom of the browser. Let's look at how to switch Web pages now, then we'll show you how to control the status bar.

For our little demo program, we need the browser to change pages whenever a button is pushed. To accomplish this, we need to use an event handling method. The **action()** method is the best place to do this, so let's look at that method in more detail:

```
public boolean action(Event evt, Object arg) {
      if (evt.target instanceof Button) {
```

```
        linkClip.play();
        fetchLink((String)arg);
        return true;
    }
    return super.handleEvent(evt);
}
```

This method handles mouse and keyboard actions for us. The first thing it does is check to see if the **target** of the action is a **Button** or not. If it is, we play a sound file and call the **fetchLink()** method that we created to actually go to other sites. We will cover the sound stuff in a minute. Right now, let's look at the **fetchLink()** method and see how we instruct the browser to grab other pages:

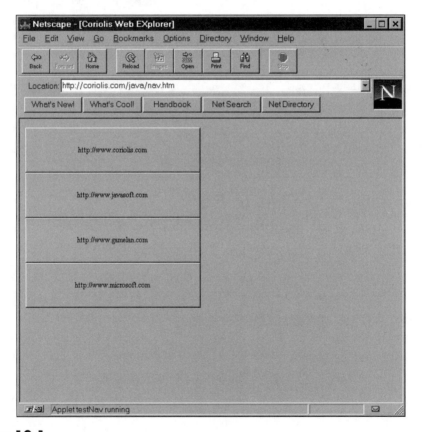

Figure 10.1

Running the testNav applet.

```
void fetchLink(String s) {
    URL tempURL = null;
    try { tempURL  = new URL(s); }
    catch(MalformedURLException e) {
        showStatus("Malformed URL Exception has been thrown!");
    }
    getAppletContext().showDocument(tempURL);
}
```

This method accepts a string representation of a URL, changes it into a URL object, then calls the **showDocument**() method that really does the work. We are forced to use a **try...catch** operation when we are creating a URL because it throws exceptions. In particular, it throws the **MalformedURLException**. Basically, if the URL string you are trying to turn into a URL object is poorly constructed, you will get an error. For example, if you leave off the "http://" part, you will get this error.

Once the URL is properly created, we call the **showDocument**() method that actually belongs to the browser. This is not an applet method. You can figure this out because we are calling the **getAppletContext**() method at the beginning of the line. This method returns the object representation of the browser which has its own methods, variables, and so on.

Changing the Status Bar

If you look at the **action**() method again, you will notice that we make an interesting method call whenever there is an error. Here is that line:

```
showStatus("Malformed URL Exception has been thrown!");
```

You can also code this operation like this:

```
getAppletContext().showStatus("Malformed URL Exception has been thrown!");
```

To some people, this is easier to read because it becomes immediately apparent which object is accepting the **showStatus**() method.

Changing this text at key times is a great way to interact with the user because the status bar is a consistent object across many applications so they expect it to be there and they expect useful information from it. For a little test, try and make the status bar display the link for any button that the mouse pointer is moving over.

Playing Sounds

For loading and playing sounds from within an applet we have two options. First, we can use the **play()** method of the applet that loads and plays the given sound right away. Second, we can load an applet into an **AudioClip** object using the **getAudioClip()** method and play the sound whenever we want. It's up to you to decide if the sounds should be loaded before they are played, or loaded and played at the same time.

To use the **play()** method, you invoke the method, sending the URL of the sound file you want as an argument. Or, you can split the URL into two pieces. The first piece would be a URL representing the code base, and the second argument would be the file name and directory relative to the code base. Here are the declarations for these methods:

```
play(URL);  // This is the full URL of the sound file you want to play
play(URL, String);  // This is the call that uses a base URL and a string
                    // representing the file name.
```

The other option we have for playing sounds is to load them into an object first. To do this we will create an **AudioClip** object and use the **getAudioClip()** method to load the sound file into the audio object. Once the sound file is loaded, we call the **play()** method of the **AudioClip** object to hear the sound. Here are the declarations and calls to handle sounds in this manner:

```
getAudioClip(URL); // This requires a fully-qualified URL that points to a
                   // sound file
getAudioClip(URL, String); // This is the call that uses a base URL and a
                           // string representing the file name.
```

To declare an **AudioClip** object, just follow this code:

```
AudioClip myClip;
```

Then, to load in the image do this:

```
myClip = getAudioClip(soundURL);
```

Finally, here's the call needed to play the file:

```
myClip.play();
```

You can also stop or loop the sound clip with these methods:

```
myClip.stop();
myClip.loop();
```

If a sound file being requested cannot be found, the **AudioClip** object will be set to null. No exception will be raised, but if you then try to play, stop, or loop the file, an exception will be thrown.

Displaying Images

One other key area we need to cover is the quick and painless use of images within applets. Images are just as easy to download as sounds. Here is a little sample applet that downloads an image and blasts it onto the screen:

```
import java.awt.*;
import java.applet.*;

public class testImg extends Applet {
    Image testImage;

    public void paint(Graphics g) {
        g.drawImage(testImage, 0, 0, this);
    }

    public void init() {
        testImage = getImage(getDocumentBase(), "sample.gif");
    }
}
```

This is an extremely simple program but it illustrates how easy downloading images is. The syntax for downloading images is almost identical to what we used for downloading sounds.

The syntax for declaring an image object is :

```
Image myImage;
```

And the syntax for the **getImage**() method is:

```
getImage(URL); // Downloads the image that resides at the given
               // fully-qualified URL
```

```
getImage(URL, String); // The URL is the code or document base,
                       // and the string is the directory and file name
                       // for the image relative to the code base
```

These image methods will support whatever format the browser supports.

11

Event Handling

Event Handling

11

Whether you use Java to write applications or applets, you'll need to master the art of handling events.

Every time you perform an action while running a Java application, such as clicking a mouse button or dragging a window, an event occurs. But, of course, events can also be triggered by internal actions that occur within a program. Many of the common events that occur in Java programs are handled by classes in the AWT package we discussed in Chapter 9. However, we decided to give events a chapter of their own because of their importance. This way, we can focus on events without being sidetracked by GUI creation issues.

We'll start by introducing the basics of how events are handled in Java. Then we'll present the **Events** class, which is used to derive objects for handling events in Java programs. As you'll see, this class defines a number of instance variables and methods to help process the different types of events that can occur in a Java program. After we cover the essentials of the **Events** class, we'll dig in and look at some of the specific methods that are triggered when events occur. As we explore different types of events, we'll present a number of programming examples to illustrate different techniques available for processing events.

Introducing Events

In the ticker tape applet we created in Chapter 2, the program scrolled a line of text across the applet space. If you click the mouse button on top of the applet while it is running, the scrolling text will stop and then start when the mouse is clicked again. These mouse clicks cause events to occur. In our applet, the event was caused by pressing down the mouse button. Here is the portion of code responsible for halting the scrolling text:

```
// Handle mouse clicks
   public boolean handleEvent(Event evt) {
      if (evt.id == Event.MOUSE_DOWN) {
         if (suspended) {
            ttapeThread.resume();
         } else {
            ttapeThread.suspend();
         }
      suspended = !suspended;
      }
      return true;
   }
```

The key to the inner workings of this error handler method (**handleEvent**()) is the argument **evt**. It is declared as an object of the **Event** class, a special class that Java provides for processing events. In our code, we simply check the **id** instance variable to make sure a **MOUSE_DOWN** event has occurred. If so, we either resume or suspend the applet.

Event Types

Events in Java can be split into three main groups: *mouse, keyboard,* and *system events.* All of these events can be handled very similarly. Java events are actually objects derived from their own classes, as we saw in the applet example we just discussed. This method of handling events makes perfect sense when you realize the power you gain from being able to manipulate an event as an object. In other programming languages, events only trigger certain methods, which limits you to receiving very little information about the current state of the system. You also cannot pass the event on to another handler, which you can do with Java.

The Event Class

Let's take a close look at the **Event** class so we can use it throughout this chapter. This class has many variables and methods that can be used for finding out information about an event that has occurred, such as where and when the event has happened, and who it has happened to. Many of the variables give us status information, such as if the Shift or Page Up key was pressed when the event has occurred.

Table 11.1 presents the variables defined in the **Event** class and Table 11.2 presents the methods. Later in this chapter you'll learn more about how to apply them. The variables that are listed in all capital letters represent static values that

Table 11.1	Variables Defined in the Events Class
Variable	**Description**
SHIFT_MASK	The shift modifier constant. This is an integer that indicates if the Shift key was down when the event occurred. This variable is used to process keyboard events.
CTRL_MASK	The control modifier constant. This is an integer that indicates if the Ctrl key was down when the event occurred. This variable is used to process keyboard events.
ALT_MASK	The alt modifier constant. This is an integer that indicates if the Alt key was down when the event occurred. This variable is used to process keyboard events.
HOME	Represents the Home key.
END	Represents the End key.
PGUP	Represents the Page Up key.
PGDN	Represents the Page Down key.
UP	Represents the Up arrow key.
DOWN	Represents the Down arrow key.
LEFT	Represents the left arrow key.
RIGHT	Represents the right arrow key.
F1 ... F12	Represents one of the function keys.
ESC	Represents the escape key.
WINDOW_DESTROY	Represents the event that occurs when a user tries to close a frame or window.
WINDOW_EXPOSE	Represents the event that occurs when part of your application has been covered by another application and the second app is removed.
WINDOW_ICONIFY	Represents the event that occurs when a window is minimized.
WINDOW_DEICONIFY	Represents the event that occurs when a window is restored from a minimized state.
WINDOW_MOVED	Represents the event that occurs when the window is moved.
KEY_PRESS	Represents the event that occurs when any key on the keyboard is pressed down.
KEY_RELEASE	Represents the event that occurs when any key on the keyboard is released.
MOUSE_DOWN	Represents the event that occurs when a mouse button is pressed down.
MOUSE_UP	Represents the event that occurs when a mouse button is released.
MOUSE_MOVE	Represents the event that occurs when a mouse button is moved across a part of the application or applet.

continued

Table 11.1 Variables Defined in the Events Class (continued)

Variable	Description
MOUSE_ENTER	Represents the event that occurs when a mouse enters a component.
MOUSE_EXIT	Represents the event that occurs when a mouse exits a component.
MOUSE_DRAG	Represents the event that occurs when the mouse button is down and the mouse is moved.
LIST_SELECT	Represents the event that occurs when an option is selected from within a list object.
LIST_DESELECT	Represents the event that occurs when an option is de-selected from within a list object.
GOT_FOCUS	Represents the event that occurs when a component gains the focus.
LOST_FOCUS	Represents the event that occurs when a component loses the focus.
Target	Holds an object that was the "target" of an event.
When	Indicates the precise time when an event occurred.
Id	Indicates the type of event.
X	The x coordinate of the event.
Y	The y coordinate of the event.
Key	The key that was pressed in a keyboard event.
Arg	An arbitrary argument.

Table 11.2 Methods Defined in the Events Class

Method	Description
translate(int, int)	Translates an event relative to the given component. This involves translating the coordinates so they make sense within the given component.
shiftDown()	Checks to see if the Shift key is pressed; returns true if it is pressed.
controlDown()	Checks to see if the Control key is pressed; returns true if it is pressed.
ToString()	Returns the string representation of the event's values.
metaDown()	Checks to see if the meta key is pressed. Returns true if it is pressed. The meta key is different for each operating system. On a PC, the meta key is the Alt key and on a Mac, the meta key is the Apple key.

correspond to certain events and conditions. We will use these values to compare events that occur in our applications so that we can tell what event has occurred.

Mouse Events

Now that you are familiar with the **Event** class, let's look at some of the methods that are triggered when an event happens. The first ones we'll discuss are the mouse events. These events are probably the most common ones that you will need to check for. The methods for processing these events can be placed in several different places in your program. At the highest level, you can override the events of the GUI elements themselves. For example, you can create your own button class by extending the **Button** class. Then, you can override the default mouse events with your own code. The next option is to place a button or multiple buttons on a panel and override a button's mouse events. With this scenario, you must use **if** or **switch** statements to detect which button is pressed.

The final option is to override the mouse events of the applet or frame you are using for the entire program. This method gets difficult when you have complex UI environments. Let's take a close look at each of the mouse events in detail.

MOUSEDOWN()

Clicking on a mouse button creates two distinct events, **mouseDown** and **mouseUp**. The **mouseDown** event occurs when a button is initially pressed and the **mouseUp** event occurs when a button is released. Why are two events required? Often, you will want to perform different tasks when a button is pressed and when it is released. For example, consider a standard screen button. If you press a mouse button while you are over the screen button, the button should look like it has been depressed. The button would remain in this "down" state until the mouse button is released.

The **mouseDown()** method accepts three arguments:

```
public boolean mouseDown(Event, int, int) {}
```

The first argument is an **Event** object that holds all the information about the event that has occurred. The second and third arguments are the x and y coordinates representing where the event took place. The values stored in these arguments are the same as the values stored in the **x** and **y** variables found in the **Events** class.

Here is an example that uses the **mouseDown()** method. It illustrates that the x,y coordinate values set by this method are the same as the values stored in the x,y instance variables contained in the **Events** class:

```
import java.awt.*;

class testEvents extends Frame {
    Panel P1;

    testEvents() {
        super("Test Events");
        P1 = new Panel();
        setLayout(new FlowLayout());
        P1.setBackground(new Color(255,255,255));
        add(P1);
        resize(300,200);
        show();
    }

    public boolean mouseDown(Event evt, int x, int y) {
        System.out.println("X, Y = " + x + ", " + y);
        System.out.println("Event X, Y = " + evt.x + ", " + evt.y);
        return true;
    }

    public static void main(String args[]) {
        testEvents TE = new testEvents();
    }
}
```

MouseUp()

The **mouseUp()** event method is implemented in the exact same way as the **mouseDown()** event method. When you are creating routines that respond to simple mouse clicks this is usually the place to put the code. Why here instead of in a **mouseDown** event method? Well, think about how people use an interface. Is it more natural for a mouse click event to occur the instant the button is pressed, or when it is released? If you look at how other programs work, you will notice that most, if not all, don't respond until the mouse button is released.

You should follow this paradigm for two reasons. First, it represents the standard way of processing mouse clicks and you do not want to create an interface that seems inconsistent to the user. Second, it gives the user an opportunity to change his or her mind. After all, how many times have you started to press a button in a program only to change your mind, move the mouse off the button, and *then* let go?

Here is the declaration for the **mouseUp()** method:

```
public boolean mouseUp(Event, int, int) {}
```

Once again, we are given three arguments—an **Event** object, and two integers that give us the x and y coordinates of the event.

MOUSEMOVE() AND MOUSEDRAG()

The **mouseMove()** event method is used to constantly give feedback when the mouse pointer is over a component. The **mouseDrag()** event method tells us the same thing, but only while one of the mouse buttons is pressed. Whenever the mouse is being moved over your component, one of these methods will constantly be called. Be careful not to put code in these methods that takes too long to execute. If you do, you may see some performance degradation in your program.

Here are the declarations for the **mouseMove()** and **mouseDrag()** event methods:

```
public boolean mouseMove(Event, int, int) {}
public boolean mouseDrag(Event, int, int) {}
```

Again, three arguments are used; an **Event** object, and two integers that represent the x and y coordinates where the event occurs.

Here is a very simple program that responds to mouse movement and dragging by displaying the location of the event in the title bar:

```
import java.awt.*;

class testEvents extends Frame {

    testEvents() {
        super("Test Events");
        resize(300,200);
        show();
    }

    public boolean mouseMove(Event evt, int x, int y) {
        setTitle("mouseMove at: " + x + ", " + y);
        return true;
    }

    public boolean mouseDrag(Event evt, int x, int y) {
        setTitle("mouseDrag at: " + x + ", " + y);
        return true;
    }

    public static void main(String args[]) {
        testEvents TE = new testEvents();
```

```
    }
}
```

As you can see, it is extremely easy to respond to mouse events. You may notice that in this example and in the previous one, you cannot exit out of the program. Basically, what you need to do is check for another event, a system event that tells you that the user is trying to close the window. This is a very easy thing to look for, but we did not want to confuse the code with extra methods. Later in this chapter we'll show you how to check for system events.

MOUSEENTER() AND MOUSEEXIT()

These two events come in handy for certain situations. For example, if you want to provide feedback to the user when he or she moves the mouse pointer into or out of your components, you may want to display a message in a status bar. You can get basically the same effect by checking for the **mouseMove**() method, but this method gets called many times while the mouse is over a component and the **mouseEnter**() and **mouseExit**() methods get called only once. The declarations for these event methods are:

```
public boolean mouseEnter(Event, int, int) {}
public boolean mouseExit(Event, int, int) {}
```

These methods are also useful for keeping track of how long a person keeps their mouse over a certain component. For example, assume you were creating a game and you wanted to cause an event to occur if the player keeps the pointer over the "fire" button for too long. You could then respond with a sound or message. Here is an example that checks the time at which the user moves the mouse onto the applet and if the user stays for more than two seconds, the status bar displays an error message. When the user leaves the applet space and returns, the message returns to normal.

```
import java.applet.*;
import java.awt.*;
import java.util.*;

// testNav Class
public class testTime extends Applet {
    Button B1;
    long downTime;
```

```
public testTime() {
    setLayout(new FlowLayout());
    B1 = new Button("Click Me!");
    add("Center", B1);
}

public boolean mouseEnter(Event evt, int x, int y) {
    downTime = evt.when;
    return true;
}

public boolean mouseExit(Event evt, int x, int y) {
    downTime = 0;
    return true;
}

public boolean mouseMove(Event evt, int x, int y) {
    if ((evt.when - downTime) > 2000) {
        B1.setLabel("Too Long!");
    } else {
        B1.setLabel("Click Me!");
    }
    return true;
}

public void init(){
    testTime TT = new testTime();
}

} // End testNav
```

Keyboard Events

Handling keyboard events is similar to handling mouse events. The big difference is that when you process a mouse event, you have only one mouse button to work. On the other hand, the user can press one of many possible keys, so processing keyboard events requires an extra step. The two methods you can use, **keyDown()** and **keyUp()**, are very similar to the **mouseDown()** and **mouseUp()** event methods. The only difference is that the keyboard events *do not* generate a location where the event has occurred. Instead, they generate an integer value representing the key that was pressed.

KEYDOWN() AND KEYUP()

Here are the declaration statements for the **keyDown()** and **keyUp()** event methods:

```
public boolean keyDown(Event, int) {}
public boolean keyUp(Event, int) {}
```

The integer argument stores the numeric value of each key on the keyboard—the ASCII equivalent of a key. Java offers us a simple technique for converting this ASCII value to a character representation; we simply cast the integer to a **char** and there we have it. Here is a simple example:

```
public boolean keyDown(Event evt, int key) {
    System.out.println("Value = " + key + ", character = " + (char)key);
}
```

This little code snippet simply waits for a key to be pressed then prints the numeric value of the key and the character representation of that value.

If you look back at the variables defined in the **Event** class (Table 11.1), you'll notice all of the key representations. These values represent the keys that do not belong to the standard ASCII character set, including keys like Home, Page Up, and the function keys. Here's a simple code example that waits for you to press the **F1** key to get help and the Ctrl-x combination to quit the program:

```
import java.awt.*;

class testKeys extends Frame {

    testKeys() {
        super("Test Keys");
        resize(300,200);
        show();
    }

    public boolean keyDown(Event evt, int key) {
        if (evt.controlDown()) {
            if (key == 24) {
                System.exit(0);
                return true;
            }
        }
        if (key == Event.F1) {
            setTitle("No help here!");
            return true;
        }
        return false;
    }
```

```
    public boolean keyUp(Event evt, int key) {
        if (key == Event.F1) {
            setTitle("Test Keys");
            return true;
        }
        return false;
    }

    public static void main(String args[]) {
        testKeys TK = new testKeys();
    }
}
```

Hierarchy of Events

Now that you've seen how to create event handlers for specific events, let's look at how you can create event handlers that capture everything in one central location. Why would you want to do that? Assume that you have an applet that uses a set of buttons that perform related operations. You can create separate event handlers for each control individually, or you can create an event handler that captures all the events at one location and then uses the information in the **Event** object to determine what happened to a certain control.

If you recall from Chapter 9, we created an applet with four buttons. Each button had a caption that represented a URL for a Web site. When a button is pressed, the event handler of the applet, not the buttons themselves, processes the event. This "centralized" approach makes the events easier to process; however, sometimes it can get a little crowded, especially if you have many components that must respond differently to certain events. In these cases it is up to you to decide where to handle the events.

If you do not handle an event at the component level, make sure that a system is in place to hand that event off to the container the particular control resides in. Let's create a little program that has two buttons in a frame. In the first example we will use a standard button and catch its events with the frame. In the second example we will create our own button by subclassing the **Button** class and adding our own event handler to that button. Here is the first example:

```
import java.awt.*;

class testEvents extends Frame {
    myButton B1;
    myButton B2;
```

```
       testEvents() {
          super("Test Keys");
          setLayout(new FlowLayout());
          add(new Button("Hello!"));
          add(new Button("Goodbye!"));
          resize(300,200);
          show();
       }

       public boolean mouseDown(Event evt, int x, int y) {
          if (evt.target instanceof Button) {
             System.out.println((String)evt.arg);
             return true;
          } else {
             return super.mouseDown(evt, x, y);
          }
       }

       public static void main(String args[]) {
          testEvents TK = new testEvents();
       }
}
```

In the second example we create our own event handler:

```
import java.awt.*;

class testEvents extends Frame {
    myButton B1;
    myButton B2;

    testEvents() {
       super("Test Keys");
       setLayout(new FlowLayout());
       B1 = new myButton("Hello!");
       B2 = new myButton("Goodbye!");
       add(B1);
       add(B2);
       resize(300,200);
       show();
    }

    public static void main(String args[]) {
       testEvents TK = new testEvents();
    }
}
```

```
class myButton extends Button {

    myButton(String s) {
        super(s);
    }

    public boolean mouseDown(Event evt, int x, int y) {
        System.out.println((String)evt.arg);
        return true;
    }
}
```

Processing System Events

Not only can you decide where to place your event handlers, Java also gives you options for capturing events. Instead of creating separate event handlers for each type of event, you can also create a single centralized event handler that accepts all events and then figures out what they are and which components are responsible for generating them.

For processing system-related events, Java provides **handleEvent()** and **action()**. The **action()** method captures all of the standard mouse and keyboard events. The **handleEvent()** method handles all of those and more. It can also catch all the system messages that might be sent to your program.

If you have several different methods in your code that all catch the same event, you need to know what order the methods will be fired in. For example, assume you have a class that has a **mouseDown()** method, an **action()** method, and a **handleEvent()** method. If the user clicks the mouse button, which method will get called? The first method to get called will be the **handleEvent()** method—the mother of all event handlers. If it does not handle the event, the event will be passed on to the **action()** method. Finally, if the **action()** method does nothing with the event, the event is passed on to the **mouseDown()** method.

With this knowledge in hand, you can better direct the flow of operations in your code. You can even handle events in multiple locations. The key here is to do something with the event, then pass it on as if it were never processed. In the case of the event methods, you would usually return a value of true at the end of a method where you handled an event. If you change the return value to false, you will see that the event continues down the chain. Here is a sample applet that illustrates this technique:

```
import java.applet.*;
import java.awt.*;

public class testEvents4 extends Applet {
    Label L1 = new Label();
    Label L2 = new Label();
    Label L3 = new Label();

    public testEvents4() {
        setLayout(new GridLayout(2, 3));
        add(new Label("handleEvent()"));
        add(new Label("action()"));
        add(new Label("mouseMove()"));
        add(L1);
        add(L2);
        add(L3);
    }

    public boolean handleEvent(Event evt) {
        if (evt.id == Event.MOUSE_MOVE) {
            L1.setText("" + evt.when);
            this.action(evt, evt.target);
            return super.handleEvent(evt);
        } else {
            return false;
        }
    }

    public boolean action(Event evt, Object arg) {
        L2.setText("" + evt.when);
        return true;
    }
    public boolean mouseMove(Event evt, int x, int y) {
        L3.setText("" + evt.when);
        return true;    }

    public void init(){
        testEvents TN = new testEvents();
    }
} // End Application
```

Try switching some of the return statements and see what happens. Figure 11.1 shows the applet in action. The applet consists of six **Label** controls. They are arranged in a grid. The top three labels list the three methods we are handling. The three lower labels show the time at which the last event of the respective type took place.

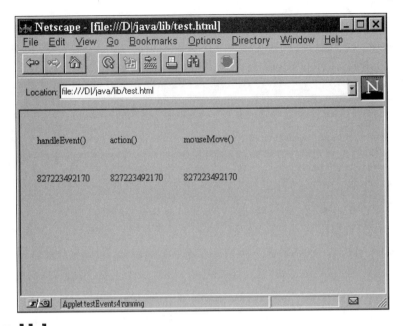

Figure 11.1

The sample events applet.

ACTION() METHOD

The **action**() method is useful for responding to a multitude of user actions. It will capture any events that are caused directly by the user. For example, it will catch mouse clicks, but it will not catch system calls. Here is the declaration for the **action**() method:

```
public boolean action(Event, Object) {}
```

HANDLEEVENT() METHOD

The **handleEvent**() method is probably the most versatile of the event handling methods. It can catch all the standard user interface events as well as system events. The ability to catch system events is crucial to larger, more complex programs. It is also essential to applications. Without the ability to catch system events, applications would never know when the user has pressed any of the title bar buttons or selected any of the title bar options.

Here is the declaration for the **handleEvent**() method:

```
public boolean handleEvent(Event) {}
```

You probably have seen this method in use in several of our example programs. When the user of an application clicks on the close icon for your application, it sends a message indicating that the close icon has been pressed. This message comes in the form of **WINDOW_DESTROY**. We need to catch this event and then tell the application to quit. Here is a code snippet that will do just that:

```
public boolean handleEvent(Event evt) {
   if (evt.id == Event.WINDOW_DESTROY) {
      System.exit(0);
      return true;
   } else {
      super. HandleEvent(evt);
      return false;
   }
}
```

This simply checks the event **id** variable to see if it equals the static variable **WINDOW_DESTROY** defined in the **Event** class. If we receive this event message, we tell the application to close by calling the **exit()** method of the **System** class.

Java Note

Problems with Processing Events

Java does not handle all events very well yet. In particular, the current Java interpreters often make mistakes or do not respond correctly to all events. The most common errors involve the mouse event methods. Sometimes the parent objects do not receive any stimulation when they should. For example, if you place a button in the middle of an applet, you should be able to catch all the mouse events that happen to the button with an event handler belonging to the applet. This *should* work, but in practice it is a little flaky.

12

Streams and
File I/O

Streams and File I/O

12

It's now time to learn the ins and outs of how streams are used in Java to perform a variety of I/O operations.

What good is a program that has no means of communicating with the outside world? If you think about it, most programs you write follow a simple pattern of getting data from a user, processing the data, and presenting the user with the results in one format or another. Java arranges the world of input/output (I/O) into a system of byte *streams*. A byte stream is essentially an unformatted sequence of data which can come from or be sent to a number of different sources including the keyboard, screen, file, and so on. To help you process input and output streams in your programs, Java provides special streams in the **System** class as well as other custom classes including **InputStream** and **OutputStream**.

In this chapter we'll show you how to use the **System** class and the java.io package to perform different types of stream I/O from reading strings typed in at the keyboard to writing data to files. After we introduce the three streams supported by the **System** class we'll examine the other key stream processing classes including **InputStream**, **OutputStream**, **BufferedInputStream**, **BufferedOutputStream**, **ByteArrayInputStream**, **ByteArrayOutputStream**, **DataInputStream**, **DataOutputStream**, **FileInputStream**, **FileOutputStream**, and others.

Introducing the System Class

The **System** class is responsible for providing access to the three main streams: **System.in**, **System.out**, and **System.error**. All input streams are derived from **System.in**, which is responsible for reading data. All of the output streams are derived from **System.out**, which is responsible for sending out data in one form

321

or another. The last stream is **System.error**, which is an output stream derived from **System.out**. As its name implies, **System.out** handles the errors that occur while I/O operations are performed.

To use the streams implemented by the **System** class, you must import the javio.io package:

```
import java.io.*;
```

Here's a simple program that uses **System.in** and **System.out** to read and write a string of text:

```
import java.io.*;

public class ProcessALine {
    public static void main(String arg[]) {
        // Bring in the stream from the keyboard and pipe it to DataInput
        DataInputStream aDataInput = new DataInputStream(System.in);
        String aString;

        try {
            // Continue to read lines from the keyboard until ^Z is pressed
            while ((aString = aDataInput.readLine()) != null) {
                // Print the line out to the screen
                System.out.println(aString);
            }
        } catch (IOException e) { // Check for I/O errors
            System.out.println("An IOException has occurred");
        }
    }
}
```

The **System.in** stream is used to create an input stream object called **aDataInput**. This object is created as an instance of the **DataInputStream** class. The advantage of this class is that it contains methods like **readLine()** for processing input streams. In fact the work of reading a string is accomplishing using a single line of code:

```
while ((aString = aDataInput.readLine()) != null)  ...
```

The **readLine()** method will continue to read characters from the input stream until a Ctrl-Z character is encountered, which terminates the input stream. (Thus, when you run this program, make sure that you enter a Ctrl-Z at some point to tell the program to stop reading characters from the input stream.)

Checking for Errors

One important feature you'll find in our sample program is simple error handling code implemented with the **try ... catch** clause. When performing I/O stream operations, you must check for possible I/O errors. Notice that in our program, a **try** clause is used to check *both* the stages of reading and writing to a stream. If an error occurs, an **IOException** error is thrown and the **catch** clause will be executed.

Different Flavors of Streams

With the multitude of possible forms your data can come in and be sent out with, it's no wonder that Java offers a variety of stream handlers that can be implemented. Each stream type is capable of combining other stream types to handle unique situations. For example, if you want to buffer data that is being read from a file so that it may be read all at once, you could use a statement like this:

```
InputStream aStream =
    new BufferedInputStream(new FileInputStream("C:\foobar.txt"));
```

This line would bring in the data from a file, buffering it in a stream called **aStream**. Then, the data could be accessed all at once by using **aStream**. This technique could be very valuable in applications that need to read data all at once instead of having to read chunks and perform multiple read operations.

Understanding the Basics of Inputting and Outputting

All data that you manipulate in the form of strings and numbers, be it an integer or a double, must be transformed into a stream (bytes) in order for the information to be interpreted by the computer and the devices that use the data. This is considered *outputting* the data verses *inputting* the data. Likewise, if a user needs to understand the data, unless they read machine language, we need to convert it to a useful format by manipulating it with one of the input streams. Figure 12.1 shows the process of how data is converted and processed with both input and output streams.

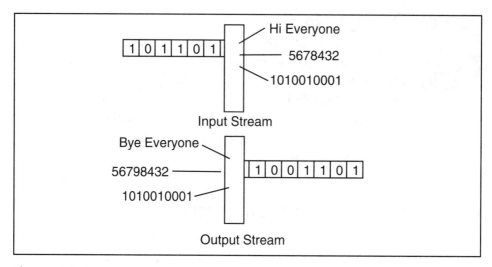

Figure 12.1

A graphical example of converting data for input and output streams.

InputStream and OutputStream Classes

In addition to the **System** class, Java provides other classes for handling stream input and output including **InputStream** and **OutputStream**, which are abstract classes responsible for the basic declarations of all the input and output streams that we'll be exploring next. All streams created from these classes are capable of throwing an **IOException** that must be dealt with by "re-throwing" it or handling it. To declare and create an object using **InputStream** or **OutputStream** you would use statements like the following:

```
InputStream aStream = getStreamFromASource();
OutputStream aStream = getStreamToASource();
```

In both declarations, the methods *getStreamFromSource()* and *getStreamToASource()* are any methods that returns a stream. The stream returned by the method will be assigned to the object *aStream*. All information passed to and from the streams must be in the form of bytes. Table 12.1 presents the key methods defined in **InputStream** and Table 12.2 presents the methods defined in **OutputStream**.

Table 12.1   Key Methods Defined in the InputStream Class

Method	Description
available()	Returns the number of bytes available in the stream without invoking a block.
close()	Closes the stream.
mark(int)	Marks the current position in the stream.
markSupported()	Returns a true/false value to indicate if the stream supports marking capabilities.
read()	Reads bytes from the stream.
read(byte[])	Reads bytes from the stream and places them in an array.
read(byte[], int, int)	Reads a specified number of bytes from the stream and places them in an array starting at a specified index position.
reset()	Sets the stream to the last mark.
skip(long)	Skips a designated number of bytes in the stream.

Table 12.2   Key Methods Defined in the OutputStream Class

Method	Description
close()	Closes the stream.
flush()	Clears the stream, forcing any buffered bytes to be written out.
write(int)	Writes *n* number of bytes to the stream.
write(byte[])	Writes an array of bytes to the stream.
write(byte[], int, int)	Writes an array of bytes of a specified size, starting at a specified index position.

Here's an example of an application that uses the **OutputStream** class to derive another class for performing a simple output operation:

```java
import java.io.*;
import java.net.*;
import java.awt.*;

public class mrsServer extends Frame {
    TextArea serverScreen;

    mrsServer() {
        super("Server Application");
        serverScreen = new TextArea("mrsServer's Screen:\n", 10, 40);
        add("Center", serverScreen);
        pack();
        show();
```

```
ServerSocket mrsServer = null;
Socket socketReturn = null;
// Assigns the variable rawDataOut to the class OutputStream
OutputStream rawDataOut = null;

try {
    mrsServer = new ServerSocket( 10, 2 );
    socketReturn = mrsServer.accept();
    serverScreen.appendText( "Connected to the mrsServer" );

    // Creates an instanceof the class OutputStream named
    // rawDataOut
    // rawDataOut receives the stream from the Socket socketReturn
    rawDataOut = socketReturn.getOutputStream();
    DataOutputStream DataOut = new DataOutputStream(rawDataOut);

    DataOut.write( 5 );
} catch( UnknownHostException e ) {
} catch( IOException e ) {
}
}
```

BufferedInputStream and BufferedOutputStream Classes

These classes are used to implement streams responsible for collecting data from a source that brings in data at a slower rate than the recipient. Then, the chunks of data collected may be delivered in larger, more manageable blocks than in the manner they were received. This proves beneficial for file systems and networks, where the connection depends on a device for transmission.

Here are the declarations for these classes:

```
InputStream aStream = new BufferedInputStream(getStreamFromASource());
OutputStream aStream = new BufferedInputStream(getStreamToASource());
```

In both declarations, a stream is returned to the parent class, **InputStream** or **OutputStream** depending if it is incoming or outgoing. The methods *getStreamFromSource()* and *getStreamToASource()* can be any methods that return a stream. The stream that the method returns will be buffered as the information comes in and is appended to the object **aStream**. All information passed to and from the streams must be in the form of bytes. Table 12.3 presents the

Table 12.3 Key Methods Defined in the BufferedInputStream Class

Method	Description
available()	Determines the number of bytes available in the stream without invoking a block.
mark(int)	Marks the current position in the stream.
markSupported()	Returns a true/false value to indicate if the stream supports marking capabilities.
read()	Reads bytes from the stream.
read(byte[], int, int)	Reads a specified number of bytes from the stream and places them in an array starting at a specified index position.
reset()	Sets the stream to the last mark.
skip(long)	Skips a designated number of bytes in the stream.

Table 12.4 Key Methods Defined in the BufferedOutputStream Class

Method	Description
flush()	Clears the stream, forcing any buffered bytes to be written out.
write(int)	Writes *n* number of bytes to the stream.
write(byte[], int, int)	Writes an array of bytes of a specified size, starting at a specified index position.

key methods defined in **BufferedInputStream** and Table 12.4 presents the methods defined in **BufferedOutputStream**.

Here's an example of an application that uses the **BufferedInputStream** class to derive another class for performing a simple input operation:

```
import java.io.*;

// Reads from a file
public class  ReadAFile extends Object {
   ReadAFile(String s) {
      String line;
      FileInputStream fileName  = null;
      // Assigns the variable bufferedInput to the class
      // BufferedInputStream
      BufferedInputStream bufferedInput = null;
      DataInputStream dataIn = null;

      try {
         fileName = new FileInputStream(s);
         // Creates an instance of the class BufferedInputStream named
         // bufferedInput
```

```
        // bufferedInput receives the stream from the FileInputStream
        // fileName as it is read
        bufferedInput = new BufferedInputStream(fileName);
        dataIn = new DataInputStream(bufferedInput);
    }
    catch(FileNotFoundException e) {
        System.out.println("File Not Found");
        return;
    }
    catch(Throwable e) {
        System.out.println("Error in opening file");
        return;
    }

    try {
        while ((line = dataIn.readLine()) != null) {
            System.out.println(line + "\n");
        }
        fileName .close();
    }
    catch(IOException e) {
        System.out.println("Error in reading file");
    }
}

// Where execution begins in a stand-alone executable
public static void main(String args[]) {
    new ReadAFile(args[0]);
}
}
```

ByteArrayInputStream and ByteArrayOutputStream Classes

These streams create a new stream from an array of bytes to be processed. They are used to perform the reverse operations of what most of the streams do. To declare and create an object from these classes you would use statements like the following:

```
InputStream aStream = new ByteArrayInputStream(getStreamFromASource());
OutputStream aStream = new ByteArrayInputStream(getStreamToASource());
```

The methods used above, *getByteArrayFromSource()* and *getByteArrayToASource()* can be any methods that returns a byte array. The array is passed through the **ByteArrayInputStream** class and a stream is created from it. The stream that was converted from the class returns a value and is assigned to the object **aStream**. All information passed to and from the streams must be in the form of bytes. Table 12.5 presents the key methods defined in **ByteArrayInputStream** and Table 12.6 presents the methods defined in **ByteArrayOutputStream**.

Here is a hypothetical example that uses a **ByteArrayInputStream** class. If you wanted to compile this program, you would need to supply a method to fill the array of bytes, **anArrayOBytes**:

Table 12.5 Key Methods Defined in the ByteArrayInputStream Class

Method	Description
available()	Returns the number of bytes available in the stream without invoking a block.
read()	Reads bytes from the stream.
read(byte[], int, int)	Reads a specified number of bytes from the stream and places them in an array starting at a specified index position.
reset()	Sets the stream to the last mark.
skip(long)	Skips a designated number of bytes in the stream.

Table 12.6 Key Methods Defined in the ByteArrayOutputStream Class

Method	Description
reset()	Resets the current buffer so that it may be used again.
size()	Returns the current size of the buffer.
toByteArray()	Returns a copy of the input data.
toString()	Converts input bytes to a string.
toString(int)	Converts input bytes to a string, sets the selected byte's first 8 bits of a 16 bit Unicode to hibyte.
write(int)	Writes *n* number of bytes to the buffer.
write(byte[], int, int)	Writes an array of bytes of a specified size, starting at a specified index position.
writeTo(OutputStream)	Writes the buffered information to another stream.

```
import java.io.*;

// Reads from a file
public class  Byte2String extends Object {
   Byte2String(String s) {
      byte[] anArrayOBytes;
      …
      //fills the anArrayOBytes with data
      …
      try {
         // Creates an instanceof the class InputStream named byteDataIn
         // byteDataIn receives the stream from the ByteArrayInputStream
         // anArrayOBytes
         InputStream byteDataIn = new ByteArrayInputStream(anArrayOBytes);
      }
      catch(IOException e) {
      }
      …
      // perform some process with the stream
   }

   // Where execution begins in a stand-alone executable
   public static void main(String args[]) {
      new Byte2String(args[0]);
   }
}
```

DataInputStream and DataOutputStream Classes

All methods defined in these classes are actually declared in an interface named **DataInput**. To declare and create a **DataInputStream** or **DataOutputStream** object you would use statements like the following:

```
DataInputStream aStream = new DataInputStream(getStreamFromASource());
DataOutputStream aStream = new DataOutputStream(getStreamToASource());
```

Notice in both declarations the need to declare the class type, **DataInputStream** or **DataOutputStream**, instead of type **InputStream** or **OutputStream**. The methods *getStreamFromSource()* and *getStreamToASource()* can be any methods that return a stream. Once the stream is passed to the **DataInputStream** or **DataOutputStream** object, the methods declared in the interface can be applied to the stream. Table 12.7 presents the key methods defined in **DataInputStream** and Table 12.8 presents the methods defined in **DataOutputStream**.

Table 12.7 Key Methods Defined in the DataInputStream Class

Method	Description
read(byte[])	Reads an array of bytes from the stream.
read(byte[], int, int)	Reads a specified number of bytes from the stream and places them in an array starting at a specified index position.
readBoolean()	Reads a boolean from the stream.
readByte()	Reads a 8-bit byte from the stream.
readChar()	Reads a 16-bit character from the stream.
readDouble()	Reads a 64-bit double from the stream.
readFloat()	Reads a 32-bit float from the stream.
readFully(byte[])	Reads bytes from the stream, blocking until all bytes are read.
readFully(byte[], int, int)	Reads bytes from the stream, blocking until all bytes are read. The starting point to begin reading and the maximum number of bytes to read are passed as parameters.
readInt()	Reads a 32-bit integer from the stream.
readLine()	Reads a line from the stream until an \n,\r,\n\r \, or EOF is reached.
readLong()	Reads a 64-bit long from the stream.
readShort()	Reads a 16-bit short from the stream.
readUTF()	Reads a UTF formatted string from the stream.
readUTF(DataInput)	Reads a UTF formatted string from a specific stream.
readUnsignedByte()	Reads an unsigned 8-bit byte from the stream.
readUnsignedShort()	Reads an unsigned 8-bit short from the stream.
skipBytes(int)	Skips a designated number of bytes in the stream, blocking until finished.

Table 12.8 Key Methods Defined in the DataOutputStream Class

Method	Description
flush()	Clears the stream, forcing any buffered bytes to be written out.
size()	Returns the number of bytes in the stream.
write(int)	Writes *n* number of bytes to the stream.
write(byte[], int, int)	Writes an array of bytes of a specified size, starting at a specified index position.
writeBoolean(boolean)	Writes a boolean to the stream.
writeByte(int)	Writes an 8-bit byte to the stream.
writeBytes(String)	Writes a string of bytes to the stream.

continued

Table 12.8   Key Methods Defined in the DataOutputStream Class (Continued)

Method	Description
writeChar(int)	Writes a 16-bit character to the stream.
writeChars(String)	Writes a string of chars to the stream.
writeDouble(double)	Writes a 64-bit double to the stream.
writeFloat(float)	Writes a 32-bit float to the stream.
writeInt(int)	Writes a 32-bit integer to the stream.
writeLong(long)	Writes a 64-bit long to the stream.
writeShort(int)	Writes a 16-bit short to the stream.
writeUTF(String)	Writes a UTF formatted string to the stream.

Let's revisit our example of the client application once more to demonstrate the use of a **DataInputStream**:

```
import java.io.*;
import java.net.*;
import java.awt.*;

public class mrClient extends Frame {
    mrClient() {
        super("Client Application");
        TextArea clientScreen = new TextArea("mrClient's Screen:\n", 10, 40);
        add("Center", clientScreen);
        pack();
        show();
        Socket mrClient = null;
        InputStream rawDataIn = null;

        try {
            mrClient = new Socket( InetAddress.getLocalHost(), 10 );

            rawDataIn = mrClient.getInputStream();
            // reads in the stream for the InputStream rawDataIn and pipes
            // it to DataIn
            DataInputStream DataIn = new DataInputStream(rawDataIn);
            // the array of bytes is then read from the stream
            clientScreen.appendText( "mrClient receives -  " +
            DataIn.read() );
        } catch( UnknownHostException e ) {
        } catch( IOException e ) {
        }
    }
}
```

Here the stream used with the **Socket** object, **mrClient**, is piped from the **InputStream** to the **DataInputStream**. The bytes are then read from the stream, **DataIn**, and appended to the text box with this line:

```
clientScreen.appendText("mrClient receives -  " + DataIn.read());
```

By simply changing the method, we can read any type of data that resides in the stream. For example, if we wanted to read a stream of chars, we would use a statement like this:

```
clientScreen.appendText("mrClient receives -  " + DataIn.readChar());
```

FileInputStream and FileOutputStream Classes

The most common use for these streams is to apply them to a file to be read from and written to. Here are the declarations for these classes.

```
InputStream aStream = getStreamFromASource();
OutputStream aStream = getStreamToASource();
```

In both declarations, the methods *getStreamFromSource()* and *getStreamToASource()* can be any methods that return a stream. The stream that the method returns is assigned to the object **aStream**. All information passed to and from the streams must be in the form of bytes. Table 12.9 presents the key methods defined in **FileInputStream** and Table 12.10 presents the methods defined in **FileOutputStream**.

Table 12.9 Key Methods Defined in the FileInputStream Class

Method	Description
available()	Returns the number of bytes available in the stream without invoking a block.
close()	Closes the stream.
finalize()	Closes the stream when the garbage collector is invoked.
getFD()	Returns the file descriptor of the file associated with the stream.
read()	Reads bytes from the stream.
read(byte[])	Reads into an array of bytes from the stream.
read(byte[], int, int)	Reads a specified number of bytes from the stream and places them in an array starting at a specified index position.
skip(long)	Skips a designated number of bytes in the stream.

Table 12.10	Key Methods Defined in the FileOutputStream Class
Method	**Description**
close()	Closes the stream.
finalize()	Closes the stream when the garbage collector is invoked.
getFD()	Returns the file descriptor of the file associated with the stream.
write(int)	Writes *n* number of bytes to the stream.
write(byte[])	Writes an array of bytes to the stream.
write(byte[], int, int)	Writes an array of bytes of a specified size, starting at a specified index position.

Here is a practical example of how you can use the **FileOutputStream** and **FileInputStream** classes:

```
import java.io.*;

public class WriteAFile {
   WriteAFile(String s) {
      write(s);
   }

   // Writes to a file
   public void write(String s) {
      // Assigns the variable writeOut to the class FileOutputStream
      FileOutputStream writeOut = null;
      DataOutputStream dataWrite = null;

      try {
         // Creates an instanceof the class FileOutputStream named writeOut
         // writeOut receives the stream from the File designated in the
         // variables
         writeOut = new FileOutputStream(s);
         dataWrite = new DataOutputStream(writeOut);
         dataWrite.writeChars("This is a Test");
         dataWrite.close();
      }
      catch(IOException e)  {
         System.out.println("Error in writing to file");
       }
      catch(Throwable e)  {
         System.out.println("Error in writing to file");
       }
      finally {
         System.out.println("\n\n.....creating a backup file.");
```

```
        try {
            // Recreates an instanceof the class FileOutputStream named
            // writeOut
            // writeOut receives the stream from the File named
            // "MyBackup.sav"
            writeOut = new FileOutputStream("MyBackup.sav");
            dataWrite = new DataOutputStream(writeOut);
            dataWrite.writeChars("This is a Test");
            dataWrite.close();
        }
        catch (IOException e) {
                System.out.println("Error in writing backup file");
        }
    }
}
// Where execution begins in a stand-alone executable
public static void main(String args[]) {
    new WriteAFile(args[0]);
}
}
```

The variable **writeOut**, which is of type **DataOutputStream**, is actually used twice in this example: once to write the file specified by the user and again to write a file MyBackup.sav.

FilterInputStream and FilterOutputStream Classes

These are classes that act as channels for streams to be passed through. As a stream is passed through the shell, a hierarchy of stream containers are created to perform some processing of bytes as the methods are passed along with it. This structure allows for a chaining effect of shells to break up a complicated task into small steps. Here are the declarations for these classes:

```
FilterInputStream anotherStream = new FilterInputStream(aStream);
FilterOutputStream anotherStream = new FilterOutputStream(aStream);
```

In both declarations, the methods *FilterInputStream()* and *FilterOutputStream()* require that a stream be passed to each method. In return, a stream is assigned to the object named **anotherStream**. Table 12.11 presents the key methods defined in **FilterInputStream** and Table 12.12 presents the methods defined in **FilterOutputStream**.

Table 12.11	Key Methods Defined in the FilterInputStream Class
Method	**Description**
available()	Returns the number of bytes available in the stream without invoking a block.
close()	Closes the stream.
finalize()	Closes the stream when the garbage collector is invoked.
getFD()	Returns the file descriptor of the file associated with the stream.
read()	Reads bytes from the stream.
read(byte[])	Reads an array of bytes from the stream.
read(byte[], int, int)	Reads a specified number of bytes from the stream and places them in an array starting at a specified index position.
skip(long)	Skips a designated number of bytes in the stream.

Table 12.12	Key Methods Defined in the FilterOutputStream Class
Method	**Description**
close()	Closes the stream.
flush()	Clears the stream, forcing any bytes to be written out.
write(int)	Writes n number of bytes to the stream.
write(byte[])	Writes an array of bytes to the stream.
write(byte[], int, int)	Writes an array of bytes of a specified size, starting at a specified index position.

Here is an example of how a **FilterOutputStream** class can be manipulated at different stages without actually changing the original stream from the **OutputStream**:

```
import java.io.*;
import java.net.*;
import java.awt.*;

public class mrsServer extends Frame {
    TextArea serverScreen;

    mrsServer() {
        ... // perform functions previous to opening the socket
        try {
            mrsServer = new ServerSocket( 10, 2 );
            socketReturn = mrsServer.accept();
```

```
        OutputStream stageOneDataOut = socketReturn.getOutputStream();
        FilterOutputStream stageTwoDataOut = new
        FilterOutputStream(stageOneDataOut);
        // perform some operations on stageTwoDataOut stream
        ...
        FilterOutputStream stageThreeDataOut = new
        FilterOutputStream(stageTwoDataOut);
        // perform some operations on stageThreeDataOut stream
        ...
        FilterOutputStream stageFourDataOut = new
          FilterOutputStream(stageThreeDataOut);
        // write the data from stageFourDataOut
        ...

    } catch( UnknownHostException e ) {
    } catch( IOException e ) {
    }
    ...
}
```

LineNumberInputStream Class

This class allows for line numbering of each line processed through the stream. It is useful for determining which lines errors have occurred on. To declare and create an object from this class, you use a statement like the following:

```
LineNumberInputStream aStream =
  LineNumberInputStream(getStreamFromASource());
```

In the declaration above, the method *getStreamAFromSource()* retrieves a source stream that is assigned line numbers. The stream that the method **LineNumberInputStream**() returns is assigned to the object **aStream**. Table 12.13 presents the key methods defined in **LineNumberInputStream**.

Here is a real world example of how the **LineNumberInputStream** class can be used:

```
import java.io.*;

// Reads from a file
public class  ReadAFile extends Object {
    ReadAFile(String s) {
        String line;
        FileInputStream fileName  = null;
        // Assigns the variable bufferedInput to the class
```

```
BufferedInputStream
    BufferedInputStream bufferedInput = null;
    DataInputStream dataIn = null;

    try {
        fileName = new FileInputStream(s);
        // Creates an instanceof the class LineNumberInputStream named
        // parsedData
        // parsedData receives the stream from the FileInputStream
        // fileName as it is read
        LineNumberInputStream parsedData = new
        LineNumberInputStream(fileName);
        dataIn = new DataInputStream(parsedData);
    }
    catch(FileNotFoundException e) {
        System.out.println("File Not Found");
        return;
    }
    catch(Throwable e) {
        System.out.println("Error in opening file");
        return;
    }

    try {
        while ((line = dataIn.readLine()) != null) {
            // adds the current line number to the beginning of every line
            System.out.println(parsedData.getLineNumber() + ": " + line +
              "\n");
        }
    fileName .close();
    }
    catch(IOException e) {
        System.out.println("Error in reading file");
    }
}

// Where execution begins in a stand-alone executable
public static void main(String args[]) {
    new ReadAFile(args[0]);
}
}
```

As the stream is passed to the **parsedData** stream, a line number is assigned to each line in the stream. The line number is then added to the line before printing the line to the browser.

Table 12.13	Key Methods Defined in the LineNumberInputStream Class
Method	**Description**
available()	Returns the number of bytes available in the stream without invoking a block.
getLineNumber()	Returns the current line number of the stream.
mark(int)	Marks the current position in the stream.
read()	Reads bytes from the stream
read(byte[], int, int)	Reads a specified number of bytes from the stream and places them in an array starting at a specified index position.
reset()	Sets the stream to the last mark.
setLineNumber(int)	Sets the current line number.
skip(long)	Skips a designated number of bytes in the stream.

PipedInputStream and PipedOutputStream Classes

These classes allow for pipe-like connection between two threads to allow for safe communication between a shared queue. For this technique to be effective, both threads must implement the class. To declare and create objects from these class, you use statements like the following:

```
PipedInputStream aThreadStreamIn =
    PipedInputStream(getStreamFromASource());
PipedOutputStream aThreadStreamOut = PipedOutputStream(aThreadStreamIn);
```

In both declarations, they must be implemented in the threads to ensure a data stream is not being written to by the other thread. The stream that the method returns is assigned to an **aThreadStreamIn** or **aThreadStreamOut** object. Table 12.14 presents the key methods defined in **PipedInputStream** and Table 12.15 presents the methods defined in **PipedOutputStream**.

Table 12.14	Key Methods Defined in the PipedInputStream Class
Method	**Description**
close()	Closes the stream.
connect(PipedOutputStream)	Connects the stream to a **PipedOutputStream** of the sender.
read()	Reads bytes from the stream.
read(byte[], int, int)	Reads a specified number of bytes from the stream and places them in an array starting at a specified index position.

Table 12.15	Key Methods Defined in the PipedOutputStream Class
Method	**Description**
close()	Closes the stream.
connect(PipedInputStream)	Connects the stream to a PipedInputStream of the intended recipient.
write(int)	Writes *n* number of bytes to the stream.
write(byte[], int, int)	Writes an array of bytes of a specified size, starting at a specified index position.

PrintStream Class

This class is most commonly used to create an instance of the **System** class, where the methods **print()** and **println()** are referenced as class variables for use in the **System.out** and **System.err** calls. The most common output device for this class is the screen. The declaration for the **PrintStream** class is:

```
PrintStream aStream = new PrintStream( getStreamFromASource());
```

Along with this class accepting the **write()**, **flush()**, and **close()** methods, it supports a slew of print methods that will handle just about every I/O operation you will need to perform. Most often, an object created from this class will be used like this:

```
System.out.print(aStream);
System.out.println(aStream);
```

The only difference between the two calls is that the second call appends a return character to the end of the stream. Table 12.16 presents the key methods defined in **PrintStream**. Here is a simple example of how the **PrintStream** class can be used to return a line that was typed in by the user:

```
import java.io.*;

public class ProcessALine {
    public static void main(String arg[]) {
        DataInputStream aDataInput = new DataInputStream(System.in);
        String aString;

        try {
        // A Control Z exits
          while ((aString = aDataInput.readLine()) != null) {
```

```
            System.out.println(aString);
        }
    } catch (IOException e) {
        System.out.println("An IOException has occurred");
    }
  }
}
```

Table 12.16   Key Methods Defined in the PrintStream Class

Method	Description
checkError()	Flushes the stream and returns a boolean in the event of an error.
close()	Closes the stream.
flush()	Clears the stream, forcing any bytes to be written out.
print(Object)	Prints an Object.
print(String)	Prints a String.
print(char[])	Prints an array of chars.
print(char)	Prints a char.
print(int)	Prints an Integer.
print(long)	Prints a long.
print(float)	Prints a float.
print(double)	Prints a double.
print(boolean)	Prints a boolean.
println()	Prints a newline chatacter.
println(Object)	Prints an Object with a newline appended to the end.
println(String)	Prints a String with a newline appended to the end.
println(char[])	Prints an array of chars with a newline appended to the end.
println(char)	Prints a char with a newline appended to the end.
println(int)	Prints an integer with a newline appended to the end.
println(long)	Prints a long with a newline appended to the end.
println(float)	Prints a float with a newline appended to the end.
println(double)	Prints a double with a newline appended to the end.
println(boolean)	Prints a boolean with a newline appended to the end.
write(int)	Writes n number of bytes to the stream.
write(byte[], int, int)	Writes an array of bytes, starting point to begin writing, n number of bytes to write.

PushbackInputStream Class

This class causes the stream to reaccept a byte that was passed to it by the **InputStream**. By forcing the byte back to the delivering **InputStream**, you can reread the byte as if it had never been read. To declare a stream as **PushbackInputStream** and instaniate it, you could type the following:

```
PushbackInputStream aStream =
    new PushbackInputStream (getStreamFromASource());
```

The *getStreamFromASource()* method can be any method that returns a stream. The stream that the method is assigned to the object **aStream**. All information passed to and from the streams must be in the form of bytes. Table 12.17 presents the key methods that are defined in **PushbackInputStream**.

SequenceInputStream Class

This class allows for two streams to be seamlessly joined. This is especially useful when creating an exception that would pick up where it left off last in a transfer. To declare a stream as type **SequenceInputStream** and instaniate it, you would type the following:

```
InputStream aStream = new SequenceInputStream(firstStream, secondStream);
```

In the declaration, **firstStream** is appended to the **secondStream** to create a single seamless stream, **aStream**. Table 12.18 presents the key methods defined in **SequenceInputStream**.

Table 12.17	Key Methods Defined in the PushbackInputStream Class
Method	**Description**
available()	Returns the number of bytes available in the stream without invoking a block.
markSupported()	Returns a true/false value to indicate if the stream supports marking capabilities.
read()	Reads bytes from the stream.
read(byte[], int, int)	Reads a specified number of bytes from the stream and places them in an array starting at a specified index position.
unread(int)	Returns a char to the stream as if it had not been read in the first place.

Table 12.18 Key Methods Defined in the SequenceInputStream Class	
Method	**Description**
close()	Closes the stream.
read()	Reads bytes from the stream.
read(byte[], int, int)	Reads a specified number of bytes from the stream and places them in an array starting at a specified index position.

StringBufferInputStream Class

This class is very similiar to the **ByteArrayInputStream** class. The difference is that it combines an array of char types into a stream. Note, an array of chars is actually a string. To declare and create an object from this class, you use a statement like the following:

```
InputStream aStream = new StringBufferInputStream(String);
```

The classes declared here passes a string through the **StringBufferInputStream** class and a stream is created from it. The stream that was converted from the class returns a value and is assigned to the object **aStream**. Table 12.19 presents the key methods defined in **StringBufferInputStream**.

Here is another hypothetical example, but this time a **StringBufferInputStream** class is used. (You may have recognized this example earlier when we introduced the **ByteArrayInputStream** class. We decided to reuse the sample program because of the similarity between the two classes.)

Table 12.19 Key Methods Defined in the StringBufferInputStream Class	
Method	**Description**
available()	Returns the number of bytes available in the stream without invoking a block.
read()	Reads bytes from the stream.
read(byte[], int, int)	Reads a specified number of bytes from the stream and places them in an array starting at a specified index position.
reset()	Sets the stream to the last mark.
skip(long)	Skips a designated number of bytes in the stream.

```java
import java.io.*;

// Reads from a file
public class  Char2Stream extends Object {

  Char2Stream(String s) {
      String aCommonString = "The quick brown fox jumped over the lazy dog";
      try {
          // Creates an instanceof the class InputStream named charDataIn
          // charDataIn receives the stream from the
          // StringBufferInputStream aCommonString
          InputStream charDataIn = new
          StringBufferInputStream(aCommonString);
      }
      catch(IOException e) {
      }
      ...
      // perform some process with the stream
  }

  // Where execution begins in a stand-alone executable
  public static void main(String args[]) {
      new Char2Stream(args[0]);
  }
}
```

The stream is piped through the **StringBufferInputStream** class before being sent to the **InputStream** object, **charDataIn**. This technique converts the string of characters into a sequence of bytes so that they can be used in a stream. The stream then can be passed to any of the **InputStreams** to be manipulated later in the program.

13

Networking
with Java

Networking with Java

Java supports a number of classes and methods so that you can make connections to the Internet and perform a variety of operations from processing Web content to transferring files.

Since you are reading this book, it's likely that you are connected to the Internet in one way or another. And after writing a few Java applets, you're probably aware that networking plays a key role in the development of Java. So, whether you are just stepping into the world of networking or you already realize what a pain networking can be, this chapter should help you use Java to connect your applications to other resources via networks.

We'll begin by examining the basics of how networking works across the Internet. As you'll see, the two key networking components for the Internet are protocols and ports. We'll then show you how to use special classes defined in the java.net package to set up network sockets and support client/server network communications. We'll also show you how to use the URL class to access content from the Web. In the last part of the chapter, we'll look at techniques for communicating between applets.

Understanding the Basics of Networking

You may not be aware of it, but you already know the basics of computer networking, especially if you use a telephone. A telephone provides a means for two or more people at different locations to talk back and forth. In order for voices (data) to be sent back and forth, a *protocol* is used that defines how each party will interact with each other. In the case of a telephone, the protocol involves speaking into a transmitter and listening to a receiver.

When it comes to computer networks that connect with the Internet, the set of key protocols that are used include:

- TCP/IP
- SMTP
- FTP
- HTTP
- NNTP
- Finger
- WhoIs

Let's take a few moments and discuss the basics of each of these protocols.

TCP/IP

The full name of this protocol is *Transmission Control Protocol/Internet Protocol*. It was proposed as a standard in 1973 but was not adopted as a standard until 1982. TCP/IP serves as a hardware-independent protocol for allowing different types of networking systems to connect and send data back and forth. Actually, TCP/IP consists of a collection of different protocols.

The Unix operating system was the first major OS to incorporate this protocol for network communications. With the proliferation of the Internet, this protocol has become widely used for both Internet connections and for networking computers in local area networks. To take advantage of Java's networking capabilities, you'll need to have a TCP/IP connection to the Internet. Fortunately, newer PC operating systems, such as Windows NT, are incorporating TCP/IP into the system. If you are using an older operating system like Windows 3.1, you'll need to make sure TCP/IP has been set up properly on your computer.

SMTP

SMTP stands for *Simple Mail Transfer Protocol*. It is the protocol that is used by email programs such as Eudora to send and receive email. The communications work of handling email is actually controlled by three protocols: SMTP, POP3, and MIME. The primary protocol used to process email is SMTP.

FTP

FTP stands for *File Transfer Protocol*—the protocol that allows files to be transferred from one computer to another across the Internet. This protocol is the most widely used, since most Internet users spend a majority of their time transferring files. Programs that automate the process of sending and receiving files for you use this protocol behind the scenes to make sure that all data is transferred correctly.

HTTP

HTTP stands for *Hyper Text Transfer Protocol*—the protocol that drives the World Wide Web. Since you've probably written countless HTML documents, you already know that information is processed on the Web in the form of hypertext links. HTTP ensures that Web content is transferred correctly from a server to a client computer so that information can be displayed in the correct format. Web browsers like Netscape live and die by the HTTP protocol. You've probably used this protocol numerous times since Web addresses are usually specified by first including the HTTP protocol (for example, http://www.coriolis.com).

NNTP

NNTP stands for *Network News Transfer Protocol.* If you have ever been involved with an Internet newsgroup, you've probably used this protocol hundreds of times, without ever knowing it existed. NNTP works behind the scenes to deliver messages from newsgroups that you belong to.

Finger

Imagine having a finger so large that you could reach out and touch anyone who is connected to the Internet to see if they are currently available. This might sound a little ridiculous, but this is the goal of the Finger protocol. With this protocol, you can "finger" an Internet user to obtain information that the user has declared as public. Some of this information might include the user's full name, mailing address, phone number, and so on.

WhoIs

If you live in a big city and you want to locate someone, you can go to a phone book and look the person up. On the Internet, you can use the WhoIs protocol to do your detective work for you. As long as a person, organization, or company is registered with the Internet address assignment agency (InterNIC), this protocol will give you the information you need.

The Client/Server Model

Using our simple phone analogy, let's investigate the concepts of client/server technology—the driving force that makes networks like the Internet come to life. At one time or another, we've all stood by the phone in anticipation waiting for a call to come in. The caller has the option to pick up the phone at any time and make the call. When they do, we can pick up the phone after a few rings to complete the connection. Since we are the party who is waiting for the call, we operate as the *server*. The person making the call, on the other hand, operates as the *client*, since by making the call, he or she is simply "requesting information" from us—the server.

Computers connected in a network pass information back and forth in the form of *messages*. The computer, acting as the client, sends messages to the server. The server processes the messages and returns information in the form of messages back to the client.

Ports of Interest

In addition to performing complex calculations quickly, today's computers are great at performing multiple tasks at the same time. (Or at least they create the illusion that they can, as we learned in Chapter 8 when we explored threads.) Computers connected to the Internet as servers can provide many services at once. They do this by using *ports* that link up different channels set up at a single address. A computer may set up a port with a number between 0 and 65535, known as a 16-bit number. Each request that comes in from a client requires a port specification as shown in Figure 13.1. If the server has a service running for that port, it is addressed with a certain message defined by the protocol. Currently, ports have been established for the default protocols. For example, port 80 is reserved for HTTP, port 21 is reserved for FTP, port 119 is reserved for News, and so on. The set of key protocols and their associated ports are listed in Table 13.1.

Table 13.1   Key Internet Protocols and Their Associated Ports

Protocol	Port
HTTP	80
FTP	21
NNTP	119
WhoIs	43
SMTP	25
Finger	79

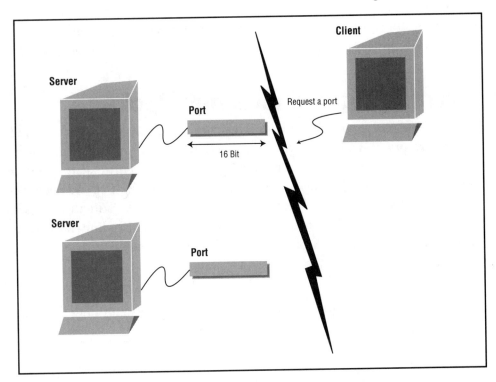

Figure 13.1

Processing a request from a client.

Establishing New Ports and Protocols

You can create your own ports and protocols for the Internet—in fact new ones are being established for the Internet all the time. Just remember that the basic principal behind a network is to be able to communicate; thus, standards are needed. To make sure that everyone follows standard practices for setting up communication links on the Internet, a system of *Request for Comments* (RFCs) have been established. RFCs are documents that are submitted for the purpose of defining specifications or the guidelines for the Internet. For example, the FTP protocol was submitted and reviewed by many Internet developers and users until it was officially adapted as RCF0959. This particular document presents all of the specifications for the protocol. If you were to create a protocol, you could submit it for review and it to would go through the process of being reviewed. Think of it as a bill on Capitol Hill on its windy path to becoming a law. There are many chances for it to be vetoed along the way.

Introducing the java.net Package

As we've explored topics like creating GUI interfaces, controlling threads, and writing exceptions, we've seen that Java's developers put a lot of care into creating packages and classes to handle important activities. Fortunately, when it comes to networking, the Java developers came through again. The java.net package provides several classes for handling key Internet protocols. With these classes, you can perform a number of Internet related operations, including transferring files, setting up and controlling mail servers, creating search agents, processing Web content, and much more.

The structure of the java.net package is shown in Figure 13.2. Table 13.2 provides a summary description of each key class. To understand how these key

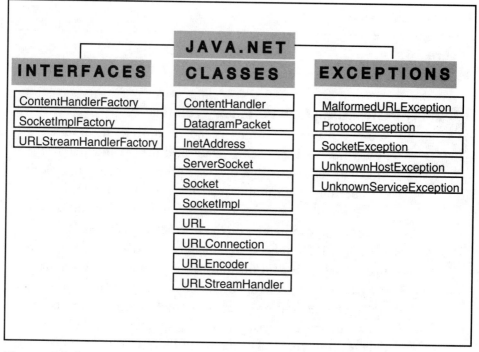

Figure 13.2

The structure of the java.net package.

Table 13.2   The Main Classes in the java.net Package

Class	Description
ContentHandler	This is an abstract class that processes data in a specific format from a stream and creates an appropriate object.
InetAddress	Used to process an Internet address.
ServerSocket	Used to set up a connection-oriented server socket.
Socket	Used to set up a socket for a client.
SocketImpl	Used to create a specific implementation of a socket.
URL	Used to set up a URL.
URLConnection	Used to set up a connection to a URL.
URLStreamHandler	Used to manage data read from or written to a URL.

classes operate, you'll need to be familiar with the client/server model of networking and how sockets are used to facilitate network communications. Because of their complexity and depth, we won't cover every class in detail; but we will cover the essentials so that you can use some of these classes to develop network-capable Java applets and applications.

Networking Applications

Although you may only be creating Java applets right now, opportunities will emerge for creating more powerful distributed programs, especially as Java compilers get better at generating more tightly compiled code. The incredible flexibility and power that Java's portability provides across multiple platforms allows you to create programs for wide distribution. As you gain more experience developing with Java, you'll find yourself building applications that perform networking related tasks that were never possible in the past using traditional languages like C and C++. The key is learning how to exploit the client/server model of developing networked applications.

Working with Internet Addressing

Before we jump in and start using some of the java.net classes to set up client/server communications, you'll need to know the basics of TCP/IP Internet addressing. Actual Internet addresses are represented using a series of four numbers separated by dots. Here's an example:

```
189.12.49.123
```

Each number must be in the range from 0 to 255.

Since you should already have your own Internet address, you can easily determine what it is by using the **InetAddress** class defined in the java.net package. This class provides five key methods as listed in Table 13.3.

To see how the **InetAddress** class can be used, let's write a simple Java program that checks your local computer and displays your Internet address:

```
import java.net.*;  // Must be included to use the InetAddress class

public class checkMyIP {
  public static void main(String args[]) {
    InetAddress localA = null;
    try {
        // Returns the name of the local address
        localA = InetAddress.getLocalHost();
    }
    catch {
    }
    system.out.println("The local address is " + localA);
  }
}
```

First notice that the **import** statement is used to include the classes from the java.net package. The variable **localA** is declared as type **InetAddress**. A call to the method **getLocalHost()** returns the address of the local host computer. Notice that no parameters are provided.

Table 13.3   The Key Methods in the InetAddress Class

Method	Description
getHost()	Returns the name of the host being stored by the **InetAddress** class. An example would be *coriolis.com*.
getAddress()	Returns the numerical address of the host being stored by the **InetAddress** class.
getLocalHost()	Returns the name of the local host.
getByName()	Returns the name of the host specified by a supplied argument to this method.
getAllByName()	Returns a list of addresses for the host name provided as an argument to this method.

The Role of the Client

A client application interacts with other clients to perform certain functions through *sockets*. In order for a client to communicate to other clients, a server must be established for connection. The server is discussed later in the chapter, but for now all you need to know is that a client requires a server to make a connection from which all communication originates.

Creating a Socket

A socket provides a means for information to flow to and from a computer, much like the way a wall socket provides a channel for electricity to flow through. To initiate a socket, the client application must create an instance of the **Socket** class. This is a class that Java provides to facilitate Internet communications. It uses Internet protocol (IP) addresses and port numbers. The IP address indicates with which computer you want to establish communication. Here is an example of how a socket object is created using the **Socket** class:

```
Import java.net.*;
...
Socket mrClient = null;
```

First, notice that the package java.net must be imported so that you can access the **Socket** class. Here the socket object, **mrClient**, is declared and set to null. To initialize **mrClient**, you use a statement like the following:

```
mrClient = new Socket(165.247.88.17, 10);
```

This code creates an instance of the **Socket** class with an IP address of 165.247.88.17 and a port value of 10.

Using Sockets

After creating the gateway for data to enter your program, you need to create a repository for the data to come and go. Streams provide a method of reading and writing data to a socket. For our example and most uses, we'll need two separate streams. The first stream is an input stream and calls a method to receive the information from the socket. The second stream is used to send data out from the socket:

```
InputStream rawDataIn = mrClient.getInputStream();
OutputStream rawDataOut = mrClient.getOutputStream();
```

The first statement instantiates the object **rawDataIn** as type **InputStream**. Any data that flows to the client, **mrClient,** will be stored in **rawDataIn.** The other stream is the **OutputStream.** As you might have guessed, this stream is responsible for passing the data from the client. If you recall from Chapter 12, the Input/OutputStream is difficult to parse all data through because not all of the data processed is just simple bytes. To use some of the more complex data types available in Java, we need to pass our stream through the **DataInput** and **DataOutput** interfaces. This allows for more control over the data that is to be received and sent. (For more information on this technique, refer to Chapter 12.) To pass both the incoming and outgoing data through the **DataInput** and **DataOutput** interfaces, you'll need to use code like the following:

```
DataInputStream DataIn = new DataInputStream(rawDataIn);
DataOutputStream DataOut = new DataOutputStream(rawDataOut);
```

An InputStream/OutputStream is used because of the extensive ability to manipulate more complex streams than simple bytes. For example, you can test the stream to see if it is at the end of a line by using a **readLine**() method. This method explicitly checks for *returns, newlines,* and *return-newline* combinations in a string of characters read from the stream.

Creating a Sample Client Application

Now that you've been introduced to the basics of how client applications communicate using sockets and IP addresses, let's write a sample Java program that creates a socket object and reads in data:

```
import java.io.*;
import java.net.*;  // Must be included to use Socket class
import java.awt.*;

public class mrClient extends Frame {
    mrClient() { }
    mrClient(String s) {
        // Create the text display for the application
        super("Client Application");
        TextArea clientScreen = new TextArea("mrClient's Screen:\n", 10, 40);
        add("Center", clientScreen);
```

```
pack();
show();

Socket mrClient = null;
InputStream rawDataIn = null; // Setup the input and output streams
OutputStream rawDataOut = null;

try {
  mrClient = new Socket(s, 10 );    // Create the socket object

  rawDataIn = mrClient.getInputStream();
  rawDataOut = mrClient.getOutputStream();
  // Create a data input stream
  DataInputStream DataIn = new DataInputStream(rawDataIn);
  // Create a data output stream
  DataOutputStream DataOut = new DataOutputStream(rawDataOut);
  int Value = DataIn.readInt();  // Read in data from the socket
  clientScreen.appendText( "mrClient receives -  " + Value + "\n" );

  switch(Value) {    // Determine which value has been obtained
  // from the socket
   case 1:
     clientScreen.appendText("Your Number 1");
     DataOut.writeInt( 1 );
     break;
    case 2:
     clientScreen.appendText("Your Number 2");
     DataOut.writeInt( 2 );
     break;
    case 3:
     clientScreen.appendText("Your Shakey");
     DataOut.writeInt( 3 );
     break;
   case 4:
     clientScreen.appendText("Your a loser");
     DataOut.writeInt( 4 );
     break;
   case 5:
     clientScreen.appendText("This is my lucky number!");
     DataOut.writeInt( 5 );
     break;
   default:
     clientScreen.appendText("What was your Number?");
     DataOut.writeInt( 6 );
   }
   mrClient.close();    // Close the socket
}
```

```
// Handle exceptions that have occurred
catch( UnknownHostException e ) {
    clientScreen.appendText("Can't find Server");
  }
  catch( IOException e ) {
    clientScreen.appendText("an IO Error has occurred");
  }
}

public static void main( String args[] ) {
    new mrClient(args[0]);
  }

  // Handle events that have occurred
  public boolean handleEvent(Event evt)
  {
    switch(evt.id)
    {
      System.out.println(evt.target.toString());
      case Event.WINDOW_DESTROY:
      {
        System.out.println("Exiting...");
        System.exit(0);
        return true;
      }
    }
  return true;
  }

}
```

When you run this code, remember to pass the address of the computer to connect to. Otherwise, you will throw an **ArrayOutOfBoundsException**. In this case, you should pass the address of your local computer as the command line argument. A sample output produced by the program is shown in Figure 13.3.

Most of the interesting code is found in the **mrClient()** constructor. After setting up an introductory message, the constructor declares objects that will be used for creating a socket and the input and output streams:

```
Socket mrClient = null;
InputStream rawDataIn = null;    // Set up the input and output streams
OutputStream rawDataOut = null;
```

Figure 13.3
Output produced by the client application.

Next, notice the **try** statement that comes before the line of code that creates the socket object, **mrClient:**

```
try {
   mrClient = new Socket(s, 10);    // Create the socket object
...
```

Because all sockets, as well as streams, are capable of throwing **IOExceptions**, it is good practice to check for an IOException when creating a socket and using the socket to perform critical operations such as sending and receiving data. (For more information on exceptions, review Chapter 11.)

The next set of statements perform the actual reading and writing to the socket. In the line shown next, **DataIn** is the reference to the **DataInput** which is linked to the **InputStream** of the socket:

```
int Value = DataIn.readInt();
```

In this case, the integer **Value** receives the value of the **DataIn** at that instance and clears the buffer. There are other types of data that may be read from the stream these are discussed further in Chapter 12. Once the data has been read from the socket, we use a **switch** statement to check the input and display an appropriate message. After the input data has been processed, the **close()** method is called to close the socket.

Networking Concerns

When communicating across a network, certain factors should be taken into consideration. In a perfect world, all users would have a fast connection with no lag. Unfortunately that "perfect" world doesn't exist, so you must take the bandwidth of your connections into consideration. To optimize your applications, the use of return codes allows for quick transmission of integers or small clauses that have more complicated procedures attached to them on either side. In our example, the receiving and returning of integers actually fall into a **switch** statement that performs a more complicated task. The following line is responsible for sending the integer "5" to **DataOutputStream** interface:

```
DataOut.writeInt( 5 );
```

From here, the data is passed through the interface and converted to bytes for the OutputStream to be able to handle the data.

Bring on the Server

Now that we have the client under our belt, we need to learn how to connect to another application. This is accomplished by having the client connect to a server. Essentially, a server is a computer that provides a service for others to utilize. The server is set to listen to a particular port. Once a client requests information on that port, the server springs into action.

For setting up and controlling servers, Java provides a counterpart to the **Socket** class called the **ServerSocket** class. Objects created from this class do not connect to an address like socket objects do. Instead, a server socket object creates a port for another socket to plug in to. To declare a variable of the **ServerSocket** class, you use a statement like the following:

```
ServerSocket mrsServer = null;
```

Then, you can create an instance of the **ServerSocket** class by supplying the appropriate parameter to the class' constructor:

```
mrsServer = new ServerSocket( 10 );
```

This line creates an instance of a **ServerSocket** class named **mrsServer**. The object, **mrsServer**, is initialized with a port setting of 10. Essentially, the server is now set up to listen for incoming sockets at port 10. In addition to specifying the port, you can set a time limit. Here's an example:

```
mrsServer = new ServerSocket(10, 5);
```

Once you have created an object of type **ServerSocket**, you must put the server in motion by using the **accept()** method. This method effectively places a hold on the program until a socket comes along to connect to the server. So, it would be wise to place this method call in a thread if you want to perform other functions while you are waiting for a socket to connect to the server. Once a socket shows up, the **accept()** method returns a socket. Then, the server operates just like the client, by allowing sockets to communicate back and forth.

Creating a Sample Server Application

Let's combine everything we know about clients and servers and create a program that uses both the **ServerSocket** and **Socket** classes. This program will create a server socket object and then wait for a client object to connect up. Once the client connects, the server will try to read data from the client. Here's the complete program:

```java
import java.io.*;
import java.net.*;
import java.awt.*;

public class mrsServer extends Frame {
    TextArea serverScreen;

    mrsServer() {
        super("Server Application");
        serverScreen = new TextArea("mrsServer's Screen:\n", 10, 40);
        add("Center", serverScreen);
        pack();
        show();

        ServerSocket mrsServer = null;    // Initialize the server socket
        Socket socketReturn = null;       // Initialize the client socket
        InputStream rawDataIn = null;
        OutputStream rawDataOut = null;
```

```java
try {
    mrsServer = new ServerSocket( 10 );  // Create the server object
    socketReturn = mrsServer.accept();  // Wait for the client
                                        // socket to come in
    serverScreen.appendText( "Connected to the mrsServer \n" );

    rawDataIn = socketReturn.getInputStream();
    rawDataOut = socketReturn.getOutputStream();
    DataInputStream DataIn = new DataInputStream(rawDataIn);
    DataOutputStream DataOut = new DataOutputStream(rawDataOut);
    DataOut.write( 5 );
    int Value = DataIn.read();

    switch(Value)
    {
    case 1:
      serverScreen.appendText("You sent me Number 1");
      break;
    case 2:
      serverScreen.appendText("You sent me Number 2");
      break;
    case 3:
      serverScreen.appendText("You sent me Number 3");
      break;
    case 4:
      serverScreen.appendText("You sent me Number 4");
      break;
    case 5:
      serverScreen.appendText("You sent me Number 5");
      break;
    default:
      serverScreen.appendText("What was your Number?");
    }

    }
    catch( UnknownHostException e ) {
      clientScreen.appendText("Can't find Server");
    }
    catch( IOException e ) {
      clientScreen.appendText("an IO Error has occurred");
    }
}

public static void main( String args[] ) {
    new mrsServer();
}
```

```
     // Handle events that have occurred
     public boolean handleEvent(Event evt)
     {
       switch(evt.id)
       {
         System.out.println(evt.target.toString());
         case Event.WINDOW_DESTROY:
         {
            System.out.println("Exiting...");
            System.exit(0);
            return true;
         }
       }
       return true;
       }
}
```

This program is essentially an extension of the client example we created earlier. A sample output is shown in Figure 13.4. This time around we added server capabilities by using the **ServerSocket** class. The key code is found in the **mrsServer()** constructor. As you start to read this code, you might want to compare it with the code found in the **mrClient()** constructor from the previous example.

The first two important lines in **mrsServer()** declare the variable **mrsServer** of type **ServerSocket** class and **socketReturn** of type **Socket**:

```
ServerSocket mrsServer = null;   // Initialize the server socket (server)
Socket socketReturn = null;      // Initialize the client socket
```

In addition to the **ServerSocket**, we must declare a socket that is returned when

Figure 13.4

Output produced by the server application.

we connect to another socket. In the following lines of code, we create an instance of the **ServerSocket** class and initialize the port to 10. Then, the **accept()** method is called to instruct the program to wait for the incoming socket. The returning socket will be assigned to **socketReturn**:

```
try {
   mrsServer = new ServerSocket( 10 );  // Create the server object
   socketReturn = mrsServer.accept();   // Wait for the client socket to come in
```

In the event of a connection, the server will write a "5" to the socket stream and not to the server socket stream. After this occurs, the server will attempt to read data from the client, and the data will be processed by the server by displaying an appropriate message.

Web Content Only Please

If communicating across the Internet to access Web content is your only concern, Java has a few special classes for you—**URL** and **URLConnection**. You can use these classes for creating objects to read, manipulate, and write Web content. Here is the syntax you use to declare a Uniform Resource Locator (**URL**) variable:

```
URL aURL = null;
```

In this case, **aURL** is the name of the variable being declared. To create and initialize an object you would use a statement like this:

```
aURL = new URL(http, www.coriolis.com, 80, index.html);
```

This line passes the **URL** class four parameters including the Internet protocol, Web address, Internet port, and the name of an HTML file to access. Although we are using four arguments with this constructor call, other variations are available including:

```
URL(String protocol, String host, String file);
URL(URL context, String spec);
URL(String spec);
```

Since the **URL()** constructor is called to create an object based upon a value, you should use **try...catch** statements to check for errors that might occur. This will allow you to check for a **MalformedURLException** that could be thrown whenever a URL is not specified properly.

Once a URL object has been created, you can easily use it to access Web content. Let's look at an example that grabs a file and prints it to the screen:

```java
import java.io.*;
import java.net.*;

public class GrabAFile {
    BufferedInputStream holdingRoom1;
    String holdingRoom2;

    GrabAFile() {
    }

    GrabAFile( String userURL ) {
        URL aURL;
        InputStream rawDataIn;
        DataInputStream refinedDataIn;
        int aCharDataIn;

        try {
            aURL = new URL(userURL);
            rawDataIn = aURL.openStream();
            holdingRoom1 = new BufferedInputStream( rawDataIn );
            refinedDataIn = new DataInputStream( holdingRoom1 );

            while((aCharDataIn = refinedDataIn.read() ) >= 0 ) {
                    System.out.print((char)aCharDataIn);
            }

            System.out.print( refinedDataIn );
        }
         catch( MalformedURLException e ) {}
         catch( IOException e ) {}
         catch( Exception e ) {}
    }

    public static void main(String args[]) {
        new GrabAFile(args[0]);
    }
}
```

First, this code declares and initializes a URL object as explained earlier. Then, we open a stream for the input. To do this we declare an object as type **InputStream** and assign it a variable. Then, we make reference to the method

openStream() using the name of the object of type URL we wish to connect to the input stream.

Using the URLConnection Class

Another class worth mentioning when reading and writing data to a URL is the **URLConnection** class. This class is an abstract class and must be subclassed to implement the methods that are contained within it. It offers an abundance of useful methods for extracting data from files and setting up properties for writing to a URL.

To utilize any of the methods available in the **URLConnection** class, you first declare a variable of type **URLConnection** as shown here:

```
URLConnection anotherURL;
```

Next, you need to open the connection to an instance of an existing URL. To accomplish this task, you would use a statement like this:

```
anotherURL = aURL.openConnection();
```

The variable, **anotherURL**, is declared as type **URLConnection** as shown in the previous statement. The variable **aURL** in the call, **aURL.openConnection**(), is an object instantiated as type **URL**. The method **openConnection**() creates an object of type **URLConnection** and establishes a connection between the remote object declared in the URL. Let's look at an example where we extract the content type of the file being accessed:

```
import java.net.*;

public class GrabInfo {

    GrabInfo() {
    }

    GrabInfo( String userURL ) {
        URL aURL;
        URLConnection anotherURL;
```

```
        try {
            aURL = new URL(userURL);
            anotherURL = aURL.openConnection();
            anotherURL.connect();
            System.out.print(anotherURL.getContentType() + "\n\n");
        } catch( MalformedURLException e ) {
        } catch( Exception e ) {
        }
    }

    public static void main(String args[]) {
        new GrabInfo(args[0]);
    }
}
```

Here we call the method **getContentType**() defined in the **URLConnection** class and print out what was returned from the object. This method can be extremely useful for determining file types. If you need a more thorough check of a file type, try the method **guessContentTypeFromStream**() and apply it to the previous example by passing the stream to it.

Networking between Applets

Situations may arise where you want applets on the same Web page to be able to communicate with each other. For example, if you want a certain event to occur in an applet when another applet reaches a point in an animation, you could have the animation applet send a message to the other applet at the appropriate time. The only limitation for this type of communication is that both applets must be present on a page to communicate back and forth. Currently, there is no way to have one applet send information to another applet on another page. Hopefully, this feature will be added in the near future.

Passing Information to a Fellow Applet

Let's write some Java code that allows one applet to communicate with another. After you compile and run the code, you should see the responses shown in Figures 13.5 through 13.7. One of the applets is named Gentleman and the other is named Lady.

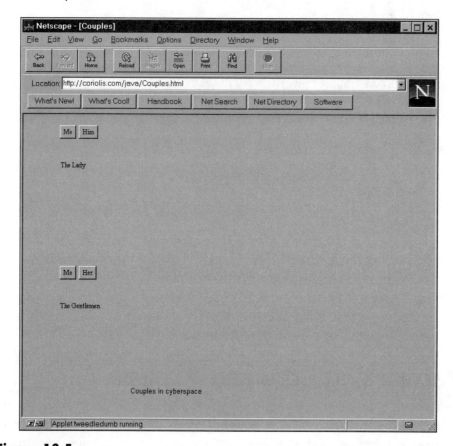

Figure 13.5

A shot of the opening screen showing the two applets.

This example can quickly be modified to perform even more complex tasks with little or no effort. But first, let's discuss exactly what is taking place. The first applet, the Lady, looks like any other applet except for the **handleEvent**() method:

```
public boolean handleEvent(Event evt)
{
  if (evt.target instanceof Button) {
    if("Him".equals(evt.arg))
    {
      Gentleman tweedledee=
        (Gentleman)getAppletContext().getApplet("tweedledee");
      if ( tweedledee != null) {
        return  tweedledee.handleEvent(evt);
      } else {
```

```
      return false;
   }
 }
}
else if("Me".equals(evt.arg))
{
   str ="You Clicked!!";
   repaint();
   return true;
}
else if("Her".equals(evt.arg))
{
   str ="Hello Mister!!";
   repaint();
   return true;
}
```

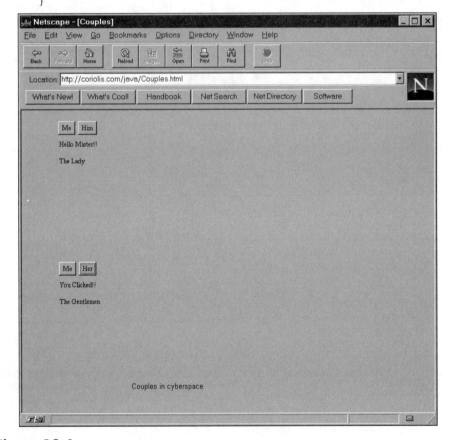

Figure 13.6

A shot of the Gentleman applet's Me button pressed and the Her button pressed.

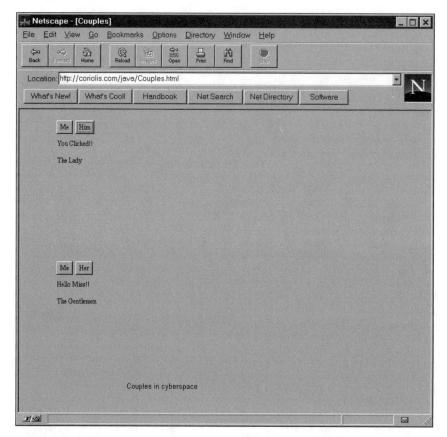

Figure 13.7
A shot of the Lady applet's Me button pressed and the Him button pressed.

```
        return super.handleEvent(evt);
}
return super.handleEvent(evt);
}
```

The actual communication code is found in the second **if** statement. The first line actually retrieves the applet named tweedledee. This applet is named within the declaration of an applet in the HTML file named Couples:

```
<applet code="Gentleman" name=tweedledee width=187 height=232></applet>
```

Using the methods **getApplet()** from the **AppletContext** class and the **getAppletContext()** from the **Applet** class, we create an interface in which to call the methods of the **Gentleman** class and apply it to the applet itself. This allows us to control the applet by calling it with the name of the variable and the name in the **<applet>** tag assigned to it. In this case, **tweedledee** controls the applet from within the **Lady**.

Now we need to make sure when calling handling events that we make reference to the particular event:

```
// From the Lady
return  tweedledee.handleEvent(evt);

// From the Gentleman
else if("Him".equals(evt.arg))
   {
     str ="Hello Miss!!";
     repaint();
     return true;
   }
```

In the event that a user clicks the "Him" button from the "Lady" applet, the Gentleman must address the event that will be passed to it. Otherwise, the **evt** object will slip by without being acted upon. The same goes for the Lady addressing the events that will occur in the Gentleman. Everything here is just reversed for the other applet to communicate in the reverse direction.

Java Note

Which Came First ... the Chicken or the Egg

When compiling the two source files for our applets listed at the end of this chapter, it is important to remember that both source files must be typed in and saved before compiling one or the other. This is because both reference each other's class file. When no class file is present, as in the event of requiring a class in both directions, the Java compiler reads the source file and compiles it from the definitions within. This would be comparable to a deadlock when relating this situation to threads.

The complete code for the Lady applet is:

```
import java.awt.*;
import java.applet.*;
```

```
public class Lady extends Applet
{
      String str = "";

    public void init()
    {
      Button a = new Button("Me");
      Button b = new Button("Him");
        add("East", a);
        add("West", b);


    }

public boolean handleEvent(Event evt)
{
  if (evt.target instanceof Button) {
      if("Him".equals(evt.arg))
      {
Gentleman tweedledee=
(Gentleman)getAppletContext().getApplet("tweedledee");
        if ( tweedledee != null) {
          return  tweedledee.handleEvent(evt);
        } else {
          return false;
        }
      }
      else if("Me".equals(evt.arg))
      {
         str ="You Clicked!!";
         repaint();
         return true;
      }
      else if("Her".equals(evt.arg))
      {
         str ="Hello Mister!!";
         repaint();
         return true;
      }
      return super.handleEvent(evt);
}
return super.handleEvent(evt);
}
      public void paint(Graphics g) {
```

```
        g.drawString(str, 60,50);
        g.drawString("The Lady", 60, 80);
    }
}
```

And here is the complete code for the Gentleman applet:

```
import java.awt.*;
import java.applet.*;

public class Gentleman extends Applet
{
    String str = "";

    public void init()
    {
        Button a = new Button("Me");
        Button b = new Button("Her");
        add("East", a);
        add("West", b);

    }

public boolean handleEvent(Event evt)
{
    if (evt.target instanceof Button) {
        if("Her".equals(evt.arg))
        {
            Lady tweedledumb= (Lady)
                getAppletContext().getApplet("tweedledumb");
            if ( tweedledumb != null) {
                return tweedledumb.handleEvent(evt);
            } else {
                return false;
            }
        }
        else if("Me".equals(evt.arg))
        {
            str ="You Clicked!!";
            repaint();
            return true;
        }
        else if("Him".equals(evt.arg))
        {
            str ="Hello Miss!!";
```

```
        repaint();
        return true;
    }
    return super.handleEvent(evt);
}
return super.handleEvent(evt);
}
    public void paint(Graphics g) {
        g.drawString(str, 60,50);
        g.drawString("The Gentleman", 60, 80);
    }
}
```

THE COUPLES.HTML FILE

```
<HTML>
<HEAD>
<TITLE>Couples</TITLE>
</HEAD>
<BODY>
<applet code="Lady" name=tweedledumb width=187 height=232></applet>
<br>
<br>
<applet code="Gentlemen" name=tweedledee width=187 height=232></applet>
Couples in cyberspace
</BODY>
</HTML>
```

Appendix A

Online Java Resources

Online Java Resources

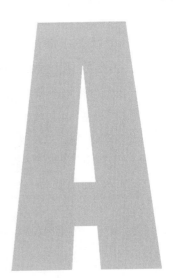

The amount of Java information available on the Web is incredible. You can find source code, applets, documentation, white papers, and many other useful resources. This appendix provides a description of all the best stuff we could find at press time. Make sure you use your favorite Internet search engines to keep looking for new resources. Send us an email if you find something that is not on this list, or if you have a site with an applet on it. We would love to see what you are working on and learn how this book has helped you to create Java applications and applets.

Java Programming Tools

Site: Javasoft - Sun's main Java site
Location: http://www.javasoft.com
Description: This is the best site to look for official information, documentation, and tools. From this site, you can download the Java Developer's Kit, check out the online documentation, or get licensing information. The applets aren't exactly earth-shattering, but this site is the best place to go to get *accurate* information from the creators of Java.

Site: Javamaker
Location: http://net.info.samsung.co.kr/~hcchoi/javamaker.html
Description: Javamaker is a neat little programming environment. It isn't extremely refined, but it is useful for programmers who prefer to use command-

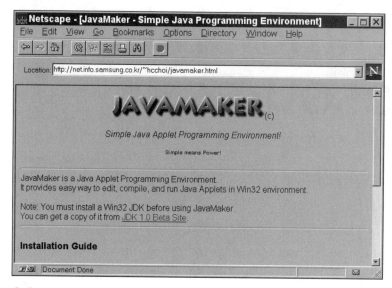

Figure A.1

The Javamaker home page.

line programming environments over some of the new visual environments. Figure A.1 shows the Javamaker home page.

Site: Diva
Location: http://www.inch.com/~friskel/rant.htm
Description: Diva is a visual design environment for Java. For being out so fast, It provides some impressive features. Diva will let you layout buttons and panels and a few other controls. Then, it automatically builds Java code for you, including event handling methods. Although Diva is not extremely robust at this time, it can help you create bigger applications in less time, especially when you are working with the AWT. The one drawback with Diva is that it requires that you use precisely laid out controls, which limits you from using the Layout Managers.

Site: Black Star's Link
Location: http://www.blackstar.com
Description: Black Star has taken a very creative approach to Java development. They have set up a CGI link that allows files on a user's local system to be compiled on their site. This is great for programmers who are working with operating systems that do currently support a Java compiler.

Site: Roaster Home Page
Location: http://www.natural.com/pages/products/roaster/flyer.html
Description: Roaster is the first Java compiler available for the Mac. It was just announced as this book was going to press, so we did not have time to fully test it out. Because of the popularity of Java, you can expect to see many more development tools for Mac programmers in the near future.

Site: Symantec's Java Central
Location: http://cafe.symantec.com
Description: Café is one of the first commercial Java development packages. It is an add-on to Symantec's C++ system. If you like Symantec C++, you will like Café. A Mac version of Café, called Caffeine is also in the works.

Site: Kalimantan Compiler
Location: http://www.dstc.edu.au/projects/kalimantan/
Description: Kalimantan is a collection of basic tools designed to simplify the task of constructing Java applications and applets. Kalimantan builds on the Sun-supplied Java API with a graphically-oriented interface. Kalimantan works under Solaris 2.4 and up, and Windows '95.

Kalimantan is bundled with the teikade (formerly known as dejava) tools from PFU Limited. We strongly suggest that you use both tools since each neatly complements the other, together forming a fairly complete programming environment.

The environment is inspired by the Smalltalk programming environment but tailored to specifically support programming in Java.

Archival Sites

Site: Gamelan
Location: http://www.gamelan.com
Description: If you could only visit a single site to get all your Java information, Gamelan should be it! That may sound a little extreme, but this site, as shown in Figure A.2, is both full of content and a joy to use. It is one of the few Web sites that has been able to use frames and applets in a way that is not overbearing. The site currently boasts over two thousand links to applets, tools, and source code! The resource links are categorized and are based on a very intuitive hierarchy. This is also an excellent place to submit your own applets for others to see and hopefully admire.

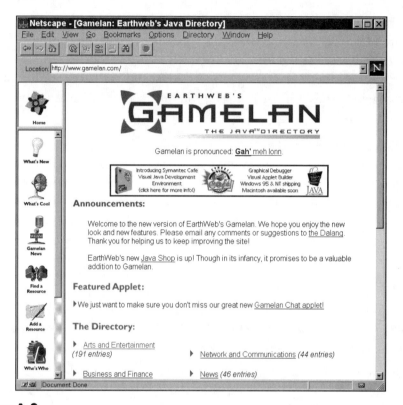

Figure A.2

Gamelan's Java applet resources.

Site: AltaVista Java Searching
Location: http://altavista.digital.com/
Description: Alta Vista is a killer search engine that lets you search for Java applets by name. The search engine has catalogued thousands of Java enabled pages and it parses out the name of the applets for you to view.

Site: Jump on Java
Location: http://www.coriolis.com/java
Description: This site was built by the authors of this book to feature both applets created by other developers and information about Java-related Coriolis Group books, including sample chapters and technical notes. We run a contest with prizes given out each week for the best applet. In addition, you'll find links to the best Java resources and development tools. Visit the site and let us know what you think. And when you create your next killer applet, submit it to the contest!

Figure A.3

The Coriolis Group's Jump on Java Web site.

Site: JARS—Java Applet Rating Service
Location: http://www.jars.com
Description: This site, as shown in Figure A.4, has based its existence on becoming the defacto rating service for Java applets. So far, they have done pretty well. You will see many sites with the JARS logo and a "Top 5% Java Applet" sign.

Site: The Java Boutique
Location: http://weber.u.washington.edu/~jgurney/java/
Description: This is a great site to look for information about using applets on your Web page. It does not really cover Java programming techniques, but from a pure implementation point of view, it is a "must-see" site.

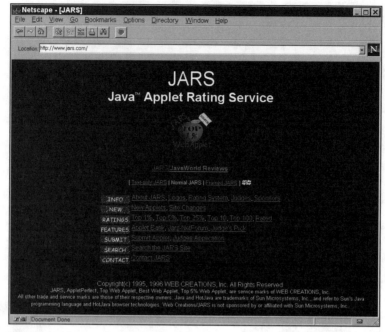

Figure A.4

The Java Applet Rating Service (JARS).

Site: Chilly's Java Collection
Location: http://cecil.cac.psu.edu/~chilly/applets/
Description: This is just a fun little site with some good links.

Cool Stuff

Site: Café Del Sol
Location: http://www.xm.com/cafe/
Description: We could write a description of this site shown in Figure A.5 but it would not sound as near as good as their own, so here it is: "Deep within the bowels of Sun Microsystems, Inc. lies a lab... the New Media Marketing lab. In addition to many other responsibilities the members of this lab are charged with the task of developing Java programs. These programs, innocently known as applets, are occasionally released... bringing much joy and happiness to the virtual world. Those with a keen eye can spot these applets on Web pages and in CDs released by the developers within New Media Marketing lab.

The Café del Sol is the first bit of the 'outside world' the applets see. Here they congregate, compile amongst themselves, and finally (with the permission of their creators) venture out amongst the other Kilo-Mega-Gigabytes that whiz by the Café del Sol, Sun Microsystems, and every other place on the Internet. But here they reside first; here in their primal stages. If you are fortunate enough to have found the Café del Sol, then you are welcome to look around, investigate the applets, and basically get your fill of Java."

Site: Netscape's Java Applet Page
Location: http://home.mcom.com/comprod/products/navigator/version_2.0/ java_applets/index.html
Description: What can we tell you about this site except that when Netscape does someting, you need to be aware of it. They don't feature a lot of resources, but what is featured is typically pretty good.

Site: Dimension X
Location: http://www.dimensionx.com/dnx/java.html
Description: Dimension X is creating some of the coolest applet technologies on the Web. They have an awesome VRML environment that was written en-

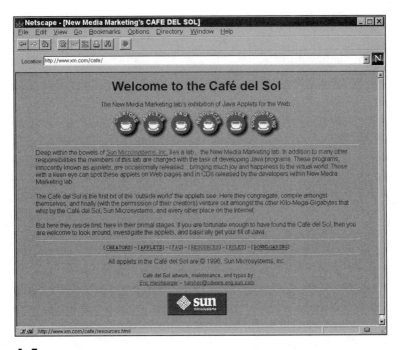

Figure A.5
Café Del Sol Java site.

Figure A.6

Netscape's Java page.

tirely in Java called Liquid Reality. They also have several other applet creation utilities that do very specific, but very useful activities. For example, they have a Java program that helps create animator applets and another program that interfaces with the IRC protocol. By the time you read this they will probably have many more cool things! Figure A.7 shows a sample of the Dimension X Web site.

Site: Sun User's Group - Java Site
Location: http://www.sug.org/java-sig.html
Description: This Java site belongs to the official Sun User's Group (SUG). It is extremely comprehensive and has some really cool content as well. It is also the home of the Java Special Interests Group (Java SIG). Make sure you join their mailing list to get the latest information.

Site: The Coffee Pages
Location: http://answer.questions.com/date/960101/date.html
Description: Any description of this site as shown in Figure A.8 could not possibly do it justice so you need to go there and see it for yourself!

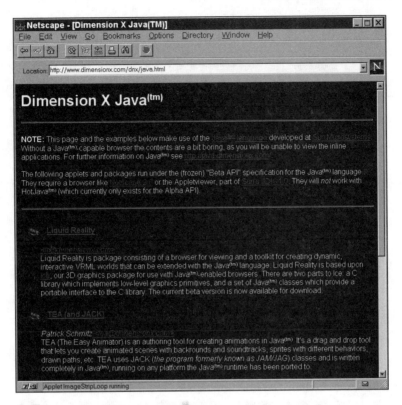

Figure A.7

Dimension Liquid X.

Publications

Site: JavaWorld

Location: http://www.xm.com/cafe/

Description: *JavaWorld* is a new online magazine devoted to, guess what, Java! It features many good articles and links to more resources. The *zine* is set up similar to a traditional magazine with press releases, features, columns, reviews, and so on. This site is a good place to hang out to find out the latest news on the Java industry. Figure A.9 shows the latest issue.

Figure A.8

The Coffee Pages Web site.

Figure A.9

The *JavaWorld* online magazine.

Appendix B

Java Database
Connectivity
(JDBC)

Java Database Connectivity (JDBC)

As we were finishing the manuscript for this book, the developers of Java announced the release of the SQL API specifications. This next step in the evolution of Java may have a huge impact on how programmers use Java to build applications. The problem with Java so far is that it is not mature and robust enough to be used for developing large scale, real-world applications. For example, you probably wouldn't consider using Java to create a company-wide client/server system. But with the introduction of the Java Database Connectivity feature (JDBC), Java is on its way to offering everything developers need to implement database schemes that are fast enough for everyday use.

By implementing a database standard for Java developers to follow, Sun has really helped Java's chances of becoming a language that will be used extensively in the future. To maintain as much of its cross-platform capabilities as possible, Sun is pushing a generic SQL database access framework. This will provide a uniform interface that can run on top of different database systems. This means that the tools you use in Java should always look the same, but the drivers that actually connect to the databases can be anything you want. As new database standards emerge, the JDBC will be able support them as soon as the appropriate low-level drivers are written.

Of course, keep in mind that the specifications for the new JDBC standard have just begun and they are likely to evolve in the near future. This first draft of the specifications is designed to help developers create database drivers more than it is designed to help database users.

In this appendix, we'll introduce you to this new technology so that you can get a sense of how this powerful database API is evolving. You can think of it as sneak preview of what is to come. At this stage, we don't recommend that you create any huge database applets or applications based on this API. You should first experiment with it and become familiar with it so that when the 1.0 version of the API is released you will be ready to jump right into it with both feet.

Introducing the Database API

At the time of this writing, Version 0.5 of the API was introduced. By the time your read this chapter, a newer version may be available. Make sure you check out the Javasoft Web site (www.javasoft.com) from time to time to look for new developments. If you are inexperienced with SQL database technology, we suggest you pick up a good SQL tutorial book. We couldn't possibly cover the entire SQL system in one chapter, so we will assume that you have at least a basic understanding of SQL.

The Java Database Connectivity (JDBC) API is based on four simple ideas. First, it offers an *environment* that provides a support structure for connecting to a database (or multiple databases). Next, it provides a *connection* that initiates contact and communication between a client and a server. Third, it accepts *statements* for specifying parameters for performing queries and searching databases. Finally, it returns a *result set* that stores the results of a query performed by a statement.

Security Issues

One of the strong suits of Java is its robust security measures. The JDBC API should be just as secure. If you use a database from within an applet, it will have the same constraints as file handling: *You will only be able to connect to a database that is on the server from which the applet was called from.* However, security "certificates" may be used to allow trusted applets to have more access.

One area of security that may be problematic involves using a database that can store binary large objects (BLOBs). These structures can store anything including images, video, animation, and unfortunately viruses. It is feasible that a misguided hacker could use a database system to transfer a virus or other harmful bit of native code onto any system through the use of a BLOB. This possibility will undoubtedly be looked at by the developers of the JDBC API but you should realize that potential dangers exist for using distributed database systems in general. As you start to make use of this technology in building your own applications, keep your eyes open for potential security problems.

The Database Classes

Let's look at the classes and methods that make up the current JDBC API. The key classes included:

- Environment
- Connection
- Driver
- ResultSet
- Statement

The Environment Class

The **Environment** class is used as a backdrop for all the other operations we wish to perform within our database. We also use this class to determine which type of driver/database combination we will be using. At this time, only the standard JDBC driver is available, but there will soon be drivers for many different database connectivity systems. Here is the declaration for this class:

```
public Environment();
Environment myEnv = New Environment();  // sample declaration statement
```

The methods for the **Environment** class are listed in Table B.1.

The Connection Interface

The **connection** interface is used to create driver-specific classes that can be used to interact with each different driver in exactly the same way. The **connection** interface and any classes that implement this interface will have the static vari-

Table B.1   The Methods for the Environment Class

Method	Description
getConnection(String, Properties)	This method initiates the connection to the database that is in the form of a URL passed through the **String** argument. It will try and make this connection by cycling through each registered database driver. The **Properties** argument contains user information such as an ID and password.
getConnection(String, String, String)	This method is identical to the one above, except that the **Properties** argument has been split up into its parts; strings representing the user ID and password.
getDrivers()	This method returns an enumeration of all the currently available JDBC drivers. Calling this method is a good way to check if a particular driver is loaded and if not you could try and download it by calling the **loadDriver()** method.
loadDriver(String)	This method tries to load a new driver. The string passed specifies the full classname (including the .class) of the driver we want to try and load. The method returns a boolean value indicating the success or failure of the load.
registerDriver(Driver)	This method registers new drivers when they are downloaded.

Table B.2   Variables Used with the Connection Interface

Variable	Value
TRANSACTION_NONE	0
TRANSACTION_READ_UNCOMMITTED	1
TRANSACTION_READ_COMMITTED	2
TRANSACTION_REPEATABLE_READ	3
TRANSACTION_SERIALIZABLE	4
TRANSACTION_VERSIONING	5

ables and methods listed in Tables B.2 and B.3. Keep in mind that the variables are all static variables belonging to the interface. They are used for setting and checking the status of database read methods.

The Driver Interface

The **driver** interface is used by database driver developers. You will not need to use it unless you are creating your own drivers. However, all JDBC drivers will need to implement the methods listed in Table B.4.

Table B.3 Methods Used with the Connection Interface

Method	Description
close()	This method frees up resources linked to the current connection. These resources can be garbage collected eventually, but it is better to do it manually to avoid memory problems.
commit()	This method commits the stored SQL statements to be queried.
createStatement()	This method simply returns a database SQL object.
getTransactionIsolation()	This method returns an integer value representing the isolation level of the connection.
isClosed ()	This method returns a boolean value that indicates if the database is closeed or not. A closed database can occur due to a call to the **close()** method or through an error with the connection.
isReadOnly()	This method checks the read-only status of the connection. The return value is a boolean.
nativeSQL(String)	This method takes a standard SQL query and converts it into a query in the form of a string that is ready for the driver specific to this class. This method is necessary if you are using a database driver that uses proprietary SQL calls.
prepareCall(String)	This method is very similar to **prepareStatement()** but it returns a **CallableStatement** object which is a call to a stored SQL procedure. Once again, the **String** argument is simply the SQL query you wish to send.
prepareStatement(String)	This method returns a **PreparedStatement** object which is a pre-compiled SQL statement. This type of statement increases query speed in large databases. The **String** argument is simply the SQL query you wish to send.
rollback()	This method will negate all the queries that are stored in the queue.
setAutoCommit(Boolean)	This method tells the database driver that all SQL statements will automatically be executed as they are prepared. Otherwise, each statement is put into a list that is not sent until the **commit()** method is called.
setReadOnly(boolean)	This method sets the read-only attribute for the connection. This method cannot be called during the middle of a transaction.
setTransactionIsolation(int)	This method sets the transaction isolation level. The integer being sent can be represented by one of the interface variables listed above. Once again, this method cannot be called in the middle of a transaction.

Table B.4 The Methods Used with the Driver Interface

Method	Description
connect(String, Properties)	This method returns a **Connection** object that can then be used to create queries. The **String** argument is the URL of the desired database and the **Properties** argument is used to pass arbitrary information, usually username and password.
getMajorVersion()	This method returns an integer that represents the major version number of the driver.
getMinorVersion()	This method returns an integer that represents the minor version number of the driver.

The ResultSet Interface

The objects you will use to actually interact with database information will be implementations of the **ResultSet** interface. From this level, you will be able to read an incredible number of different types of data. Look near the end of the chapter for information on the SQL data types. The methods defined in this interface are listed in Table B.5.

Table B.5 The Methods Used with the ResultSet Interface

close()	This method closes the result set so that its resources can be recycled.
getBigInt(int)	This method accepts a column number as an argument and returns a **long** value.
getBinary(int)	This method accepts a column number as an argument and returns an array of **byte** values.
getBit(int)	This method accepts a column number as an argument and returns a **boolean** value.
getChar(int)	This method accepts a column number as an argument and returns a **String** object.
getColumnCount()	This method returns an integer representing the number of columns in the database.
getDate(int)	This method accepts a column number as an argument and returns a **Date** value. (**Date**, **Time**, and **Timestamp** are three more new data classes introduced with the SQL package.)
getDecimal(int, int)	This method accepts a column number and scale value as arguments and returns a **Numeric** value.
getDouble(int)	This method accepts a column number as an argument and returns a **double** value.
getFloat(int)	This method accepts a column number as an argument and returns a **float** value.
getInteger(int)	This method accepts a column number as an argument and returns an **integer** value.
getLongVarChar(int)	This method accepts a column number as an argument and returns a **String** object.
getNumeric(int, int)	This get method is a little different. First, we have two arguments. The first is the column number and the second is the scale of the value—the number of decimal point to the right to use for accuracy. The return value for this method is a little different also. Instead of getting a standard data type, you get a new object, **Numeric**. **Numeric** objects can be used to retrieve various types of numeric values and parse out the type later. This method is great for dealing with databases where you are not sure of some column data types.
getReal(int)	This method accepts a column number as an argument and returns a **float** value.
getRowCount()	This method counts the number of total rows in this result set.
getRowNumber()	This method returns an integer representing the current row number in the result set.
getSmallInt(int)	This method accepts a column number as an argument and returns a **short** value.
getTime(int)	This method accepts a column number as an argument and returns a **Time** value.
getTimestamp(int)	This method accepts a column number as an argument and returns a **Timestamp** value.

continued

Table B.5   The Methods Used with the ResultSet Interface (Continued)

getTinyInt(int)	This method accepts a column number as an argument and returns a **byte** value.
getVarChar(int)	This method accepts a column number as an argument and returns a **String** object.
isNull(int)	This method returns a boolean value that tells us if the column at the given **integer** is null or not.
next()	This method advances to the next record in a result set. It returns true if the next record is available or false if the end of result set is reached.

The Statement Interface

The **Statement** interface is used for executing queries that will result in a **resultSet**. The methods defined in this interface are listed in Table B.6.

Table B.6   The Methods Used with the Statement Interface

Method	Description
cancel()	This method can be used in a threaded program to stop the execution of a query that is being processed by another thread.
clearWarnings()	This method clears the warnings from the queue.
close()	This method closes all resources associated with a **statement** object.
execute(String)	This is method is the counterpart to **executeQuery()**. It is used to perform statements on the database that write to it rather than read. The return value is an integer representing the new total number of rows for the database.
executeQuery(String)	You will probably use this method more than any other for retrieving information from a database. Its sole argument is a **String** that holds a standard SQL query. After this method executes successfully, a **resultSet** object is returned.
getMaxFieldSize()	This method returns an integer value that indicates the limit in bytes on how much data can be sent as part of any one single field.
getMaxRows()	This method returns an integer value that indicates the maximum number of rows that can be returned as part of a **resultSet**.
getWarnings()	This method returns error information relating to the current statement either being executed or has executed. This can be a single or multiple errors of the **SQLWarning** type.
setMaxFieldSize(int)	This method sets the maximum number of bytes that can be transferred with any single field.
setMaxRows(int)	This method is used to set the maximum number of rows that can be received as part of a **resultSet** from a query.

The Numeric Class

The **Numeric** class can be used to represent SQL values from a database before they are transferred to a Java data type. This class is useful for performing operations on SQL specific data that will be returned to the database and will not be needed in a Java-centric data type.

This class includes its own simple math functions as well. However, whenever you perform a mathematical operation with one or more **Numeric** objects, you will always receive another **Numeric** object as the return type. Table B.7 describes the methods found in this class.

The **Numeric** object is quite a bit different than using our standard data types, so let's look at a few simple code snippets that illustrate the use of the **Numeric** class:

```
Numeric x, y, z, result;
boolean bool;

x = new Numeric(5, 0);              // x = 5 (integer)
y = new Numeric(5.0, 1);            // y = 5.0 (double)
z = new Numeric(2.5, 4);            // z = 2.5000 (double)
result = x.add(y);                  // result = 10
result = y.subtract(z);             // result = 2.5
result = z.multiply(z);             // result = 6.2500
bool = y.greaterThan(z);            // bool = true
bool = x.lessThanOrEquals(z);       // bool = false
```

The Date Class

One type of data element that Java does not support very well are dates and times. Since these are improtant parts of the SQl database system, Sun created three new data type classes. The constructors and methods for these classes are presented in Table B.8.

The Timestamp Class

The **Timestamp** data type is the **Time** and **Date** data types mixed together and put on steroids. You can use it to represent times down into the nanosecond range as well as the date. The constructor for this class is:

```
Timestamp(int, int, int, int, int, int, int);
```

Table B.7   The Methods Used with the Numeric Class

Method	Description
add(Numeric)	Adds the given **Numeric** value to the current one. The result is a third **Numeric** object.
divide(Numeric)	Divides the given value into the current value.
Environment(double, int)	Creates a double style object.
Environment(int, int)	Creates an integer-based representation of the database value.
Environment(String, int)	Creates a string representation of the value with the integer being the scale of the numeric accuracy.
equals(Object)	Returns true if the numeric value matches the objects value; otherwise, it returns false.
greaterThan(Numeric)	Returns a boolean value.
greaterThanOrEquals(Numeric)	Returns a boolean value.
lessThan(Numeric)	Returns a boolean value.
lessThanOrEquals(Numeric)	Returns a boolean value.
multiply(Numeric)	Performs a multiplication operation.
subtract(Numeric)	Same as **add()** but performs subtraction.

Table B.8   The Constructors and Methods Used with the Date and Time Classes

Method	Description
Date(int, int, int)	The constructor for the **Date** class. The three integer arguments represent the year, month, and day, respectively.
toString()	This is the only method available to the **Date** class. It returns a string representation of the date.
Time(int, int, int)	The constructor for the **Time** class. The three integer arguments represent hours, minutes, and seconds, respectively. The **Time** class uses 24-hour military time.
toString()	This is the only method available to the **Time** class. It returns a string representation of the time.

The list of integer arguments include the year, month, day, hour, minute, second, and nanoseconds. The only method provided in this class is **toString()**, which returns a string representation of the date and time stored in the object.

SQL Data Types

When accessing SQL databases your programs will come into contact with data types that do not exist as standard data types in Java. For this reason, the JDBC will automatically *map* the SQL data type to the closest Java data type. If you want to handle this yourself, you can actually cause data types to be mapped into many possible Java types. Table B.9 presents the set of SQL data types used along with their corresponding Java data types.

After examining Table B.9, you're probably wondering about the **InputStream** data types that are listed. They are an object that can be used to stream data into a program as needed. Sometimes a database will have fields that store huge amounts of data like blobs that if we tried to download them into a **resultSet** we

Table B.9 The Set of SQL Data Types Along with Their Corresponding Java Types

SQL Data Type	Java Object Type
Char	String
VARCHAR	String
LONGVARCHAR	InputStream
NUMERIC	Numeric
DECIMAL	Numeric
BIT	boolean
TINYINT	Integer
SMALLINT	Integer
INTEGER	Integer
BIGINT	Long
REAL	Float
FLOAT	Float
DOUBLE	Double
BINARY	byte[]
VARBINARY	byte[]
LONGVARBINARY	InputStream
DATE	Date
TIME	Time
TIMESTAMP	Timestamp

would run out of memory and have to wait a very long time for the data to come across the Net. The **InputStream** class works by reading the data in manageable chunks that the system can handle.

JDBC URL Usage

A few of the classes and methods we described in the previous section use **String** objects that represent URLs. These URLs are quite different than the standard URLs used for Web and FTP navigation. This part of the JDBC API is not set in stone yet so watch out for big changes here.

As it stands now, here is the syntax for a JDBC URL:

```
jdbc:<subprotocol>:<subname>
```

The *subprotocol* should name the type of database protocol you are running SQL through. The *subname* will represent more detailed information that the subprotocol can use to locate a specific server or database.

The *subname* can further be refined to include information about the location of a secondary server on a LAN. Here is an example of this:

```
jdbc:odbc://ntserver:80/web
```

If this looks confusing, don't panic yet. Wait for the full release and hopefully some more detailed documentation from Sun. Also, we expect that there will be a tremendous number of tools available to aid in this sort of development. For example, the development environments that Symantec and Borland are working on will undoubtedly aid in database application and applet development.

Eventually, we may have protocol naming services, much like the dynamic naming services we have now for Web sites. So, you may be able to use a simple name that points to your server over the Web by resolving the name with a naming service. At this point, Sun is going to start a registry that people can register their drivers with.

JDBC Code Examples

Here are a couple of simple classes that illustrate how the database system will work. Note that because we don't have easy access to a SQL server that you and we can connect to, the URLs in these samples are provided for example purposes only.

Retrieving Information from a Database

This first example shows you how to use the SQL package to create database queries for retrieving information. In particular, we use the **Connection, Statement,** and **ResultSet** classes.

```java
import java.net.URL;
import java.sql.*;

class readDatabase {

  public static void main(String args[]) {
    try {
      // Create a URL specifying an ODBC database
      String url = "jdbc:odbc:coriolis";
      // Connect to the database
      Connection con = Environment.getConnection(url, "username", "password");
      // Create and execute a SQL SELECT statement
      Statement stmt = con.createStatement();
      ResultSet rs = stmt.executeQuery("SELECT a, b, c, d, key FROM
        Table");
      // Step through the result
      while (rs.next()) {
        // get the values from the current row:
        int a = rs.getInteger(1);
        Numeric b = rs.getNumeric(2);
        char c[] = rs.getVarChar(3).tocharArray();
        boolean d = rs.getBit(4);
        String key = rs.getVarChar(5);
        // Now print out the results:
        System.out.print(" key=" + key);
        System.out.print(" a=" + a);
        System.out.print(" b=" + b);
        System.out.print(" c=");
        for (int i = 0; i < c.length; i++) {
          System.out.print(c[i]);
        }
        System.out.print(" d=" + d);
        System.out.print("\n");
      }
      stmt.close();
      con.close();
    } catch (java.lang.Exception ex) { ex.printStackTrace(); }
  }
}
```

Writing to a Database

In this example we are using classes from the SQL package to write data to a database:

```
import java.net.*;
import java.sql.*;

class writeDatabase {
  public static void main(String args[]) {
    try {
      // Create a URL specifying an ODBC database
      String url = "jdbc:odbc:coriolis";
      // Connect to the database at that URL.
      Connection con = Environment.getConnection(url, "username", "password");
      // Create a prepared statement to update the third field in a
      // row in the "Table" table.
      PreparedStatement stmt = con.prepareStatement( "UPDATE Table1 _
        SET a = ? WHERE key = ?");
      // First use the prepared statement to update the "count" row.
      stmt.setInteger(3, 34);
      stmt.setVarChar(2, "count");
      stmt.execute(); //Executes the query and update
      stmt.close();
      con.close();
    } catch (java.lang.Exception ex) { ex.printStackTrace(); }
  }
}
```

Index

T

U

V

JAVA
PROGRAMMING LANGUAGE HANDBOOK

REFERENCE CARD

Java Interpreter Command-Line Options

`a [options] sourcefile`

sspath *path*—Specifies the path Java uses to look up classes. The path rides the default or the one set by the CLASSPATH environment variable if set.

-checksource—When a compiled class is loaded, this option causes the fication time of the class bytecode file to be compared to that of the class ce file. If the source has been modified more recently, it is recompiled and ew bytecode file is loaded.

ug—Allows the Java debugger (jdb) to attach itself to this Java session. **-debug** is specified on the command line, Java displays a password which be used when starting the debugging session.

x—Sets the startup size of the memory allocation pool (the garbage col-heap) to x. The default is 1 megabyte of memory. x must be > 1000 bytes.

x—Sets the maximum size of the memory allocation pool (the garbage col-heap) to x. The default is 16 megabytes of memory. x must be > 1000 bytes.

syncgc—Turns off asynchronous garbage collection. When activated, rbage collection takes place unless it is explicitly called or the program out of memory.

rify—Turns verification off.

x—Sets the maximum stack size that can be used by Java code in a to x. Every thread that is spawned during the execution of the program d to Java has x as its Java stack size. The default units for x are bytes. x e > 1000 bytes. You can modify the meaning of x by appending either the k" for kilobytes or the letter "m" for megabytes. The default stack size is obytes ("-oss 400k").

—Sets the maximum stack size that can be used by C code in a thread to x. hread that is spawned during the execution of the program passed to Java s its C stack size. The default units for x are bytes. x must be > 1000 bytes. n modify the meaning of x by appending either the letter "k" for kilobytes or er "m" for megabytes. The default stack size is 128 kilobytes ("-ss 128k").

rbose—Causes Java to print a message to stdout each time a class file is

—Runs the verifier on all code.

segc—Causes the garbage collector to print out messages whenever it emory.

remote—Runs the verifier on all code that is loaded into the system via loader. **verifyremote** is the default for the interpreter.

Compiler Command-Line Options

r that converts byte-code (.java) into pseudo-code (.code).

`[options] filename.java`

-classpath *path-of-classes*—Specifies the path the Java compiler uses to look up classes. If declared in the options, the default environment variable is overridden. Directories are separated by semicolons.

-d *directory*—Specifies the destination of compiled classes.

-g *debugger*—Enables debugging capabilities of java.

Javap

Breaks down the class file revealing public methods and variables passed to it.

`javap [options] class`

-c—Prints out disassembled code, i.e., the instructions that comprise the Java bytecodes, for each of the methods in the class.

-l *variables*—Prints out line and local variable tables.

-p—Prints out the private and protected methods and fields of the class in addition to the public ones.

JDB - Debugger

`jdb`

breakpoints—Sets a breakpoint in a class. The source file line number must be specified, or the name of the method. (The breakpoint will then be set at the first instruction of that method.)

clear—Removes breakpoints.

cont—Continues execution.

dump—Dumps an object's instance variables. Objects are specified by their object ID (a hexadecimal integer). Classes are specified by either their object ID or by name. If a class is already loaded, a substring can be used, such as Thread for java.lang.Thread. If a class isn't loaded, its full name must be specified, and the class will be loaded as a side effect. This is needed to set breakpoints in referenced classes before an applet runs.

exceptions—When an exception occurs for which there isn't a catch statement anywhere up a Java program's stack, the Java runtime normally dumps an exception trace and exits. When running under jdb, however, that exception is treated as a non-recoverable breakpoint, and jdb stops at the offending instruction. If that class was compiled with the -g option, instance and local variables can be printed to determine the cause of the exception.

help or **?—**Displays the list of recognized commands with a brief description.

print—Browses Java objects. The **print** command calls an object's **toString()** method—so it will be formatted differently depending on its class.

threads—Lists the current threads.

where—Dumps the stack of either a specified thread, or the current thread (which is set with the thread command). If that thread is suspended (either because it's at a breakpoint or via the suspend command), local (stack) and instance variables can be browsed with the print and dump commands. The up and down commands select which stack frame is current.

JAVAH - C Header File Creator

`javah [options] sourcefile`

-classpath *path*—Specifies the path javah uses to look up classes. Overrides the default or the CLASSPATH environment variable if it is set. Directories are separated by semi-colons.

-d *directory*—Sets the directory where javah saves the header files or the stub files.

-o *outputfile*—Concatenates the resulting header or source files for all of the classes listed on the command line into outputfile.

-stubs—Causes javah to generate C declarations from the Java object file.

-td *directory*—Sets the directory where javah stores temporary files. By default, javah stores temporary files in the directory specified by the %TEMP% environment variable. If %TEMP% is unspecified, javah checks for a %TMP% environment variable. And finally, if %TMP% is unspecified, javah creates the directory C:\tmp and stores the files there.

-verbose—Causes javah to print a message to stdout concerning the status of the generated files.

JAVADOC - Documentation Generator

`javadoc [options] sourcefile`

-classpath *path*—Specifies the path javadoc uses to look up the .java files. Overrides the default or the CLASSPATH environment variable, if it is set. Directories are separated by semicolons.

-d *directory*—Specifies the directory where javadoc stores the generated HTML files.

-verbose—Causes the compiler and linker to print out messages about what source files are being compiled and what object files are being loaded.

Applet Viewer

-debug—Starts the applet viewer in the Java debugger (jdb) which allows you to debug applets.

Comments

C Style: `/* Comments here… */`

C++ Style: `// Comments here…`

Java Documentation Style: `/** Comments and tags here… */`

To process these style of comments, run the Javadoc program with your *.java file as an argument.

Class Tags Used for /** ... */ Style Comments:

@see *classname*— Adds a hyperlinked "See Also" to your class.

@see *fully-qualified—classname*—Also adds a "See Also" to the class, but this time you need to use fully qualified class name like "java.awt.window."

@see *fully-qualified—classname#methodname*—Also adds a "See Also" to the class, but now you are pointing to a specific method within that class.

@version *version-text*—Adds a version number that you provide.

@author *author-name*—Adds an author entry.

Method Tags Used for /** ... */ Style Comments:

@param *paramter-name description*...—Used to show which parameters the method accepts.

@return *description*...—Used to describe what the method returns.

@exception *fully-qualified-classname description*... —Used to add a "throw" entry that describes the type of exceptions this method can throw.

Identifiers

Identifiers should always begin with a letter of the alphabet, either upper or lower case. The only exception to this rule is the underscore symbol (_) and the dollar sign ($) which may also be used.

Reserved Keywords

Abstract	boolean	break	byte
byvalue	cast	catch	char
Class	const	continue	default
do	Double	else	extends
final	finally	float	for
future	generic	goto	if
implements	import	inner	instanceof
int	interface	long	native
new	null	operator	outer
package	private	protected	public
rest	return	short	static
super	switch	synchronized	this
throw	transient	try	var
void	volatile	while	

Data Types

Type	Negative Minimal	Positive Maximal
byte	-256	255
short	-32768	32767
int	-2147483648	2147483647
long	-9223372036854775808	9223372036854775
float	1.40239846e-45	3.40282347e38
double	4.94065645841246544e-324	1.79769313486231
boolean	False	True

Character Escape Codes

Character Combination	Standard Designation	Descripti
\	<newline>	Continua
\n	NL or LF	New Line
\b	BS	Backspa
\r	CR	Carriage
\f	FF	Form Fe
\t	HT	Horizont
\\	\	Backslas
\'	'	Single Q
\"	"	Double
\xdd	0xdd	Hex Bit
\ddd	0ddd	Octal Bi
\uddd	0xdddd	Unicode

Variable Declaration

```
datatype identifier = [value];

int i;           // Declare an integer variable
byte i, j;       // Declare two byte variable
int a=7, b=a;    // Declare and initialize two
float f=1.06;    // Declare and initialize a flo
String name="Tony"; // Declare and initialize a
```

Array Declaration

```
datatype identifier[] [= {value list}];
datatype[] identifier [= {value list}];

int nums[];  // Declare an open-ended array
int[] nums;  // Same as line above
// Declare an array of a fixed size
int nums[] = new int[200];
// Declare array having 6 elements and assign v
int nums[] = {1,2,3,4,5,6};
```

Assignment Operators

=	Simple Assignment
+=	Assignment with addition
-=	Assignment with subtraction
*=	Assignment with multiplication
/=	Assignment with division
%=	Assignment with modulo
&=	Assignment with bitwise AND

(Continued on next page)